Turkey Between East and West

New Challenges for a Rising Regional Power

EDITED BY

Vojtech Mastny and R. Craig Nation

Westview Press

A Member of the Perseus Books Group

Copyright © 1996 by Westview Press, A Member of the Perseus Books Group

Published in 1996 in the United States of America by Westview Press, Inc., 5500 Central Avenue, Boulder, Colorado 80301-2877, and in the United Kingdom by Westview Press, 12 Hid's Copse Road, Cumnor Hill, Oxford OX2 9JJ

Library of Congress Cataloging-in-Publication Data
Turkey between East and West : new challenges for a rising regional power / edited by Vojtech Mastny and R. Craig Nation.
    p. cm.
  Includes bibliographical references (p.) and index.
  ISBN 0-8133-2420-3   0-8133-3412-8 (pbk)
  1. Turkey—Foreign relations. 2. Turkey—Foreign economic relations. 3. Turkey—Politics and government—1980- . I. Mastny, Vojtech, 1936- . II. Nation, R. Craig.
DR477.T79 1996
327.561—dc20   95-39563
                                                                                  CIP

The paper used in this publication meets the requirements of the American National Standard for Permanence of Paper for Printed Library Materials Z39.48-1984.

10   9   8   7   6   5   4   3   2

Contents

Tables

Preface

The modern Turkish Republic was born at the end of the First World War as the negation of the collapsing Ottoman empire. Its founder, Mustafa Kemal (Atatürk), abandoned the ancient imperial capital, Istanbul, in favor of Ankara, replaced the Ottoman constitutional monarchy with republican institutions under the guidance of a single ruling party, launched a radical secularization campaign, and made clear his desire to adapt the new Turkey to the ways of the West.

During the cold war era Turkey appeared to be firmly anchored to Europe. As a pillar of the NATO alliance in a highly sensitive region it was considered to be an essential strategic partner. The tradition of single party rule was abandoned, and though the domestic environment remained troubled, movement toward political pluralism seemed to be inexorable. From the early 1960s, the goal of gradual association with the European Community was placed on the agenda. This period also saw hundreds of thousands of Turks permanently relocate in western Europe as a migratory work force, giving rise to a host of new and complex social and interpersonal interactions. The opening of the Turkish economy during the 1980s, associated with prime minister Turgut Özal, integrated the national economy more closely with western markets and gave rise to something of an economic boom. Özal himself spoke of his country, somewhat unguardedly, as "the Japan of West Asia."

The optimistic sense of future prospects to which these dynamics gave rise was naturally transferred to evaluations of Turkey's potential role in the post-Cold War environment. The breakup of the USSR eliminated a centuries-old common border with a centralized Russian state and seemed to transform Turkey's strategic situation. The emergence of newly independent states of Turkic and Islamic heritage in Central Asia and the Caucasus created a new field of interest for Turkish foreign policy and gave rise to considerable enthusiasm concerning the Turkish mission amongst the "lost cousins" of Turkestan. This enthusiasm was to some extent shared in the West, where the distinctiveness of the modern Turkish experience was highlighted. As a democratically governed secular state, Turkey was unique in the Islamic world. It possessed a dynamic market economy and was committed to integration with international markets. It was moreover a reliable international partner closely bound to the U.S.-led western security community. In this guise, Turkey was presented as a "model" to the newly emerging states of the Caucasus and Central Asia and as a "bridge" for interaction between East and West.

None of Turkey's aspirations have been abandoned and none of its prospects have disappeared. The enthusiasm of the late 1980s has nonetheless been tempered by a host of new and sometimes unexpected dilemmas. The rapid growth of the 1980s was accompanied by sharp social differentiation and by the 1990s it had given way to a deep recession with accompanying social tensions. In 1989 the European Community suspended consideration of Turkey's application for full membership and Ankara has since been pushed to the back of a line of new applicants, including the former communist states of eastern and central Europe. The rise of a politicized Islam in the form of the Welfare Party has called some of the assumptions of the Kemalist legacy into question and posed basic questions about Turkish identity. The limits of Turkey's capacity to sponsor transition in Central Asia and the Caucasus have quickly become apparent and in these regions a new geopolitical competition with the Russian Federation is well under way. Perhaps most important, the struggle against Kurdish separatism in the southeast has become a major domestic challenge that also poses fundamental questions about the character of the modern Turkish state.

The essays collected in this book accurately reflect the process of reflection to which these new challenges have given rise. The perspectives that are offered are diverse but there are several shared perceptions and unifying themes that emerge clearly and deserve to be emphasized. The contributors share the conviction that Turkey remains fully committed to a process of development, democratization, and integration with the West. What the dynamics of the post-Cold War era have made clear, however, is that there are major barriers that continue to stand in the way of fuller integration. Some of these barriers are familiar and in fact date back over centuries. Others are specific to the nature of contemporary economic and political developments. Although no one factor is likely to prove decisive taken by itself, an image of modernization in Turkey as linear movement toward attachment to a greater Europe has been to some extent discredited.

First, there is the legacy of underdevelopment, which the imbalanced growth of the 1980s did not succeed in overcoming. Turkish gross domestic product per capita remains little more than half that of the poorest members of the European Union (EU), the state carries a heavy long-term foreign debt burden, and state expenditures are extremely high (more than double the EU average). Turkey's strategic situation is also particularly complicated, with open-ended armed conflicts under way in adjacent areas such as Bosnia-Herzegovina and the Caucasus and a potentially volatile triangular relationship with its neighbors Syria and Iraq. The consequences of the severe military crackdown of 1980 continue to be felt, and despite the considerable progress made in institutionalizing democratic norms, Turkey has been exposed to sharp criticism for its alleged record of systematic human rights violations.

The contributors to this volume devote a great deal of attention to these various dilemmas but on the whole they conclude that in no case are the problems too great to be managed. Efforts to overcome the burden of underdevelopment, the challenge of strategic exposure, and an inherited democratic deficit make up much of the substance of the modern Turkish experience and the record of accomplishment is on balance impressive. The most fundamental barrier to fuller integration is rather perceived to derive from western attitudes toward Turkey and the Turks, too often informed by raw cultural prejudice and a basic lack of knowledge. This perception has been sharpened by the EU's apparent disinterest in Turkey's long-term goal of full membership, by the rise of racial violence directed against Turkish families in western Europe, and particularly by the way in which the crisis in former Yugoslavia has been managed. Rightly or wrongly, many Turks have concluded that the European great powers have tolerated or even encouraged the violence directed against the Muslim peoples of Bosnia-Herzegovina because they fear the emergence of a "Muslin state in Europe." No matter what Turkey accomplishes, some conclude, it will continue to be viewed as foreign and unassimilable by majority opinion in the West.

These conclusions are reflected in contemporary Turkey in contradictory ways. The original enthusiasm for Turkey's tutelary role in Central Asia was in part a reaction to what was perceived as rejection by the West. The domestic impact of a politicized Islam derives in part from social marginalization and exclusion but also from a search for indigenous sources of meaning and value. The same may be said for a new interest in Turkey's Ottoman past, perceived not so much as an alternative to a weakening Kemalist synthesis as a neglected source of cultural identity. The torturous Kurdish issue is likewise in part a reflection of concern for national integrity in the face of the weakening of traditional sources of domestic cohesion. The more extreme manifestations of these patterns of thought are likely to remain marginalized. Turkey nonetheless seems to be in the process of redefining itself in the post-Cold War era in a way that places more emphasis upon its cultural integrity, great power tradition, and status as the center of an autonomous geopolitical area rather than as the "peripheral extension" of a greater Europe. This does not mean turning away from Europe and all that it represents but rather accepting and seeking to come to terms with the essence of the Turkish experience as a complex amalgam of East and West.

These conclusions are reflected in the contributions to this volume in various ways. **Kemal Karpat** asserts the richness and complexity of the Ottoman legacy and argues that by nurturing this legacy democratically Turkey will reinforce its allegiance to the spirit of European civilization. **Bruce Kuniholm** looks at the factors which shaped Turkey's strategic partnership with the West after World War II and reflects on how the contradictory dynamics of integration and fragmentation in the post-Cold War era might affect that relationship in the future. **Duygu Bazoğlu Sezer** systematically analyzes Turkey's new security challenges and places special emphasis upon the disturbing implications of the "Muslim-Christian dichotomy" that seems to have opened up in the Balkans and southern Caucasus. She also notes the importance of working to overcome the legacy of hostility that has prevented a positive Greek-Turkish relationship from becoming a factor of stability in the politics of southeastern Europe. **R. Craig Nation**'s contribution takes up the theme of the Muslim peoples of Central Asia, the Caucasus, and the Balkans and discusses the ways in which their relations with Turkey have evolved in an environment embittered by regional wars and severe discontinuity.

Clement Dodd and **İlkay Sunar** look at domestic challenges to democratization. Dodd places special emphasis upon the destabilizing potential of sharpened religious consciousness and Sunar on the "authoritarian temptations" born of economic crisis, though both draw guardedly optimistic conclusions. **Ziya Öniş** draws a hopeful portrait of the evolution of Turkish development policy toward a "post-populist" model while **N. Bülent Gültekin** and **Ayşe Mumcu** examine the implications of Turkey's most significant initiative on behalf of regional development, the Black Sea Economic Cooperation project. **Heinz Kramer** looks carefully at the record of Turkey's relations with the European Community and is particularly critical of Europe's "basically reluctant or hostile approach toward Turkey" based upon a combination of "cultural prejudice and religiously motivated fear." In his carefully documented essay on the Turkish communities in western Europe **Faruk Şen** examines the sources of some of these prejudices while noting the extent to which a large Turkish community is now rooted in the West, where it makes an economic contribution of considerable importance.

All of the contributors share a sense of Turkey's enhanced importance as a strategic actor in a conflict-torn regional environment, a conviction that despite its many problems modern Turkey is destined to pursue its development as an emerging regional power, and the hope that Turkey's relations with the West will continue, as in the past, to be based upon a common purpose and shared values. Mutual respect and careful management of inevitable areas of tension will be the keys to realizing those hopes.

The idea for this book was born during the visit of His Excellency Süleyman Demirel to The Johns Hopkins University Paul H. Nitze School of Advanced International Studies Bologna Center to deliver the Gerold von Braunmühl Memorial Lecture in the spring of 1992. In February 1994 the Research Institute of the Bologna Center, directed by Professor Vojtech Mastny, sponsored an international conference on the theme *Turkey and Europe*. The papers presented at the conference, re-written and updated to take account of more recent events, constitute the substance of the present work. Assistance and collaboration in the organization of the conference was provided by the Faculty of Political Science of the University of Bologna, the *Istituto Affari Internazionali* (IAI) in Rome, and the Turkish Embassy to Italy. Generous support for the event was offered by the Foreign Ministry of the Republic of Turkey, the Marmara Bank in Istanbul, and the *Ente Nazionale Idrocarburi* (ENI) in Rome and the present volume is in large measure a product of their generosity. Special thanks are due to the staff members of The Johns Hopkins University Bologna Center who helped in the organization of the conference and the preparation of the text. Marina Ghiacci was instrumental in managing the conference on behalf of the Research Institute. Lauri Cohen was an accomplished text editor. Barbara Wiza and Arlene Binuya provided vital editorial assistance at critical moments and Laura D'Ambrosio and Karaça Mestçi graciously offered expert assistance with editing and indexing.

R. Craig Nation
Bologna, Italy

1

The Ottoman Rule in Europe From the Perspective of 1994

Kemal H. Karpat

The disintegration of the USSR in 1991 was followed by the formation of eight independent states in the Caucasus and Central Asia, six of which have a predominantly Muslim and Turkic population. All had historical relations with the Ottoman state dating back to the fourteenth century and culminating in the nineteenth century. The re-emergence of the Balkans as an area of international conflict has rekindled western interest in Turkey. The Balkans were mainly an Ottoman dominion until after the period 1878-1913 and remain of strategic, economic, and cultural interest to Turkey. In unforeseen and unpredictable ways history has revived the Turks' cultural, religious, and political legacy and interwoven it with Europe's contemporary politics. The Caucasus and Central Asia are rapidly becoming part of the global economic and political system and the western cultural sphere, not only because of their own need for survival but because they are a vital part of the emerging balance of power among Asia, Europe, and the United States. Most of the new Muslim republics of the former USSR have decided to accept the Latin alphabet, in large measure because of pressure from Turkey. Thus, the millenary relationship of the Turks of Turkey with their coreligionists in Asia, interrupted for seventy years, has been resumed in a new frame of reference.

The West saw Turkey as an oasis of stability and expected it to serve as a model of democracy, secularism, and free enterprise for the newly independent states. Turkey was envisioned as a model primarily because of its primordial historical and ethno-religious appeal to the Central Asians—which Turkey wanted to ignore in the past—but also because of its secularism, democracy, and relatively developed market economy. The

Black Sea Economic Cooperation project added additional weight to Turkey's attractiveness as a role model.

The Turkish government accepted these self-devised or assigned roles without much hesitation or reflection and without paying attention to the contradiction between the expected role and its poor record in dealing with Asia and Muslims in the past. Almost from its inception the Turkish Republic has abstained rigorously from becoming involved or even displaying interest in the history, culture, and languages of the Central Asian and Azeri peoples. Many individual Turks were greatly interested in the area but the government remained aloof for seventy years, not only towards the Turks and Muslims in Central Asia but also to those in the Balkans, lest it be accused of irredentism, pan-Turkism, and pan-Islamism.[1]

The features that make Turkey attractive as a role model were all adopted from the West. In other words, the West expected to use Turkey as a relay station to transfer these acquired western values and modes of life to the newly emerging cluster of Islamic countries in the former USSR. Had these Muslim countries of Central Asia been Christian as in the case of the Baltics—or had the West found another Muslim country to act as a better model—Turkey might have been promptly discarded. At the same time, Europe seemed ready to ignore the Turks' seven decades of relentless effort to modernize and westernize themselves, and prompt to embrace its old image of Turkey as a Muslim country likely to fall prey to fundamentalism, Islamism, or some other supposedly anti-western movement existing more in imagination than in fact.

The key consideration behind the foreign policy plans centered on Turkey in the post-Cold War period revolves around Islam. Turkey is expected and is able to play a role in Central Asia because of the Muslim faith and its shared ethnicity with the Turkic peoples of Asia and the Caucasus. Yet even though the West was prepared to consider Turkey sufficiently acculturated to western ideas of democracy, secularism, and capitalism to trust it to pass them on to Asian coreligionists, it did not accept the Turks as real partners of European culture and civilization because of their Islamic religion. Europe has never understood that Islam, which plays a key role in the life of the average Turk, has developed unique Turkish cultural and behavioral characteristics that make it more liberal than its Christian counterparts. Turkey can indeed play a role in the region only by retaining its Asian, Muslim-Turkish legacy.

The Central Asian countries seem to place great importance on their Islamic and ethnic Turkic background. The first secretary of the Communist Party of Kazakhstan, Dinmukhamed Kunaev, was emphatic about it.[2] Uzbek president Islam Karimov and his associates have stated clearly that what brought Uzbekistan close to Turkey was history, religion, and culture and because of this closeness it was willing to accept Turkey as a model. Uzbekistan has also appeared intent on reconstructing its "unique 1000 year old state structure while taking into account the effects of the immense change" which occurred in popular attitudes, culture, and mores under Soviet rule.[3] The leader of Kyrgyzstan, Askar Akaev, proposed inserting in the constitution a reference to Islam as a source of moral values and went to perform the *umra* (the off-season pilgrimage to Mecca), as did Karimov. No Turkish sultan or president, with the exception of the late Turgut Özal, ever went to Mecca while in office.

The Islamic and historical ties between Turkey, Azerbaijan, and Central Asia, along with the latter's commitment to change and modernization, provide the bricks and mortar for building a firm structure of cooperation between the Turks of Turkey and those of the newly independent states. (The dismissal of Abulfaz Elçibey as President of Azerbaijan dealt a severe blow to Turkey's position but did not eliminate the bases of future relations with Central Asia and the Caucasus.) In sum, Turkey cannot be divorced either from Islam and Turkishness or from western-style modernism. The commitment to modernism was and remains a cardinal point in the life of modern Turkey; it was stated repeatedly by Atatürk and was enshrined in the old constitution of 1924 as *inkilâpçılık* (*devrimcilik* in the new language), one of the six key principles of the republic. Today, the western ideas of modernism and progress have become an integral part of the culture of society and could not be phased out any more than Turkey could be induced to abandon Islam.

The debate about the role to be played by Turkey in Central Asia and the Caucasus went hand in hand with the controversy over the admission of Turkey as a full member into the then European Community (EC). For years the Turkish application was delayed and then was essentially rejected supposedly because of the country's low level of economic development, high rate of population growth, huge foreign debt, inflation, low tax revenue, high state expenditures, colossal state sector, human rights violations, etc. However, the main reason for the European refusal to admit Turkey into the EC was not a question of economics. As Ian O. Lesser puts it; "The fundamental issue for many Europeans is whether Europe can or should embrace an Islamic country of fifty-seven million. Significantly, the issue is being posed at a time of mounting intolerance and xenophobia in Western Europe, much of it directed against Muslim immigrants from the Maghreb and Turkey."[4]

Indeed, with the tacit approval of the Vatican, Europe has refused to accept Turkey as a true partner in the Community while warmly opening its arms to the countries of eastern Europe, a fifty-year friendship with the Turks notwithstanding. Thus, when in its interest the West invokes and magnifies Turkey's potential and qualities, but when Turkey fails to follow instructions, even if its own national interest is at stake, it is subjected to criticism and censure. The West is using the Kurdish question to bring the Turks to their knees in a manner similar to that in which it manipulated the "rights" of the Christian minorities in order to shatter the Ottoman empire. Turkish foreign policy is also at fault for its intellectual anemia. Turkey's leaders have navigated the ship of state in such a way as to remain marginal to Europe and to the Muslim Middle East, while claiming to belong to both of them. Thus, in the end the Turks remain unable and unwilling to define their position on the religious, cultural, and ethnic map of the world and to act accordingly. Turkey today is a Muslim country converted to the civilization of the West and with the zeal of a new convert is ready to proselytize its faith—secularism, democracy, ethnic nationalism—among other Muslims, a role it cannot fulfill because of its ambivalent cultural and historical position.

The Making of an Image

Turks of all ethnic and linguistic denominations started moving westward toward Europe in the third century (if not before) as though attracted by an invisible magnet. The Huns, Pechenegs, Cumans (Kipchaks), Uzes, and, finally, in the thirteenth century, Tatars (Mongols) came westward, following the route along the northern shore of the Black Sea. Most were baptized as Orthodox Christians—the main body of Cumans became Catholic—and rapidly assimilated almost without a trace into the local populations of central and southeast Europe. Those who converted to Islam after the thirteenth century conquests of the Golden Horde or before (Bulgars accepted Islam in 880) stayed in central Russia or retired east of the Urals. Religion appeared from the very start as the key factor in distinguishing, for the West, "them"—the Turks—from "us"—the Christians.

The southernmost branch of the Turks began arriving in Anatolia as nomadic tribespeople as early as the eighth century. Those who had not accepted Islam or did not internalize it as their basic identity accepted Christianity and some, such as the Karamanlıs, retained their Turkish language but were considered Greek. In 1926 these peoples were exchanged for the Turks of Greece (and Crete), some of whom were actually converted Greeks. Thus religion determined nationality. The bulk of the Turks moved into Anatolia in the tenth and eleventh centuries after their mass conversions to Islam ca. 950. After the Selçuki sultan Alparslan defeated the Byzantine emperor at Manzikert in 1071 and proceeded to conquer Jerusalem—more out of political and economic calculations than religious zeal—a negative image of Islam was reasserted with a vengeance.

By the eighth century, John of Damascus, among others, had declared that Muhammad was the enemy of Christianity, a false prophet, and that his followers pursued a path of vice, promiscuity, and decadence. Thus the Turks became part of an already existing anti-Muslim image of Islam—one that would be revived from time to time, reinforced, and perpetuated with new arguments regardless of the circumstances.[5] The fact that Turks hindered the march of the crusaders through Anatolia and that later sultans like Zangī, Nur al-Din (Saladin was his subordinate), and Qutuz forced them out of Syria and Egypt certainly did not endear the Turks to Europe.

The Turks who founded the Ottoman state moved to western Anatolia not to confront the Christians but to escape the pressure of the Mongols (Chingiz Khan's descendants). They crossed into the Balkans in 1354 to help sultan Gazi Orhan's Byzantine father-in-law gain the throne of Constantinople. In due time the early Ottoman sultans and their companions (some of whom, such as the Mihaloğulları, were of Greek origin) took the name *gazis* (holy warriors) and developed the ideology of *gazavat* (holy war) in order to justify their conquering march westward.[6] However, what the Turks conquered in the Balkans was the territory of the east Roman empire. This area was contested by Bulgarians, Serbians, and other groups which had re-established their medieval states in 1204-61 because of the fourth crusade. The crusade devastated the peninsula and the crusaders spent sixty years occupying Constantinople while trying to convert the Greeks to Catholicism. Therefore, the Turkish conquest not only liberated the Balkans from western domination and put an end to their feudal order in what is today Greece but also assured the survival of Orthodox Christianity. In this manner the Turks unwittingly became involved in the struggle between Orthodox Christianity and Rome and were eventually accused of perpetuating their schism.

The good will of the Orthodox Christians gained allies against western Christianity for the Turks and helped them secure their own rule in the peninsula. The failure of several western crusades, such as Nicopolis (1396) and Varna (1444), was due not only to the Turks' prowess as fighters but also to the animosity of the native Orthodox Christian population toward the West. Many Greeks, in particular, openly declared that they preferred "the turban of the Sultan to the tiara of the Pope." Some Greek orthodox prelates, such as Anthimos of Antioch, wrote as late as the eighteenth century that the Turkish sultan was a God-sent gift to protect and benefit the Orthodox Christians.

The Orthodox church was divided into two groups; the unionists favored union with (and submission to) Rome, while the anti-unionists, the "nationalists," sided with the Turks. The division deepened after the rulers of Byzantium accepted union with Rome at the fateful Council of Florence in 1439. This act persuaded the new Ottoman sultan, Mehmet II (1451-81), to expedite the conquest of Constantinople (1453) in order to forestall its possible occupation by the West. The Turks had thus, without any specific intent to do so, intervened in the bitter 500-year-old struggle between the eastern and western Christian churches and had prevented their fusion into a single whole—or at least it so appeared. The efforts of contemporary Greece to prevent the fusion of Turkey into Europe gives a rather ironic twist to the history of the area.

These events, publicized widely and unfavorably by Greek scholars who fled to Italy, further colored the image of the Turk as the enemy of Christendom. Greek scholars eventually reached the Muscovite court and pleaded with the czar to "liberate" the second Rome; already Ivan III had married Zoe Paleologus and staked a claim for Moscow as the third Rome. (Today, the Greek Patriarchate in Istanbul is seeking partners in Russia in the hope that a rebaptized Russia will assume its traditional role as defender of the Orthodox against the Turk and thus mask its reviving imperialist nationalism.)

The situation was aggravated further after the Venetian leadership, which for centuries enjoyed a privileged trading position in the Balkans, was replaced under pressure by the local Ottoman merchants and lords. This city-state then became the ally of the Roman church and the financier of its crusades. Venice remained an active player in Balkan and Mediterranean politics until the middle of the eighteenth century and was a major European source of information about Ottoman affairs thanks to the *bagli* (consuls) stationed in the main Mediterranean ports. In exchange, the Turks had the right to station their own representative in Italy. Catholic opposition to the Muslim and Turkish presence on their soil was so intense that the Turks had to defend their basic commercial interests in key Italian ports such as Ancona by appointing Christians as their representatives there, most of whom originated in the Balkans. In the eighteenth century the Habsburgs finally allowed Muslims to work in Vienna. Out of some ninety Ottoman commercial representations in Vienna approximately twenty were staffed by Muslims, including Turks.

For over a century and a half—that is, from the emergence of Osman's small principality in 1286 (or 1299, when he minted coins in his own name), until the conquest of Constantinople by Mehmet II—almost the entirety of Romania (Rumeli) was brought under Turkish rule.[7] After the conquest, Constantinople's position as the administrative capital of the territory of the east Roman empire was reasserted and henceforth the city assumed the Turkish name of Istanbul. (The name actually derived from the Greek "Is-t-an polis" (to the City), not "Islambol" (City of many Muslims). The Slavs called it "Tsarigrad," or "the Ruler's City," for, indeed, whomever ruled Constantinople was considered the ruler of the Balkans and Anatolia. The conquest created outrage in the Christian world, but there were many who regarded it as a divine punishment for the Greek schism from Rome. The Turks did not try to convert the Christians of the Balkans (the Bosnian and Bulgarian Bogomils and, to a large extent, the Albanians, converted voluntarily) but established a pluralistic cultural and religious system that took into consideration the mixed character of the peninsula and preserved it as such until 1878. Then, the newly established states in the Balkans embarked on a policy which was perhaps best described by Todor Zhivkov of Bulgaria as *edinstvo* (unity), implying the supremacy of the dominant ethnic group, in this particular case the ethnic Bulgarians.

Indeed, the Ottoman empire developed a well-balanced socio-economic and political structure and a pluralistic cultural-religious corporatist structure and legalized it during the reign of Mehmet II (1451-81). This was accomplished through the issuance of *kanunameler*, which were in essence secular regulations formally sanctioned by the religious *fetva*, that laid down an Ottoman constitutional order that lasted until the collapse of the empire.[8] It is clear that there was no *Byzance après Byzance*, as the Romanian historian of Greek parentage Nicolae Iorga once put it, but a new Turkish-Muslim order created specifically to suit the multi-ethnic, multi-religious structure of the Balkans and Anatolia. The reforms of the nineteenth century were simply a revision of the constitutional order of Mehmet II.[9] (In the nineteenth century Fuad Paşa created a similar multi-confessional order in Lebanon that lasted until 1975.)

Thus, the reign of Mehmet II marked the emergence of the Ottoman empire as the dominant regional power in the eastern Mediterranean. He and his successor, Beyazıt II (1481-1512), consolidated the northern flank of the empire by turning the Black Sea into a sort of Ottoman *mare nostrum*. These military moves were accompanied by the replacement of Venice and Genoa as the dominant commercial powers of the eastern Mediterranean with France and England and by the rise of a powerful Ottoman middle class of merchants and craftspeople in the service of the state.

The encounters between the Ottoman empire and western Europe during this first period (the dwindling city-states of Italy aside) were sporadic and accidental. The arrival of the Jews expelled from Spain and Portugal after 1492, who had been invited initially by Mehmet II, provided the Turks with an excellent source of knowledge about Europe and a skilled pool of professionals, merchants, and craftspeople. In the exchange of letters between Mehmet II and the Pope, Mehmet II claimed to be caesar, khan, and sultan and asked for political submission to Ottoman power. However, the Pope tried to convert the sultan to Christianity as the first condition for western rapprochement with the Turks. The exchange produced no lasting results, the painting school established by Gentile Bellini notwithstanding. The papacy remained the implacable foe of Islam and the Turks until the twentieth century when it recognized Islam as a revealed religion, an unnoticed and later forgotten act.

Ottoman Relations with Central Asia and Europe

The conquest of Hungary in 1526, the first siege of Vienna in 1529, and the annexation of Hungary and its direct administration as a *paşalık* with an appointed governor in 1541 brought the Ottoman empire into direct conflict with the Habsburgs and turned it into an active player in European politics overnight. For centuries Hungary had been the major seat of Catholicism in east central Europe and an active contender for power and influence in the Balkans. The Habsburgs developed a claim to Hungary through their usual method—marriage with Hungarian royalty. Consequently, after the death of King Louis on the battlefield at Mohács in 1526 his brother-in-law Ferdinand of Habsburg (brother of Charles V) managed to get himself elected king by the nobles of Bohemia, whom he had bribed. He was opposed by nationalist Hungarian nobles led by János Zápolyai, who subsequently turned pro-Turkish, but this did not improve the image of the Turks. Thus, the two most powerful rulers of Europe, Süleyman the Magnificent (1520-66) and Charles V (who became emperor of the Holy Roman Empire in 1519), found themselves engaged in a deadly rivalry, seemingly a contest between Christian and Muslim but in fact a struggle for power. The Ottoman-Habsburg rivalry, which continued until the end of both empires in 1918, carried extraordinary significance for the history of Europe.

Concomitant with the drive into central Europe, Süleyman faced the challenge of Persia, whose Shiite rulers, despite suffering a crushing defeat in 1514, arose again and continued to challenge the Turks. (All the Persian rulers, until as late as 1925, were of Turkish origin but religion proved stronger than ethnicity.) By conquering Syria and Egypt (1516-17) and assuming custody of the holy Muslim sites in Hicaz the Turks further consolidated their position as champions and defenders of Sunni Islam—a role begun in the eleventh century when Tuğrul bey, leader of the Selçukids, liberated Baghdad from the Shiite Buyids in 1055 and restored the caliph to his throne as the supreme head of the Muslim community. According to reliable sources, after his conquest of Syria and Egypt, sultan Selim invited caliph al-Mutawakil to Istanbul (ca. 1517) and had him transfer his caliphal title to the sultan.[10] The Ottoman sultan thus formally became the head of the Muslim community but, not being Arabs of the Prophet's Kureyish family, they never claimed to be the actual caliphs: their official title was *hilafet penahi*, or shelter of the caliphate. (This is probably why the Ottoman sultans seldom used their caliphal title until the second half of the nineteenth century, when, mainly under sultan Abdülhamid, the caliphate became a bastion against the threat of the West.) The caliph had the obligation to keep Mecca and Medina in proper condition and assure free access to all Muslims who wanted to make their annual pilgrimage—the *hac* or *umra*—to the Muslim holy lands.

The rise of Shiism as a state religion in Iran early in the sixteenth century gave the old ethnic relations between the Ottoman and Central Asian Turks a political twist. The early Islam of the Ottoman Turks was a "frontier religion" due to the dominant position of the mystic popular orders, whose language was mainly Turkish (Slavic in the Balkans) or Persian (in some quarters of Bukhara and Samarkand). This mystic, popular Islam, developed chiefly by Ahmet Yesevi (d. 1166) and his followers, resulted from incorporation of the native culture, including elements of shamanistic rituals, into the faith, although Turks remained faithful to the basic doctrine of Islam. It was this Turkified, liberal, and humanistic Islam which was brought into Anatolia by migrating Turkic tribes and was disseminated by such leading figures as Hacı Bektaş Veli, Sarı Saltuk, and Yunus Emre (whom UNESCO recognized as an important world figure). The *Saltukname* (the epic of Sarı Saltuk's exploits and the dissemination of Islam in the Balkans put into book form on the orders of Cem Sultan, the son of Mehmet II) describes Sarı Saltuk as a follower of Yesevi. Eventually Bahauddin Nakşbandi (1318-1389), linked to Yesevi, gave this Central Asian Islam a systematic, orthodox interpretation more suitable to urban areas than to the nomads among whom Yesevi mostly preached.

From the fourteenth century onwards hundreds and even thousands of Nakşbandi şeyhs preached in Anatolia and the Balkans and established their lodges (*tekke* or *zaviye*) as popular places of worship. In turn, many Turks went to the famous schools of Bukhara and Samarkand to study religion and also the natural sciences in which Central Asia excelled. The Muslim discoveries in philosophy, mathematics, and medicine attributed today to "Arabs" and "Persians" belong to the Central Asians schooled in the seminaries of the area such as Avicenna (Ibn Sina), al-Fārābī, and al-Bīrūnī. Kuşcu Ali, who established the Ottoman observatory, was a colleague and friend of Uluğ bey, the grandson of Timur lenk (Tamerlane). He was an astronomer and the ruler of Samarkand whose telescope and mathematical treatises can be seen in the museum established at his place of study.

The rise of Shiite Iran under shah İsmail (d. 1525) forced the Shaybanids—who had established their first Uzbek state under Muhammad Shayban—to seek Ottoman support. (The name Shayban is derived from Shiban, one of the descendants of Chingiz Khan's eldest son Jochi, and is indicative of a certain political imperial continuity in Central Asia.) The Kazakhs and the Uzbeks emerged as proto ethno-national groups after the Timurid empire collapsed following the death of Timur in 1405. Timur stressed the ethnic Turkic character of Central Asia and laid the foundations for the emergence of Chagatai, the Turkic *lingua franca* of the elites which gradually replaced Persian and survived in various forms until the twentieth century. Thus the Turkish-Persian confrontation which began on the linguistic-cultural level in the fifteenth century assumed a religious dimension in the sixteenth century. The Uzbek rulers (who ruled most of Central Asia), notably Abdullah II (de facto ruler after 1561) along with his uncle Pir Muhammad, sought Ottoman help against Iran, which they attacked repeatedly.

The Ottoman sultans relied heavily on the Uzbeks to keep the pressure on the Persian rulers and it was upon the Uzbek ruler's insistence that the Ottoman sultan launched an expedition into Russia in 1557-59 to open the roads of Astrakhan (conquered by Russia in 1556) to the passage of Central Asian pilgrims on their way to Mecca. Such Uzbek embassies to Istanbul, and vice-versa, continued throughout the centuries. As late as 1914 both Bukhara and Khiva, although they were forced to accept a Russian protectorate after the mid-1860s, still maintained diplomatic representatives in Istanbul; the şeyh of the Uzbek lodge in Istanbul was usually the representative of his country to the Porte. The Central Asians' diplomatic tradition was maintained even after they became "turkified" in the tradition of the republic. A relative of the last Uzbek şeyh was appointed the first ambassador of republican Turkey in Washington after Turkish-U.S. relations were established in 1930 and one of the Turkish ambassador's sons, Ahmet Ertegun, is a prominent Turkish-American figure.

The relations of the Ottoman Turks with Central Asia from roughly 1100 to 1917-18 were continuous, intense, and multifaceted. In fact, by the eighteenth and nineteenth centuries some Central Asian rulers asked the Ottoman sultan to legitimize their rule by confirming their appointment and some, such as Yakup bey (d. 1877) of Kashgar (now in Chinese Xinjiang), agreed to mint coins and cite in the *hutbe* (Friday sermon) the

Ottoman sultan's name as their superior. Today, as the historical relations between the Turks of Turkey and Central Asia are being revived, legendary traditional figures are being nationalized. Ahmet Yesevi has become a Kazakh national figure while the Uzbeks have appropriated Nakşbandi, largely because the tombs of these luminaries are located in their respective national territories. Yesevi is buried in the magnificent mausoleum built by Timur in Turkistan, Kazakhstan (now being repaired by Turkish architects with funding from Turkey) while Nakşbandi is buried in his native village near Bukhara, Uzbekistan. A Yesevi University for all Turks under the aegis of Kazakhstan was scheduled to open in Turkistan (the former Yesi, from whence Yesevi derived his name).

Extraordinary changes occurred in the cultural-religious premises that underlaid the confrontation between Turks and Europeans. Prior to 1515-41 the confrontation was not far outside the borders of the Balkans. When the scene of the struggle moved to central Europe and the western Mediterranean, however, new credence was given to the long-held papal view—expressed by Pius II, Leo X, and Pius V—that if the Turks conquered the Hungarians, then the Germans and Italians would be rapidly subdued and the Christian faith extinguished. Consequently the papacy aligned itself solidly with the Habsburgs who, in order to justify their already contested rule in western Europe and Spain, portrayed their struggle with the Turks as the fateful encounter of Christianity with Islam. The military encounter between the Ottomans and the Habsburgs acquired religious and cultural overtones reflected in the thousands of anti-Turkish books, pamphlets, plays, and paintings that flooded European book stalls.[11]

The struggle between the two ruling titans of Europe, Süleyman and Charles V, was accompanied and eventually superseded by the Reformation and the rise of France and England and their establishment of commercial-military relations with the Turks. Western writers have dismissed the contribution of the Turks to the making of a new Europe in the sixteenth century as inconsequential and self-interested. True, the Ottoman sultans supported—militarily, economically, and politically—the rise of France in order to counterbalance the Habsburgs but in the process they helped make the nation-state the basic form of political organization of the new Europe. Ultimately they themselves would accept the same form of organization.

The French-Turkish entente started under Francis I of France, who began his royal career as the champion of a crusade against the Turks but after losing the battle of Pavia in 1525 and being taken prisoner by Charles V sent his envoy Frangipani to Süleyman to ask for help. Eventually Turkish galleys travelled up the Rhone and Muslim soldiers from

Anatolia and the Balkans battled the Habsburgs to protect France's identity and independence. In 1536, the French were allowed to establish the first resident ambassadorship in Istanbul and were given extensive trading privileges, known as capitulations, and specific rights in the Christian holy places. Thus the French gained a solid foothold in the Middle East and maintained it until their final ejection from Syria and Lebanon in the period 1943-46.[12] France would constantly abuse the Turks' trust but the Turks proved unable to maintain a grudge or seek revenge against any of their enemies; in the early twentieth century nationalist writer Celal Nuri argued that Turks possessed no ability for national hatred, while the Balkan Christians based their national revival on religious hatred. (Another writer responded to Celal Nuri that noble characteristics, such as forgiving and forgetting past injustices, did not improve the Turks' image in the eyes of Europe).

In 1538 Francis I made peace with Charles V at Aigues-Mortes and promised to take part in the crusade against the Turks. However, the pressure put on the Habsburgs and the pope by the Turks gave the Protestants a respite and a certain freedom of action that aided their struggle. It also prompted Martin Luther to question the policies of the papacy. The papal effort to raise money to support the crusades against the Turks, which included Johann Tetzel's selling of indulgences, was a key factor in bringing Luther to issue the famous theses that condemned the war against the Turks as "impious resistance to the judgement of God."[13] Like Erasmus, Luther viewed the Turks as God's reminder to Europe to atone for its sins.

The role played by the Turks in relations between the "new" Europe, represented mainly by France and England, and the "old" Europe embodied in the Habsburgs and the papacy, combined with the wealth of their lands, produced some curiosity about their society and faith. Queen Elizabeth I and Süleyman the Magnificent discussed their faith, among other things, and Protestantism was likened to Islam.[14] Although the Protestants thought that the Turks' concept of faith resembled their own they were bewildered that the Turks persisted in following Islam, which in their view was "incomplete" and not "fully revealed." These talks between Elizabeth I and Süleyman culminated with the dispatching of William Harborne to Istanbul in 1578 (where he later became ambassador), the granting of trading privileges to the English such as those given the French and the Venetians, and the establishment of the Levant Company in 1581.[15] The Ottoman sultan gave the English economic aid in order to enable them to oppose the Habsburgs and to reinforce Protestantism against the papacy, thus creating a new Turkish-European relationship.

The letter from the Queen empowering the Levant Company to engage in trade expressed England's dual interest in "trade and merchandise and traffiques into lands...of the Great Turk, whereby there is good and apparent hope and likelihood both that many good offices may be done for the peace of Christendom...and also good and profitable vent and utterance may be had of the commodities of our Realme."[16] At the same time the English tried to bring the Turks into the war against Spain, hoping that the two would weaken each other so much that the true church and doctrine—that is, Anglicanism—could grow to such strength that it could suppress both of them.[17] Throughout the sixteenth and seventeenth centuries the Ottomans provided steady support for the Protestants: Calvinists were allowed to settle freely in Hungary and Transylvania.[18] This created good will towards Turks that still survives, even in the regional churches.

Along with their interest in trade within the Ottoman lands, England, France, Austria, and Venice developed a scholarly interest in Turkey. The Germans, despite the warnings of Luther, who forsook his earlier views and stated publicly that Turks and Catholics were the arch-enemies of Christendom and the flesh and spirit of the anti-Christ, were very curious about the Turks. They translated several Ottoman chronicles and dispatched Salmon Schweiggle from Tübingen to Vienna and then to Istanbul in 1575 to collect materials and information about them. The works of Richard Knolles and Ogier Ghiselin Busbecq were among the first serious writings about Turks.[19] None of these writers, mentally preconditioned as they were, liked the Turks. They were nonetheless objective and rational in describing Turkish qualities and weaknesses and suggested ways to correct the shortcomings of their own European compatriots with the ultimate purpose of defeating the Turks.[20]

In contrast to the continuous and growing European curiosity about Turks and their country the Turks made practically no move to know Europe or European society, despite several much touted exceptions such as Piri Reis' map of the Americas of 1513, probably bought from sailors in the Mediterranean. During this period the Mediterranean had become a sphere of intensive commercial and human interaction between Europeans and Turks, described by Fernand Braudel in his classic work on the reign of Phillip II.[21] Although disturbed by naval warfare—such as the inconsequential battle of Lepanto in 1571—this interaction continued well into the next centuries in the form of extensive commerce and personal relations. The first permanent Turkish embassy abroad, however, despite some short missions in the seventeenth century, was established in London only in 1793.[22]

In the sixteenth century the Turks, as described by Knolles with some timid admiration and considerable awe, were proud and sure of themselves and held the rest of the world in scorn, with a full persuasion in time to rule over all without limits or bounds. The negative image of the Turk in Europe which had arisen in the late fifteenth century had scarcely changed by the end of the seventeenth century, intensive commercial relations notwithstanding. As long as the Turks remained powerful the belief in the superiority of their system remained intact as did the arrogant pride of the sultan's court, which found Europe unworthy of much attention.

The treaty of Zsitva-Torok, signed with Austria in 1606, marked the end of the Ottoman military advance into Europe. There were a series of other Turkish conquests during the century—in the Caucasus, the Mediterranean (Crete), and Poland—but none of these was of major consequence. From the signing of the treaty in 1606 until the Küçük Kaynarca treaty in 1774 there was a balance between Europe and the Ottomans. The crushing Ottoman defeat at Vienna in 1683, despite its psychological impact, did not undermine Ottoman military might to the extent that is sometimes claimed and by 1739 the treaty of Belgrade restored Ottoman sovereignty over most of the Balkans, though not for long.

The greatest Ottoman weakness was not military capacity but rather social structure and political order. The price of maintaining the empire was a constant expansion of the statist economic system and the autocratic form of governance needed to run it. Individual freedom became more and more circumscribed. The civil or semi-civil institutions (such as guilds) were subverted by the state and only in the mystic religious brotherhood did some sense of private, inner freedom survive. Thus popular religion became the haven of freedom, although the state controlled most religious institutions through bureaucratization and manipulation.

The conflict with Russia brought Ottoman weaknesses to the surface and opened a new chapter in the Turks' relations with Europe. The eighteenth century also saw an intensification of commercial connections with Europe, especially an increased demand for agricultural commodities and other Ottoman products. The interaction between the Ottomans, both Muslim and Christian, and Europe was so intense as to induce the Ottoman sultan Ahmet III (1703-30) and his handpicked grand vizier, Nevşehirli İbrahim, to attempt to introduce a sort of state capitalism. The attempt was nipped in the bud by the urban revolution of 1730 (the first of its kind) but both Muslim and Christian individuals continued to expand a wide range of commercial relations with their European counterparts. The drive toward a commercialized agriculture intensified. A great variety of European goods, together with some influences in the fine arts, architecture, and sciences, began to enter the

Ottoman empire, notably in areas along the Mediterranean littoral. These cultural influences can be seen in the plans of buildings and even mosques, including the baroque style of the Nuru Osmaniye mosque in Istanbul, and palaces built by *ayans* (powerful local lords) in Anatolia, the Balkans, Syria, and Egypt.

Differences between Ottomans and Europeans

The treaty of Küçük Kaynarca of 1774 marked the full emergence of Russia as a world power and the rapid decline of Ottoman military power. This treaty, and those of Iaşi (1792) and Bucharest (1812), left the Ottoman lands along the northern Black Sea, including Crimea and its Muslim population, in the hands of Russia. The Ottoman trade monopoly in the Black Sea was broken and the czar received the right to make representation to the Porte on behalf of its Orthodox Christian subjects while Russia's Muslims were permitted to acknowledge the caliph as their religious head. The newly acquired rights gave both rulers the means to incite nationalist sentiments in their respective communities. Russia justified its drive into Ottoman lands as a move designed to liberate Orthodox Christians and used religion to incite resistance, thereby transforming faith into a foundation for the Balkan Slavs' nationalism. Orthodox Christianity had become a political ideology and overnight Russia had become its promoter and an immediate threat to Ottoman authority.

The emergence of Russia as a great power profoundly affected Turkish relations with Europe and placed England and France—and to a lesser extent the Habsburg empire—in the position of brokers between the sultan and the czar. Meanwhile Egypt became the scene of rivalry between France and England, and Ottoman power and prestige in the Middle East was further undermined. In 1798 Napoleon occupied Egypt, prompting the Turks to abandon the friendship with France that had helped them keep a check on the Russians and to conclude a *de facto* alliance with the British. Napoleon's armies were pushed out but Egypt became autonomous. In 1805 the rebel Turkish officer Mehmet Ali was recognized as viceroy, and he eventually obtained French support. England intervened on behalf of the Ottomans once again in the period 1839-41, driving the Russians out of the Bosphorus and restoring Ottoman sovereignty over Syria, Hicaz, and the rest of Arabia—which was occupied by Mehmet Ali's armies. In anticipation of this service London received the first of many economic privileges to be granted it by the Porte in 1838 (more were forthcoming in 1860-61) as well as a pledge that the archaic statist Ottoman economic and trade system would be liberalized. Finally, in 1840-43 Palmerston pledged to maintain the territorial integrity of the Ottoman state.

This was a fundamental foreign policy decision with far-reaching consequences for the Turks. It guaranteed the survival of the Ottoman empire but also indirectly assured the survival of the British empire and gained for England an extraordinary position of influence in Ottoman life. The Ottoman reform movement, started in 1839 in return for British help, produced fundamental changes in the Turks' culture and society.

The parameters of the Turks' new relations with Europe thus emerged early in the nineteenth century. Russia was an aggressor on the move and its aim was the Mediterranean sea. The Mediterranean was rapidly becoming the choicest market for the goods produced by England's industries as well as a strategic link to India that was coveted by both France and Russia. In 1840-42, guaranteeing the survival, integrity, and friendship of the Ottoman empire appeared to offer the British the best way to defend their interests. By this time the Turks and the British tacitly agreed that the traditional Ottoman forms of government, institutions, and socio-economic structure were dysfunctional and inadequate to meet the Russian threat. The challenge of reform was, however, con-considerable. No country in the Muslim world had experienced the industrial revolution or established a new political relationship between the state and its population in the context of the nation-state as had western Europe. Moreover the bureaucracy, the backbone of the classical Ottoman state, had developed a pragmatic, rational attitude towards the affairs of society and appeared ready to assure its survival and safeguard its position and status regardless of the cultural costs.

The sultan envisaged the state as the instrument of change but the state itself required change, particularly in its relation with the individual. The Ottoman governing elite had recognized this need for change as early as the 1780s and sultan Selim III (1789-1807), who spoke French and engaged in correspondence with the French king, was inclined to adopt France as a model, as demonstrated in his drive to centralize the government and to create a modern army under the command of French officers. However, with the French invasion of Egypt and the defeat of Napoleon, Turco-French relations cooled and England became the main influence on the Ottoman reform movement, as both promoter and critic. Indeed, the negative verdict of England about the success and sincerity of the Ottoman reforms would be accepted by the rest of Europe, often at face value, and was significant in conditioning attitudes and policies towards the Turks. Soon the historical image of the enemy of Christendom was revived and supplemented with a new view of the Turks as unwilling and unable to understand and absorb European civilization. Consequently, Europe wholeheartedly embraced czar Nicholas I's (1825-

55) characterization of the Ottoman empire as the "sick man of Europe."[23] Soon this characterization was wholeheartedly adopted by the European media. Although it has been proven wrong in almost every way it is still influential today.

Each major European country expected the Turks to undertake reforms and create a government and society much like its own. Prince Clemens Metternich advised the Ottomans not to follow the European—that is, English and French—model but to stick to their own traditions, probably in order to safeguard the multi-ethnic character of his own state. In the end both England and France became the models for the reforms, although they were in many ways unsuitable. Both were nation-states, while the Ottoman empire was a corporatist structure composed of numerous ethnic-religious communities linked to the sultan. There was no Ottoman nation with an identity of its own although the structure and identity of each major ethno-religious group could potentially enable it to become a nation. Furthermore, the two model states were diametrically opposed to the Ottomans in basic political philosophy. England viewed the nation-state as an association of free individuals imbued with civic nationalism and regarded each individual as possessed of dignity and worthy of respect—especially if they were English and belonged to the proper social set, reinforced by Anglicanism. In France the individual was liberated from the dual prison of church and state by a myth of the nation with a will of its own and by the transference of authority from the king to the state.[24] Jean Jacques Rousseau drew a picture of the nation resting upon free will with the national will depicted as a collective force to which the individual surrendered voluntarily (Atatürk had read Rousseau, and in a speech urged intellectuals to read and understand why the French philosopher had invented the fiction of "national will.") The French remained attached to the collectivity, displayed ethnic nationalism, and had a propensity for authoritarianism as well as for sharp rationalization and formal logic.

Whatever their differences, both the English and French nation-states were alike in putting the individual at the center of their political system whereas in the traditional Ottoman system the situation was dichotomous. The individual enjoyed unlimited physical and ethnic-religious freedom within the confines of his community but had no autonomy, freedom, or rights vis-a-vis the political system, although there were some limitations on the ruler's authority stemming from Islam. The common person in the traditional Ottoman community had a deeply imbedded respect for tradition, precedent, and social ranking and a pragmatic, practical outlook similar to the British. The ruling elites, on the other hand, were deeply committed to the maintenance of collectivity and faith under state supervision and thus resembled the French. The community obeyed and respected the elites to the extent that they served and maintained the faith—the famous *din-u devlet*, the unity of faith and religion.

The Ottoman modernizers deprived the state of its traditional legitimacy but retained and exercised absolute authority in the name of some haphazardly conceived idea of modernization which became in practice a form of vulgar materialism. The Turkish "modernists" did not understand that Europe continued to dislike them primarily because under their glittering costumes made in Paris and their accentless mastery of European languages they continued to be the same despots as the traditional predecessors whom they had dethroned. They saw themselves as the absolute representatives of the nation in much the same way that the old sultans saw themselves as the absolute representative of the community. They continued to act as the masters of one uniform, monolithic collectivity rather than as the representatives and spokespersons of a nation made up of free individuals. The modernizers, most of whom were bureaucrats, could not understand that blind obedience to their authority exercised on behalf of an authoritarian state had less value than the dissent of a truly free individual, regardless of that individual's faith.

The dichotomy between state and society, which existed in embryo throughout the Muslim world, developed into a major rift in the Ottoman empire because of the reforms. The reforms came to be viewed by a large group of Muslims as being destructive of faith, thus placing the state in the awkward position of betraying its mission and undermining its legacy as the custodian of Islam. The Ottoman state had always acted to defend its worldly interests with relative immunity from criticism thanks to its control of the legitimizing mechanism—that is, the office of the Şeyhulislam (created in the sixteenth century and appended to the bureaucracy). However, the Islamic revivalist movements strengthened the sense of individuality and encouraged freedom of individual inquiry in the spirit of *ictihat*, which had been the intellectual backbone of Islam in its golden age and appeared to challenge the state's supremacy. Paradoxically, the European brand of individualism that was making its way into Ottoman thought provided a considerable philosophical boost to revivalist thought despite the fact that Europe and Islam appeared to be political enemies. The edict of Tanzimat of 1839, for example, was an instrument that catered to the individual, offering guarantees of life, property, and equality regardless of faith and thus limiting the sultan's absolute authority. It clearly bore the imprint of Britain.

The Tanzimat edict was drafted and publicly read, with the consent of the ruling sultan Abdülmecid, by Mustafa Reşit Paşa, who had just returned from his post as ambassador to London. Reşit had become convinced that the Ottoman state could not survive without drastic reforms and without the backing of a strong European power, preferably England. He appeared to have persuaded the new eighteen-year-old sultan Abdülmecid (1839-61) of the wisdom of his reformist views which were shared by a westernist group in the foreign ministry. Stratford Canning (Stratford de Redcliffe), who served on several occasions as the British ambassador to the Porte during the period 1825-58 and who was exceptionally knowledgeable about Ottoman society, supported Reşit and eventually gained the friendship of the sultan and exerted a profound influence on him. (The ruler fondly called him *büyükelçi*, "great ambassador," and granted him unlimited access to his palace.) It was Canning who, anxious to strengthen the Ottoman state against Russia, persuaded the Porte to initiate the reforms by making the individual and individual freedom the centerpiece of change. He presented concrete proposals for creating "equality" among the sultan's subjects regardless of religious differences.[25] The sultan referred the equality issue to a high committee composed of religious men who advised against acceptance on the grounds that it would undermine the essence of the Ottoman empire—separation of faiths and communal cultural-religious autonomy. Canning, a good Protestant, held the view that the Ottoman state was stagnant because Islam had a strong hold on the government and that Islam, being a backward (and even false) religion, prevented progress in society and government. His proposed remedy was to free government from the hold of Islam and he elaborated on his ideas in talks with Ottoman officials at his home.[26] The refusal of the *ulema* to support his proposals convinced Canning that Islam was the cause of Ottoman decline. Thanks to the Crimean War of 1853-56 Canning's point of view eventually prevailed.

The Crimean War was preceded by the revolutions of 1848 in central Europe, and thousands of Hungarian and Polish revolutionaries under Lájos Kossuth, pursued by Austrian and Russian forces, took refuge in Ottoman lands. Sultan Abdülmecid (1839-61), backed by England, refused to surrender the revolutionaries to Austria despite threats of war. This caused the sultan and Turks in general to be portrayed by the European press as champions of freedom and civilization. This new, positive image of the Turks resulted from their courage in defying powers that were then enemies of England and France; in other circumstances this "courage" was considered "intransigence." The good impression was soon to fade but not before Europe and the Turks, for the first time in their history, entered into an alliance against Russia.

The Crimean alliance, which brought together Muslim Turks, Catholic French and Sardinians, and the Protestant British, inflicted a crushing defeat on Orthodox Christian Russia. Muslims all over the world, and especially in the Middle East (there were many Arab voluntary units in the Ottoman army) and India, became convinced that Europe headed by England was indeed a friend of Islam. Consequently the level of mistrust towards Europe dropped considerably. After 1856 European influence on the Ottoman state, which had begun as a trickle, became a torrent. Ambassador Canning, who disliked the Russians as much as Islam, had gone back to England in 1852. However, alarmed by the Menshikov Mission (A. S. Menshikov was a Russian prince sent to Istanbul to reaffirm formal recognition for the czar as protector of all Orthodox Christians), he returned to Istanbul in April 1853 and played a leading part in frustrating Russia's demands and launching the war. When the allies won the war Russia was forced to retreat—temporarily—from the Black Sea and the Romanian principalities. The Turks' part in this defeat—the memory of which continues to hurt Russian pride—has never been forgotten or forgiven. Nor did the Russians forget the spectacle of Christian Europe—Catholics and Protestants alike—allied with the "infidel" Turks against Orthodox Christian Russia, a fact which also bothered many religious English people.

The Ottoman state was a signatory of the Paris treaty and the Reform Edict of 1856, eulogized as a major act of reform. The edict had been prepared without Ottoman participation by England, France, and, partly, Austria as an intrinsic part of the peace arrangements in the treaty of Paris and the sultan had to accept it wholesale without even a chance to propose amendments.[27] In return for accepting it the Ottoman empire, after 500 years of existence as a political and religious outcast despite its physical presence in Europe, was finally accepted—unwillingly, and simply to prevent its fall to the Russians—as a partner by the "civilized" nations of Europe, made subject to international law, and expected to live up to European standards. The first and most important test of the Turks' compatibility with European civilization was the enforcement of the Reform Edict which, if shorn of a few general provisions, dealt almost entirely with the status of the Christians in the Ottoman empire. The edict sought to deprive Russia of a pretext on which to intervene in Ottoman affairs and in practice it gave the Orthodox Christians in the empire a truly privileged status and turned the European powers into their patrons, a position Russia had aspired to for a century. England had already begun opening consulates in 1843 and now had about two dozen established in the Ottoman areas inhabited by Christians and at least five offices, staffed by military officers, in the areas inhabited by Armenians. The consulates became in due time a sort of parallel government, coexisting with Ottoman administrative offices and often superseding them. The edict also aimed at creating equality between individual Muslims in a system that was built on a corporatist basis and was alien to the individualistic mode of political organization of the West.

Included in the edict were all the provisions that had been rejected by the *ulema* council. Its wholesale adoption created sharp opposition to the sultan and his advisors, who were bitterly accused of having acted under European guidance and undermining the essence of the state—*"devletin esasına halel geldi."* The objections came from both religious conservatives and progressive-minded intellectuals and led to the first organized opposition to the sultan—a secret revolutionary society—in 1859.

Although not exclusively responsible, the edict gave momentum to a profound socio-economic development which had begun after the economic liberalization in 1838 and was best represented by the Land Code of 1858. The code played a seminal role in expediting the transition of the Ottoman economic system to a capitalist economy but it also aggravated the Christian-Muslim division of the population. The Land Code sought to increase agricultural production by regularizing the chaotic situation of land ownership. Most of the arable lands in Anatolia and Rumeli were state lands and had been used for centuries as the economic basis of the military establishment and the provincial bureaucracy. Above all, they gave the government leverage for its social and political control over society. The trend toward commercialization of agriculture in a market economy, which grew consistently after 1774, led to the constant piecemeal appropriation of state lands by individuals. This did not result in the emergence of a truly feudal land system, although such a development was incipient at the end of the eighteenth century when the breakdown of the central authority led to the sudden emergence of the free agrarian private sector. Unable to reestablish its previous control over the land after 1840, the government began accepting as *de jure* owners those in possession of the land if they could produce concrete proof that their possession derived from legitimate authority. Only very flimsy evidence was rejected, whereupon the land reverted to government ownership. The Land Code of 1858 played a major role in expanding the scope of private ownership and in regularizing land relations and it indirectly stimulated the growth of an agrarian middle class.

The production end of the commercial agriculture sector—including land ownership—was dominated by Muslims, while the marketing end, which included export-import operations and offered possibilities for huge profits, was dominated by Christians. A commercial bourgeoisie rapidly arose and played a vital role in the distribution of European goods and in fostering French and British influence, including the dissemination of European dress and leisure activities.[28] The edict of 1856 sharpened the socio-economic differentiation between Muslims and Christians which came to a head in the Tuna province after its selection in the 1860s as a pilot area for reforms. The Porte appointed its most capable administrator—Mithat Paşa—as governor of the province and a huge investment reinvigorated it and enabled the Bulgarians, who were less than 50 percent of its population but to whom the government had given preference in order to show its impartiality, to emerge as a powerful group.

The social tensions inherent in such a situation soon acquired an ethno-religious and political dimension, already evident in the uprisings of the 1800s. These were not bonafide "national" uprisings but, rather, social upheavals that immediately took on political-national overtones. Nationalism proved to be an anathema to the multi-ethnic, multi-religious Ottoman empire. The Greek uprising of 1821 had the effect of ending what may be called a *de facto* Greek-Turkish coalition that began in 1453. With the rise of ethnic nationalism in the Ottoman empire—preceded by the neo-Byzantianism of the Phanariotes (1760-1821)— the Christians of the Ottoman Empire began to view Europe as a civilization that they could regard as their "own" because it was Christian; but when reminded that theirs was an often despised brand of Christianity they would invoke the universal, secular, and humanist dimensions of European civilization. The Serbian revolt in 1804 had little philosophical impact on the Ottomans but the Greek uprising of 1821 had the support of Britain. This was a warning that the old religious identity, which had been the backbone of the traditional system, was being replaced by a national identity with all that this entailed.

The Muslim popular reaction against the edict and England started soon after 1858 and became increasingly vehement as the Christian Orthodox bourgeoisie grew in size and wealth and its educated offspring became the leaders of ethnic nationalist movements. The Muslim's objections to the edict grew as did the demands of the Christians for additional rights. With the active support of Austria and Russia the situation degenerated into open revolt, first in Bosnia and Herzegovina in 1875 (this revolt was fueled by legitimate social grievances) and then in Bulgaria in 1876. These revolts, especially the one in Bulgaria, where the leaders had been educated in Russia, acquired from the very start anti-Islamic, anti-Turkish overtones. By this time the terms "Muslim" and "Turk" had become synonymous in the Balkans (as they are today). The Christian massacre of 300 Turkish villagers in Batak at the beginning of the Bulgarian uprising produced a violent reaction on the part of the local irregular Ottoman troops, who killed 2,100 innocent Bulgarians. Overnight Batak became famous. It was subject to numerous visits by missionaries (E. Schuyler, among others) and came to be cited as proof that Turks were unable to come to terms with western civilization and its corresponding values and standards.[29] The rapidly growing European dissatisfaction with the Turks intensified after the government of

Mahmud Nedim Paşa, under advice from Russian ambassador Nikolai Pavlovich Ignat'ev, announced a 50 percent reduction in interest paid to European (mostly British) holders of Ottoman bonds. The storm of indignation climaxed in William Ewart Gladstone's famous pamphlet, "Bulgarian Horrors and the Question of the East," in which he accused the Turks of killing 60,000 Bulgarians. The pamphlet reportedly sold 50,000 copies in a few days.

All of this gave an aura of legitimacy to demands for autonomy for the Balkan Christians. Lord Salisbury wrote Prime Minister Benjamin Disraeli:

> it is clear that the traditional Palmerstonian policy is at an end. We have not the power, even if we were to wish, to give back any of the revolted districts to the discretionary government of the Porte....The opportunity should...be taken to exact some security for the good government of the Christians throughout the Turkish Empire. The Government of 1856 was satisfied with promises....We must have something more than promises.[30]

The Constantinople conference, which met in December 1876, was called to find a solution to the Balkan crisis—that is to provide autonomy to the Christians.[31] The Ottoman nationalists, including the reformist Mithat Paşa, saw the conference as an attempt to dismember the Ottoman state and as a symbol of the Christians' victory over the Turks, as indicated by the name and place of the meeting. In response, the Ottoman nationalists produced the constitution of 1876, which assured the non-Muslims representation in the administration of the country and would render autonomy unnecessary. The constitution and the two parliaments which convened subsequently, in 1877 and 1878, provided the new middle classes with direct access to power and the opportunity to criticize the bureaucracy (and, indirectly, the sultan) and politically mobilized the population. It was probably the first and most important act of democratization and political westernization in the history of the Muslim world; yet the conference participants and the western press treated the constitution as a trick which was intended to derail the conference and deceive Europe.

The conference disbanded without achieving its goal but left the Ottoman government isolated and stigmatized by the accusation that it was determined to keep the Christians enslaved and oppressed forever. England realized the extremely dangerous position of the Ottoman government and made a last-minute attempt to amend the conference proposals in favor of the Porte but the nationalists in the Ottoman cabinet rejected the compromise in the belief that they had won and had enough military capability to defeat the Russians if the czar decided to launch a war. Russia promptly took advantage of the extreme isolation of the Ottoman government and attacked and defeated the Turkish troops. England declared her "neutrality" and refused even to sell weapons to the Ottoman government. However, faced with the enormity of the Russian victory, for which the English government had possibly prepared the ground, London intervened again and pushed Russia to agree to revise the San Stefano treaty, a treaty which made Russia the most influential power in the Balkans due to its overwhelming influence over Bulgaria. The treaty of Berlin of 1878, drawn up without the Ottoman delegation's participation as negotiators, allowed the sultan to preserve Macedonia and Thrace but awarded independence to Serbia, Romania, and Montenegro and gave autonomy to Bulgaria; Bosnia-Herzegovina was occupied by Austria.[32] For all practical purposes the Ottoman presence in the Balkans was eliminated and the empire reduced to the status of a secondary Middle East state. During the war, according to British consular reports, about 300,000 Muslims in the Balkans, mostly Turks, were killed and one million uprooted and forced to emigrate. Great Britain, having played the major role in both the dismemberment of the Ottoman empire and in preventing it from collapsing entirely at the hands of Russia, took Cyprus as a sort of payment, promising to defend the sultan against further Russian advances.

Behind the negative British attitude towards Turkey that commenced in the late 1860s were a number of international and domestic events not necessarily connected with each other. The rise of Germany and its defeat of France in 1870 compelled England to come closer to Russia so as to counterbalance Otto von Bismarck and his powerful army; the defeat also weakened the anti-Russian coalition led by France and worsened the strategic position of the Ottoman empire. In 1870 Russia announced that it would militarize the Black Sea, an open violation of the Paris treaty. This action, along with several other violations—including the occupation of eastern Rumeli by Bulgaria in 1885 despite the Berlin treaty provisions meant to safeguard Ottoman rights—met with no opposition by England.

On the domestic front, the question of England's relations with the Ottoman state were thrown into the political arena. General suffrage, increasing power of the press, and other such developments gave the English commoners new political weight and made them subject to the politicians' courtship. Gladstone, of the Liberal Party, wrote his famous anti-Turkish pamphlet of 1876 not out of moral indignation at the killing of the Bulgarian civilians but because the event provided him with an excellent opportunity to question the commitment of prime minister Disraeli, the Conservative Party leader, to Christian causes. Indeed, Gladstone eventually accused Disraeli, a converted Jew, of remaining silent on the fate of the Balkan Christians because of his sympathy for the Turks. The subsequent British national election of 1880 was fought mainly on the issues of British foreign policy towards the Ottoman empire and Gladstone won easily on an anti-Turkish, anti-Muslim platform.[33]

Gladstone thus became prime minister and quickly recalled Henry Layard, the British ambassador in Istanbul, who believed in maintaining the territorial integrity of the Ottoman state and who had very positive views about the Turks' prospects for and dedication to modernization and progress. The new ambassador, George Goschen, a rather abrupt person (he used the British navy to force the sultan to cede Dulcingo to Montenegro) acted under strict instructions from London to enforce immediately, among others, Article 61 of the Berlin Treaty which charged the Ottoman government with carrying out reforms in east Anatolia under British supervision.

The new sultan, Abdülhamid (1876-1909), believed that Gladstone's purpose was to set up an independent Armenia in eastern Anatolia and he did his best to frustrate the British in their pursuit of this goal. The Turkish relations with England that started on an auspicious note in 1839 thus came to an unhappy end by 1880. In place of the Palmerstonian doctrine of Ottoman integrity, England adopted the new view that the Turkish empire was doomed to disintegrate and England should oversee and try to control the collapse in such a way as to secure the best morsels of territory. The Foreign Office was prepared to let Russia take over the Turkish ports of Trabzon and fast-developing Samsun, for the czar would stimulate trade with England as he did in Crimea and along the Black Sea littoral where Odessa became the leading port. Sultan Abdülhamid immediately recognized the change in British policy and tried to pressure London to revert to the Palmerstonian policy, knowing all too well that the survival of the Ottoman empire was dependent on England. He also felt that in the long run the survival of the British empire, at least its Middle Eastern components, was tied to the continuation of the Ottoman state. Abdülhamid used an Islamic policy to put pressure on England to revert to the Palmerstonian policy, only to alienate it even further. Caught in its own imperialist ideology, Britain ignored the essential fact that special structural features made empires dependent on each other for survival. England dismembered the Ottoman empire along with France and took possession of its Arab provinces only to be dismally forced out of the Middle East two decades later by Gamal Abdel Nasser of Egypt and the Hashemites of Jordan, whose patriarch, Şerif Hussein, London had used effectively against the Turks in 1916.

The change in England's foreign policy towards the Ottomans occurred without much regard for the internal intellectual transformation of the Empire that England, paradoxically enough, had helped to accelerate and direct. Indeed, during the period of Tanzimat from 1839 to 1878 Turkish society was deeply involved in a multi-sided, forward-oriented change that made a return to the past impossible. "Ottomanism," a European-type bureaucratic centralization and its accompanying policies centered around common citizenship, was unsuccessful in keeping the Christians in the fold of the empire but succeeded in undermining the old communal system and the religious identities it nurtured. Ottomanism helped to create a degree of homogeneity and an awareness among individuals about their social, ethnic, and cultural identities. In effect it instituted a new type of political culture and was transforming the Muslims into a sort of proto-nation under the label of Islam—an Ottoman-Muslim nation in which the non-Muslims were no longer viewed as members of autonomous religious communities but as individuals belonging to minority groups whose rights and freedoms were determined by a worldly government rather than a state asserting divine legitimacy. Europe had forced the Turks to abandon their own Islamic frame of reference for dealing with and assuring the unlimited freedom of culture and religion in favor of European secular formulas that depended on elected governments.

Sultan Abdülhamid and
Islamism as an Ideology of Self Defense

The domestic and foreign policies of the reign of Abdülhamid II (1878-1909) have left a permanent mark on Turkish society and the Muslim world as a whole. It is essential to note that his policies were determined almost entirely by his perception of the European designs and plans to divide his realm and by his relentless attempts to oppose those plans and assure the survival of his state. Abdülhamid came to the throne amidst grave internal turmoil. Mithat Paşa and his followers, who had forced Abdülaziz from the throne, eventually forced Abdülhamid to promulgate a constitution in 1878 but Abdülhamid soon ousted and exiled Mithat Paşa and then suspended the constitution and parliament. He centralized all government authority in the hands of a small staff and used it to rule the country from his Yıldız palace. He has been labelled an autocratic dictator, "red sultan," and reactionary bigot by his numerous Turkish and European critics. This image of the sultan has persisted to our day despite attempts by some western scholars, such as Stanford Shaw, to point to Abdülhamid's extraordinary modernist achievements. Today he is viewed as a towering Muslim leader by a growing number of Islamist defenders in Turkey and abroad.

Abdülhamid had an extraordinarily sharp intelligence, an enormous capacity for work, and a born instinct for politics; he was also suspicious, secretive, and ruthless in dealing with his adversaries. He was a devout, sincere, practicing Muslim and believed that Islam was a forward looking religion compatible with science, technology, and progress. As an individual in his private business, however, he preferred to work with Christians (his personal doctor and banker were Greeks). He admired the Jews for their intelligence and perseverance—Arminius Vambery was his friend—but not Zionism.

His state policies were oriented toward the Muslims because, as he explained in his memoirs, in the new order of things—that is, in a state based upon the individual—the government must abide by the cultural tendencies of the majority of its subjects. The Ottoman state being made up mostly of Muslims, its government should abide by Islam, very much as the French government abided by the Catholic culture.[34] The despot thus developed individualistic views of society much in the way that his arch opponents, including the Young Turks and Atatürk, used authoritarianism in the mistaken belief that it was the only way to build a modern society and encourage emancipation.

During the initial years of his reign the empire suffered a crushing defeat in the war of 1877-78 (he wanted to avoid war with Russia but Mithat Paşa prevailed) and lost its best provinces and much of the army. He inherited a heavy foreign debt and in 1882 had to accept the authority of the Foreign Debt Administration set up by European debtor countries to collect their loans.[35] The population of the empire, meanwhile, following the loss of the Balkan provinces, consisted predominantly of Muslims whose ethnic and linguistic differences had long been superseded by their common Islamic faith and Ottoman culture. The idea of a nation-state had been formalized in the Berlin Treaty and applied rather arbitrarily to the heterogeneous Balkan society. It was obvious that if the Muslims in the Ottoman empire, especially the Arabs, adopted ethnic-linguistic identity as a principle of political organization the disintegration of the Ottoman state was inevitable.

Moreover, the sultan was well aware that the Muslims abroad, notably in India, had developed a keen sense of solidarity with their coreligionists in the Ottoman empire. Indeed the murder and ousting of millions of Muslims from their ancestral homes in the Balkans in the 1877-78 war outraged the Indian Muslims to the extent that they petitioned Queen Victoria to stop the carnage and also sent money, mobile hospitals, and even volunteers to support the Turkish effort. As early as the 1850s Muslim rulers on the periphery of the Islamic world—such as Yakup bey of Kashgar and the sultans of Ache in Sumatra and the Comoro Island in the Indian Ocean—asked the Ottoman sultan in his role as caliph to defend them against European occupation, promising in return political allegiance and unity with the Ottoman empire.

The same threat of foreign occupation and fear of loss of cultural identity generated at least twenty four militant Muslim revivalist movements in the nineteenth century in areas stretching from India (Syed Ahmet Barelvi) to Caucasia (şeyh Shamil) to Africa (Muhammad al-Sanusi). These revivalist movements also represented the search of the Muslim masses for ways to come to terms with the profound changes taking place in the socio-economic structure of the Muslim societies, while still remaining faithful to the Koran and the Prophet's Sunna. The English had become aware of the potential threat of these movements: they battled Barelvi's followers in India from 1825-35 and beyond and temporarily lost control of India during the Sepoy revolt in 1857. At that time they asked sultan Abdülmecid, as caliph, to counsel the rebels to cease their attacks on the British; the sultan obliged but met with adverse reaction from the Muslim leaders.

Sultan Abdülhamid's Islamist policy, initiated after 1878, must be analyzed within this framework. His primary aim was to maintain the integrity and independence of the Ottoman empire by creating cohesion and solidarity among his Muslim subjects, who formed about 80 percent of the population. Consequently he stressed the importance of Islam not only as a religion but also as a system of social beliefs, mode of life, and family organization shared by all Muslims. He promoted Islam not simply as a faith but as an ideology of political unity. His central idea, which was also that of the popular revivalist movements and of the Nakşbandis, the ideological spokespeople of the new Muslim middle classes, was sincere devotion to the *iman*—the faith. Abdülhamid emphasized this idea by a strict observance of Islamic customs and rituals. He, like many of his advisors, was keenly aware that Muslims at home and overseas were increasingly looking towards the caliphate as a central Muslim institution which could mobilize resistance to foreign occupation and help maintain their Muslim way of life.

The question was not one of freedom of religion. Actually, the English in India and, less so, the French in Africa had recognized Islam as a faith and allowed the Muslims to practice their rites. The Muslims of Calcutta declared India under the British to be *dar ul-Islam*—Muslim land—and the Muslims could accept British authority as long as the Raj did not prevent Islamic worship. But the goal of most Muslims was not just to obtain freedom to practice their own faith in their own land but to create an integral Muslim way of life, even though the economic and social institutions that had supported such a life in the past, such as the autonomous *vakıf* and the *imaret*, had been undermined by the global capitalist system.

Sultan Abdülhamid turned the caliphate into a centralized and universal Muslim institution with himself as the spokesman for the religious rights of the Muslims of the entire world. Once more the Turks asserted their role as the defenders of Sunni-Orthodox Islam but did not leave the caliphate to others (as in 1051) or give it a relatively neutral status (as in post 1517-20) but, rather, revitalized and politicized it in the role of representative for the entire Muslim community. The Turks were considered a regional Muslim power—the Moguls of India and Iran being others—until the nineteenth century when they became a universal Muslim state. Abdülhamid turned the caliphate into a powerful, universal Muslim institution and used it as a means to strengthen internal unity and forestall the emergence of ethnic nationalism among Muslims and to maintain the Turk's international position. He specifically dreaded a possible uprising of Kurdish nationalism based on a European definition of ethnicity.

Abdülhamid's Islamism was labelled "Pan-Islamism" by Europe and defined as a movement aimed at uniting all the Muslims in the world in a single body and at declaring *jihad* (holy war) against the West. Actually, Abdülhamid was too intelligent and sophisticated even to consider unleashing a religious war against Europe. Aside from the unlikeliness of success, Abdülhamid knew that such an action would make him an international outcast and deprive him of the protection of Europe against Russia. Thus it is easy to understand why he ignored all calls for Islamic action and refused to establish a formal Muslim union (*Ittihad-ı Islam*) or use the Ottoman diplomatic offices as outlets for propaganda and subversion. However, he did not hesitate to use these offices to collect information about overseas Muslims, to convey his personal concern about their freedom to practice the faith, and to make representations on their behalf to the proper European governments. Abdülhamid made it clear that in making such representations he was acting as caliph—that is, as the religious spokesman of the Muslims in the world—but not as their political leader, knowing full well that such representation won him political credit among Muslims. Gladstone had found his match in the ruler of an empire that every European leader expected to expire in just a few years.

Abdülhamid's ultimate purpose in enhancing the visibility and influence of the caliphate among the world's Muslims was to make the Europeans aware that a call to *jihad*, if he were forced to issue it, could pose a deadly threat to the British, French, and Russian authorities in the Muslim lands they had conquered. He did not try to incite rebellion but rather used the threat of *jihad* to put pressure on these countries not to usurp additional Ottoman territory nor interfere in the empire's domestic affairs. The sultan waged a psychological war in the awareness that the threat of *jihad* was much more effective than its activization. In large measure, Abdülhamid's so-called pan-Islamic policy developed as a reaction to the French occupation of Tunisia in 1881 and the British invasion of Egypt in 1882.

The sultan believed that England and France were ready to solve the Eastern Question once and for all by dividing the Ottoman lands among themselves, as they in fact did after World War I. At the same time, Abdülhamid still believed that England had too many interests in common with the Ottoman empire to wish for its immediate disintegration. He would thus play for time while seeking to strengthen the empire from inside. He even tried to persuade England that a strong caliphate could help the British cause. Indeed, in 1878 the viceroy of India and the British ambassador in Istanbul persuaded Abdülhamid (or they were persuaded by the sultan) that a high level embassy should be sent by the caliphate to amir Sher Ali in Afghanistan to induce him to accept British protection. The mission was unsuccessful, the amir asserting to the Ottoman envoy, Ahmet Hulusi effendi, that the English, not the Russians, were his main enemies. But the sultan continued to hope to induce Great Britain to return to its Palmerstonian policy; he clung to this hope until 1889, when Gladstone firmly dashed it. He did not hesitate to use his caliphal powers to reward his western friends—in this case the Americans, whom he perceived as having a more balanced view on religion, including Islam.

Gladstone and the French initially took the sultan's threats of Islamic *jihad* seriously and launched a virulent counterattack against him, the caliphate, and Islam that lasted well into the twentieth century. The English first challenged the legitimacy of Abdülhamid's claim to the caliphate and sought to establish an Arab caliph (they ultimately succeeded in doing so; they installed the Şerif of Mecca, Huseyin, as caliph for a short time in 1924). They also tried to undermine the caliph's influence in Africa and among Russia's Muslims. The French had begun to develop suspicions about the caliphate's threat to their rule over North African Muslims well before Abdülhamid's time. As early as 1872 they accused Istanbul of having aided the Algerian revolt of 1871—though the Bishop of Algiers had in fact engaged in a campaign of conversion. In 1881 they charged Istanbul (and they were partly right in this) with inciting the tribespeople of south Tunisia to migrate to Tripolitania and engage in guerrilla warfare against France. England regarded Colonel Urabi's revolt in Egypt in 1881 and the Mahdi's uprising of the same year in the Sudan to be a result of Istanbul's meddling, although sultan Abdülhamid disliked both militants. He had a profound antipathy towards revolutionaries regardless of their faith and devotion to Islamic causes.

Nonetheless the sultan was blamed for any unrest anywhere in the Muslim world aimed at Europeans. Russia did its best to perpetuate the image of the sultan as an inveterate enemy of Europe and its civilization and was exceptionally suspicious that the rise of nationalism among its Muslim subjects was instigated by Istanbul. Consequently, the European press forgot the Turks' past alliances with the West and began attacking the caliph, Islam, and the Turks as permanent enemies of the West and civilization. The old historical image of the terrible Turk was revived and enhanced by additional negative features. Some English, regretting their alliance with the Turks in 1853, began to advocate ousting the Turks from Europe, a view expressed publicly by David Lloyd George at the time of the First World War.

By 1890 many French and English (including Lord Curzon) came to regard Abdülhamid's Pan-Islamism more as a political scarecrow than a real threat, and some even began to consider Abdülhamid and the caliphate as a useful bulwark against the new militant, anti-colonialist, nationalist Muslim movements rising among the Muslim masses. The American ambassador persuaded Abdülhamid to send word through the Mecca pilgrims to the revolutionaries in the Philippines, telling them not to fight the Americans since these latter were opposing the Spanish rather than Islam. An American general subsequently expressed the view that the sultan's intervention in the Philippines saved the lives of 20,000 U.S. soldiers. Lieutenant Colonal John P. Finley, who for ten years had been the United States' governor of the district of Zamboanga Province in the Philippines, wrote:

> At the beginning of the war with Spain the United States Government was not aware of the existence of any Mohammedans in the Philippines. When this fact was discovered and communicated to our ambassador in Turkey, Oscar S. Straus, of New York, he at once saw the possibilities which lay before us of a holy war....he sought and gained an audience with the Sultan, Abdul Hamid, and requested him as Caliph of the Moslem religion to act in behalf of the followers of Islam in the Philippines....A telegram to Mecca elicited the fact that they not only visited Mecca in considerable numbers, but that at that very time there were Moros from Sulu in the Sacred City....The Sultan as Caliph caused a message to be sent to the Mohammedans of the Philippine Islands forbidding them to enter into any hostilities against the Americans, inasmuch as no interference with their religion would be allowed under American rule.
>
> President McKinley sent a personal letter of thanks to Mr. Straus for the excellent work he had done, and said its

accomplishment had saved the United States at least twenty
thousand troops in the field. If the reader will pause to consider
what this means in men and also the millions in money, he will
appreciate this wonderful piece of diplomacy in averting a holy
war.[36]

It was too late, however, for the caliphate to clamp down on the
militants. By 1900 Abdülhamid's brand of religious Islamism was being
overtaken by a new secular Islamic nationalism where religion became
just one source of cultural identity, though a major one—a militant
nationalism aimed at liberating the Muslims from foreign rule. That
liberation finally came, beginning with Turkey in 1919-22 and followed
by the rest of the Middle East and North Africa over the period 1943-62.
Russia's Muslims failed to achieve independence in 1920 in part because
their modernist leaders supported the Bolshevik revolution, notably in
Kazakhstan, Uzbekistan, and Azerbaijan, in the vain hope that it would
bring them economic progress, democracy, and independence—exactly
the things that Turkey would like to offer them today. The modern
Turks, whoever they were and wherever they went, appear to have been
more interested in living a good life on this earth than waiting for the
bliss of Paradise in the next.

Sultan Abdülhamid was initially cool to Germany's efforts to make
inroads into the Middle East. However, in 1889 he changed his policy
overnight, inviting the German kaiser for an official visit to Istanbul. The
reason for this about-face can be found in Gladstone's remarks to
parliament when, citing troubles in Crete, he sought to prove that Turks
were the same "cruel" and "bloodthirsty" opponents of Christians,
Europe, and European civilization that he had described with such
destructive efficacy in 1876. He did this simply to regain control of the
British government; in 1885 he had resigned in disgrace because the
Mahdi of Sudan defeated the British army and killed General Gordon of
Khartoum.

Shortly after reading Gladstone's speech to parliament (and
mistakenly attaching too much importance to it) the sultan issued his
invitation to the kaiser, who promptly accepted it and came hurriedly to
Istanbul in November 1889 despite the inclement weather that nearly
killed him with pneumonia. The die was cast. The Turks were moving
closer to Germany, although to the end of his reign Abdülhamid
conducted a neutral foreign policy. He expected a war stemming chiefly
from European conflicts and ambitions and deemed that an Ottoman
entry into such a war would not help the country. Abdülhamid's foreign
policy was pacifist, neutral, and to some extent isolationist (he also
declined to associate with Iran). He leaned slightly towards Germany and

achieved a rapprochement with Russia while maintaining cordial relations with France and England. He managed to stay on friendly terms with all the Great Powers, including Russia, but without any commitment to follow their policies; this was also republican Turkey's policy until 1939 when it allied with France and England. Abdülhamid knew that Europe would feel no real respect for a society which was ready to shed its culture, history, and personality for the sake of short-term political advantages.

The internal and international policies of Abdülhamid were successful, if success can be measured by the achievement of the goals he had set for himself: namely, to maintain the territorial integrity of the Ottoman empire and to consolidate its internal unity. The Ottoman empire lost no territory during his reign with the exception of the period 1876 to 1878, when Abdülhamid's power was limited. He also achieved successes in developing the country. He adopted to the greatest extent possible the material and scientific achievements of Europe but rejected its political ideas, notably democracy. Abdülhamid did not rescind or abolish any major reforms of the Tanzimat or any of the modern institutions. He openly advocated the adoption of science and technology; in fact, he speeded up educational reform. He encouraged the development of a transportation improvement program including the railways, supported fiscal reorganization, and stabilized the foreign debt (34 percent of the annual revenue went to pay interest and principle). He was responsible for the establishment of a series of professional schools, and literacy rose from about 5 percent to between 15-18 percent. Modern Turkish literature, which played a major role in the intellectual modernization of the Turks, developed quickly during Abdülhamid's reign and a great number of western books in all fields of endeavor were translated.[37] The press was modernized and expanded freely "within the limits of law": that is, it could publish anything but could not engage in political debate (discuss freedom, constitutionalism, the parliament, etc).

It was during his time, in part due to Abdülhamid's support for a market economy and foreign investment, that a Muslim middle class consisting of a large agrarian sector and a small commercial-manufacturing wing emerged. This class built most of the modern schools in the countryside and asked the government to supply the teachers. A sizeable Ottoman elite, made up of all the Muslim nationalities living in the Ottoman empire, emerged from this class and played a seminal role in the Turks' modernization. Notwithstanding the religious-Islamic garb clothing them, Abdülhamid's schools created a new brand of rational, pragmatic, and individualistic elite, whose mental attitude and world philosophy began to resemble that of Europe. Atatürk, Ismet İnönü, and other republican reformist leaders were the products of these modern schools. Probably the greatest development that took place during Abdülhamid's reign was the culmination of the nation-building process that had started during the Tanzimat and ended by producing what became, after the 1920s, the Turkish nation of today.

The nation was the consequence of a willful act. The ruling elite used various elements at its disposal, such as culture, language, and history, to reconstruct the old Muslim community in a new image and endow it with a new national identity, that of the Turks. The process began with the Tanzimat, received its ideological baptism during Abdülhamid's reign, and was concluded by Atatürk, who added the ethnic ingredient while unsuccessfully trying to eliminate its religious content. Sultan Abdülhamid, in his quest to maintain Ottoman territorial integrity, employed Islam in a totally new capacity—as an integrative political ideology to create what he hoped would be an Ottoman Islamic nation. The group conflicts caused by social transformation, the traditional state-society dichotomy, and the fact that the language of the state and the dominant political elite was Turkish, produced, under the cloak of religious unity, ethno-linguistic differentiation and two separate macro political social systems, one Turkish and the other Arabic. However, the most important intellectual development of Abdülhamid's reign, which occurred both despite and because of his Islamic policy, was the Turks' drive to achieve a communion with the civilization of Europe without losing their historic identity as Muslims and Turks.

The Tanzimat reformers had recognized that the reforms and close collaboration with Europe as a member of the European concert of nations compelled them to introduce foreign elements of law, social organization, ethics, art, and literature into their Turkish-Muslim society. These innovations did not destroy the Turks' basic Islamic identity—as the Muslim conservatives claimed—but forced it into a syncretic innovation. However, as long as the western and Muslim elements in this syncretism were presented as being based upon different religious foundations they could not be accepted by either the masses or the educated elite. A new framework for modernization which did not reject Islam, Islamic culture, or the Turks' well-established historical identity was urgently needed.

The issue was first tackled during Abdülhamid's reign by intellectuals such as Samipaşazade Sezai, who, as an aristocrat, had all the necessary social and political credentials to insure official trust. Sezai, among others, claimed that civilization and culture were different things. Civilization comprised mainly the material achievements of a society while culture defined the unique moral, ethical, and aesthetic characteristics of that society and was rooted in religion, among other things. In effect, Sezai claimed that if the Muslims formed a worldwide union and thus assured the survival of their culture they would then feel no inhibition in adopting the civilization of Europe and in joining the march of humanity towards a global civilization.

The culture-civilization relationship was debated extensively by Ziya Gökalp and became a cardinal point in his definition of the modern Turk. In Gökalp's view, the identity of the modern Turk rested on three pillars: Islam (in its Ottoman version), ethnicity, and modernity. Intended was modernity inspired by Europe, although Gökalp did not say this openly, speaking instead of "contemporary civilization." This three-dimensional view of modernization, which is today more or less accepted by most Turks with the exception of die-hard westernizers, was put forth first by Hüseyinzade Ali, a reformist from Azerbaijan. Gökalp's definition of identity became the basis for Turkish nationalism and has played a seminal role—both negative and positive—in Turkey's modernization. Under it, the Turks could absorb the essence of European civilization but maintain their historical identity and their faith. The Turkish reformists, however, did not follow his views but accepted ethnic nationalism and secularism (a form of governmental irreligiosity) as their policy.

Europe did not note, or care to acknowledge, the fundamental changes in the Turkish-Muslim's self-definition that occurred under Abdülhamid's reign, which had begun to move the Turks closer to Europe; Europe continued to criticize the sultan as a reactionary and bigot. This was to be expected, as democracy, individual freedoms, and rights were becoming the practical faith of Europe and the sole—almost exclusive—criterium by which it judged other societies. The Turks were seeking a *modus vivendi* for coexistence while Europe demanded a total cultural surrender, if not to Christianity then at least to democracy. Ultimately the judgement on Abdülhamid was written by the Young Turks' opposition movement which arose among the elites in the 1880s. This opposition judged Abdülhamid not on the basis of his multi-sided achievements but on the basis of a single subjective criteria: his record on freedom and democracy. The restoration of the constitution and parliament of 1876—ignored by Europe—became the linchpin of the Young Turk opposition to Abdülhamid and the reinstatement of these institutions in 1908 marked the end of his reign.

The Young Turks and Europe

The Young Turks represented a synthesis of the centuries-old Turkish relationship with Europe. They wanted to develop relations not as the representatives of an historical Ottoman state with its own traditions and identity but as young reformers who claimed to share the political values of the West and wanted to be accepted at any cost, although they soon discovered the impossibility of this desire. They began by denouncing the Islamist policy of Abdülhamid and his use of the caliphate to serve the ends of personal despotism. They concocted a doctrine of anti-religious secularism and attempted to Turkify the empire. The immediate effect of this policy was to end the *modus vivendi* established by Abdülhamid among the Muslim ethnic groups and undermine the international status quo. Austria annexed Bosnia-Herzegovina, Bulgaria declared independence, in 1911-12 the Italians occupied Libya, and eventually Albania declared itself independent—the first Muslim group in the Ottoman fold to do so. Finally, the Balkan Wars of 1912-13 ousted the Turks from Macedonia and Thrace, where more than 50 percent of the population was Turkish and Muslim.

The Young Turks envisaged the Ottoman empire as another European power with the naive expectation that it would be treated as such and would enjoy the benefits of basic western principles concerning national sovereignty and human rights. The Young Turks considered themselves to be a part of the European system of checks and balances and acted accordingly. They accepted as a truism the idea that England and France were determined to occupy the Middle East and thus sought to prevent this by siding fully with Germany. They also harbored an irredentist aspiration to recoup the Ottoman provinces in the Balkans. Increasingly pursuing a policy inspired by ethnic nationalism in hope of finding a more effective ideology than Islam to galvanize the ethnic Turks, the Union and Progress government opted for Turkism, which took the form of an expansionist Pan-Turanism aimed at Russia. Abdülhamid, while encouraging relations with and the modernist-nationalist aspirations of Russia's Muslims, had opposed Pan-Turanism and thus assuaged the czar's worst fears.

The entry of the Ottoman empire into the First World War on the side of Germany was managed by Enver Paşa and a few military officers against the wishes of the cabinet and the overwhelming majority of the population. The German kaiser had declared during his second visit to the Ottoman lands that he was a protector of the Muslims. Thus the Young Turks, with German prodding, induced caliph Mehmet V to issue the *jihad* urging the world's Muslims to rise against England, France, and Russia with the ultimate purpose of securing the victory of Germany. The war led to the final collapse of the Ottoman state after the British army, supported by some Arab tribes, defeated the Ottoman army in Palestine. History records few instances of large political entities such as the Ottoman empire brought to ruin by a few inexperienced zealots.

The Young Turks ignored the rich historical experience of the Ottoman empire, its true foundation of strength, and speeded up its disintegration because they cast aside the democracy that enabled them to come to power in 1908. They committed the army to a war that grew out of the expansionist aims of Europe. The ultimate truth was that Germany was a Christian power and the use of a *jihad* to help one Christian power fight another could only denigrate the caliphate. After failing to install Şerif Hüseyin, the amir of the holy lands of Mecca, as a credible Arab caliph, the English came to the conclusion that the Muslim world regarded the caliphate as an Ottoman-Turkish institution in the service of Islam and that it represented a perennial danger to their hold in India. Meanwhile the Young Turks disappeared from the world scene and Atatürk abolished the caliphate in 1924.

Turkey's Future

The Turks moved into the orbit of Europe gradually, first as a strong, even superior, enemy, then as an ally, and finally as a dependent client in order to ward off the Russian threat. In the process they "converted" to the civilization of Europe to retain their independence and nationhood, building for themselves a modern type of nation-state. The Turks' ideo-logical-cultural transformation is not historically unique. Many states and ethnic groups adopted a new religion and/or civilization to safeguard their existence and identity, sometimes under a new name if possible. The Bogomils of Bosnia and Bulgaria accepted Islam from the Turks in order to maintain their ethnicity and the social order threatened by both the Catholic and Orthodox churches. The Turks converted from Shamanism and even Buddhism to Islam between the sixth and tenth centuries to reassert their group identity in a new political form. After the middle of the eighteenth century they gradually accepted Western civilization in order to fight the Russians and remain independent.

The political association with the West in the nineteenth century and the concept of the nation-state made ethnicity (and faith) the foundations of a powerful new identity. The Turks thus adopted ethnicity as the basis of political organization and gained their current national identity through association with the West. The governing elites failed to understand the place of Islam in the life of their nation and committed a series of costly blunders. Yet the Turks are unique among Muslim peoples for having openly accepted modernization in its European dress as state policy. Theirs is the first example in the long encounter between Islam and the West whereby a Muslim people accepted the civilization of Europe as its guide for modernization and political identification. Was the Turkish decision a betrayal of Islam or an astute move to change in order to reinforce the identity of Muslim and Turk? I believe the latter is true.

The West has invoked the Turks' Islamic faith, whenever suitable to its own interests, as the key impediment to the Turk's full acceptance as a European partner. Some forces in Europe even hoped that modernization would be a convenient vehicle to convert the Turks to Christianity. The Christian missionaries of all denominations who invaded the Ottoman empire after the Paris peace of 1856 regarded the reforms as the beginning of the Turks' conversion to Christianity. The Islamist policy of Abdülhamid was, in part at least, a reaction to the missionaries' proselytizing. The missionaries' hopes were revived as they came to see Atatürk's reforms as a resumption of the de-Islamization process. The West, and some Turks, subscribe silently to this expectation for conversion although everything that has happened to Islam and the Turks during the past half a century has contradicted this hope.

Today Islam in Turkey is more powerful than ever and yet one of the least militant variants because it is individualized. It is strong also because religiosity or its alternatives are matters of true individual choice guaranteed by a democratic constitution. The Turks' association with Islam is a constitutive, intrinsic part of their identity and personality and a basic force which has defined their place in history. Most of the Turks who stayed outside of Islam perished and those who survived, such as the Gagauz or Chuvash, remained marginal to world history and civilization. Turks without Islam would cease to be Turks.

The Turks can play a substantial role in the emerging new world only if they remain Muslims and Turks who are democratic, individualistic, and economic-minded. They have a highly respected place throughout the Muslim world because of their historical record and the sincere devotion of their people to the faith. Average Turks are committed to the maintenance of their faith and ethnic identity. But what kind of faith? Professor Bernard Lewis was probably correct in stating that the Turks' emerging faith may be a form of Islamic Protestantism.[38]

Although Turkey has suffered a major setback in Azerbaijan and, because of this, in Central Asia, it retains a future role since the direction of development is nationalism rooted in ethnicity, language, and democratized Islam and not anti-western militancy. If Turkey is to play a role in Central Asia (and make up for its rejection by the European Community), it must improve relations with the Islamic countries, including Iran and Iraq, but without establishing a formal Islamic alliance. So far, in order to please its European allies and domestic anti-Islamist bureaucrats, Turkey has refrained from approaching potential Muslim allies.

It is high time for Turkey to use its reputation as the most advanced Islamic country to strengthen its international position and play a role as a democratic and progressive force. All this, in the long run, would facilitate the acceptance of the West in the Islamic world and help the democratization of Russia. So far the West has done its best to alienate the Muslims, including the Turkish masses. The West has not been helpful to the Muslims of Bosnia and Azerbaijan despite their just cause and Turkey's frantic efforts to assist its beleaguered friends. The West abandoned Turkey shortly after 1856 fearing that a strengthened Turkey and growing Muslim militancy against colonialism threatened its long range interests. The situation today, at the end of the Cold War, resembles the one prevailing after 1856.

Russia played a decisive role in compelling the Turks to first seek a political and then an intellectual alignment with Europe. Russia became keenly interested in the ultimate fate of the Ottoman empire after it conquered Central Asia in 1865-73 and had to deal with a large number of Muslims who became increasingly susceptible to the caliph's influence. This fear was aggravated further by the rising tide of nationalism among Russia's Muslims, especially in Kazan and Crimea. By the 1890s many Muslim students from Russia began to arrive for study in Istanbul. All this made Russia, and later the Soviet Union, exceptionally fearful that the Turks could use the Muslims of Russia to incite national revolts the way the czar had used the Orthodox Christians to undermine the sultan's rule in the Balkans. Now that fear is being revived in an Islamic garb. There are at present approximately 9,000 Central Asian students enrolled in Turkish universities and their tuition is paid by Turkey.

Today Russia has begun to view Turkey's endeavors in Central Asia, and especially in Azerbaijan, as a veiled form of Pan-Turkism and even expansionism. In the nineteenth century Russia launched Pan-Slavism rooted in Orthodox Christianity in order to undermine the Ottoman empire's existence. Unfortunately, Russia still views the world as being divided by religious differences and has accepted Orthodox Christianity as a force capable of filling the spiritual vacuum left by the collapse of communism and of consolidating national unity among Russians. The Russian Orthodox Church is quietly courting the Orthodox Christians in the Balkans, including Greece, which is looking increasingly towards Russia as the only power which can create a united Christian Orthodox front against Turkey. Boris Yeltsin's visit to Greece in 1993 may be attributed, in part at least, to Russia's attempts to create such a front and to undermine Turkey's efforts in Central Asia and even to neutralize it as an international player. All this casts very serious doubts upon Russia's willingness to become a stable democracy respectful of the independence of other nations. The well-planned subversion of the pro-Turkish regime in Azerbaijan was manipulated by Russia not only to reassert its influence in the Caucasus but also to show Muslims in the Commonwealth of Independent States that Turkey cannot serve as a model of democracy and free enterprise. As expected, Europe did little to salvage Turkey's reputation. Ultimately the role to be played by Turkey in Asia will be determined not so much by Europe as by Turkey itself, and by the ultimate stand taken by the United States in rearranging its relations with Asia and Europe.

Since Turkey's future position in Asia and among its immediate neighbors will be determined by America's world policies, how should Turkey's position versus American and European policies be defined? These policies may begin as collaborative but they are destined to become adversarial. If Turkey is able to maintain its image as a developing, progressive democracy dedicated to freedom and progress and capable of exerting influence in the Muslim world then it may be able to play a role in Asia both with the U.S. and Europe.

In any case, democracy is bound to remain a permanent feature of the Turkish system. The emergence of democracy and the establishment of individual rights and freedoms which have stemmed from it signaled the apparent victory of the individualistic philosophy of the West over the collectivist-communal philosophy of the Ottoman state. A western criterium is thus in order. Paradoxically, however, Islam could not be and was not abandoned by the modernists. It was more important than ever because it became not only the creed of the community but also the irreplaceable source of spiritual nourishment for the individual Turk. In an individualizing society everything from ethics to politics had to be individualized. In a strange and tortuous way many Turkish elites managed to accept the individualism of Europe (more in its French rather than its English form), although Europe insisted on the Turks' total surrender, either through their conversion to Christianity or their departure from Europe.

Europe did not pay much attention to democratization in the non-western world. Indeed, England and France seemed to regard democracy as uniquely western, stemming from the distinctive history, culture, and faith of the West. After World War II the United States gave democracy a universalist scope as a value that coexisted with religion without necessarily being derived from it. The American concept of democracy, as opposed to the original class-oriented British concept, was egalitarian and individualistic from the very beginning. Turkey adopted this American-type democracy in 1946-47, in large measure in order to be accepted into the European coalition of democracies that was being formed against the Soviet Union.

Turkey's modernization in all its material, moral, and spiritual aspects is possible through the acceptance of full democracy with its basic individualistic philosophy. Today, democracy in Turkey, defined by the individual's freedom to choose and participate in government, is part and parcel of the Turks' culture. Democracy has permitted the Turks to redefine their relation to Islam. It has rejuvenated Turkish society, partially freed it from the bureaucratic-militarist philosophy of statism, and allowed the Turks to seek or to redefine their true identity. Today more than ever the Turks are part of Europe because they have started absorbing its true individualistic spirit by redefining their own historical identity in European terms. The West has come to terms with the Jews because they modernized and accepted European democracy and its spirit regardless of the surviving Orthodox Jewish religious extremism. There is no reason why the West cannot come to terms with the Turks, who have done exactly the same.

Notes

1. The Turkish government began to defend the Turks in Bulgaria quite late, in 1985, because of mounting domestic pressure and after the West indicated that it was also critical of Bulgaria's actions and would use the case to stress the communist regime's violation of human rights. On the case of the Bulgarian Turks see Kemal H. Karpat, ed., *The Turks of Bulgaria* (Istanbul: Isis, 1990).

2. In an interview with the late Kunaev (he died in August 1993) at his home in Almaty early in December 1992, I asked whether he considered himself first a Kazakh, a Muslim, or a Communist. He replied that he was all of them at once but added that he believed in God. He then proudly showed the picture of his grandfather dressed in Muslim attire that was taken just after the latter returned from pilgrimage to Mecca. Kunaev added as an afterthought that he could not ignore his family ties and his own personal past and all this made him feel close to Turkey. He claimed that he was not dismissed by Mikhail Gorbachev from his post as first secretary but resigned.

3. See the declarations of Karimov and Akaev in *Foreign Broadcasting Information Service* (Central Eurasia), 27 December 1991 and 11 March 1993.

4. Graham Fuller and Ian O. Lesser (with Paul B. Henze and J. F. Brown), *Turkey's New Geopolitics* (Boulder: Westview, 1993), p. 105.

5. Brandon H. Beck's statement dramatizes the enduring power of the ancient images as follows: "Today's traveller to Turkey...will encounter personal friendliness and warmth...but he can hardly step down on the platform at Sirkeci Station...or even alight from his plane at Yeşilköy Airport without some of the images from the early writing in mind." Cited from *From the Rising of the Sun—English Images of the Ottoman Empire to 1715* (New York: Peter Lang Publishing, 1987), pp. ix-x.

6. Paul Wittek, *The Rise of the Ottoman Empire* (London: Royal Asiatic Society, 1938); Fuat Köprülü, *Les Origines de l'Empire Ottoman* (Paris: E. de Boccard, 1935) (there is a Turkish and English version of Köprülü's work); W. L. Langer and R. P. Blake, "The Rise of the Ottoman Turks and its Historical Background," *American Historical Review* XXXVII (April 1932): 468-505. For the manner in which

Turks penetrated Byzantium gradually, see R. S. Atabinen, "Les Turcs à Constantinople du Ve au XVe Siècle," *Revue d'Histoire Diplomatique* (October-December 1953): 338-364.

7. Elizabeth A. Zachariadou, *Romania and the Turks (c. 1300-c. 1500)* (London: Variorum Reprints, 1985).

8. See Halil İnalcık, *Studies and Documents on the Reign of Mehmed the Conqueror* (in Turkish) (Ankara: T.T.K., 1954) and N. Itzkowitz and C. Imber, trs., *The Ottoman Empire: The Classical Age 1300-1600* (New York: Praeger, 1973), pp. 66-75.

9. The most extensive treatment of Mehmet II, despite its shortcomings, is still Franz Babinger, *Mehmed the Conqueror and His Time* (Princeton: Princeton University Press, 1953). (There are expanded Italian, French, and English translations.)

10. The existence of such a formal transfer has been long debated. As late as the 1880s the Ottoman government issued a formal declaration that the transfer document existed and was annually viewed by the population of Istanbul. This and other related issues will be debated in the writer's forthcoming work, as is the Ottoman relationship with Central Asia.

11. This literature has been the subject of numerous studies. Probably the best and most unique source is Normal Daniel, *Islam, Europe and Empire* (Edinburgh: The University Press, 1966). See also C. D. Rouillard, *The Turk in French History: Thought and Literature, 1520-1660* (Paris: Boivin, 1940); C. Chew, *The Crescent and the Rose* (New York: Oxford University Press, 1937); J. W. Bohnstedt, "The Infidel Scourge of God: The Turkish Menace as Seen by the Pamphleteers of the Reformation Era," *Transactions of the American Philosophical Society* LVIII, no. 9 (1958).

12. Probably the best source on Turkish relations with Europe is Dorothy M. Vaughan, *Europe and the Turk—A Pattern of Alliances, 1350-1700* (Liverpool: Liverpool University Press, 1954).

13. Ibid., pp. 106-7.

14. See L. B. Baumer, "England, the Turk, and the Common Corps of Christendom," *American Historical Review* (October 1944): 26-48; S. A. Fischer Galati, "The Turkish Impact on the German Reformation, 1520-1555," Ph.D. Dissertation, Harvard University, 1949; K. M. Setton, "Lutheranism and the Turkish Peril," *Balkan Studies* III (1962): 133-66; and "Leo X and the Turks," *Proceedings of the American Philosophical Society* CXIII (1969): 367-424.

15. S. A. Skilliter, *William Harborne and the Trade with Turkey 1578-1583: A Documentary Study of the First Anglo-Ottoman Relations* (Oxford: Oxford University Press, 1977).

16. Cited from *From the Rising of the Sun*, p. 31.

17. Ibid., p. 32.

18. Halil İnalcık, "The Turkish Impact on the Development of Modern Europe," in Kemal H. Karpat, ed., *The Ottoman State and Its Place in World History* (Leiden: E.J. Brill, 1974), p. 53.

19. Richard Knolles *The General Historie of the Turks* (abbreviated title) (London: A. Jslip, 1603), though written in the Elizabethan period (probably around 1580) was published much later (1603) and went rapidly through several editions. The fifth edition was published in London in 1638 as well (a recent edition has been published in New York by the AMS Press in 1973). It served as a basis for other

writers who provided information for additional years. For instance, Paul Rycaut, consul in Izmir, brought Knolles' history up to 1687. See also O. Ghiselin Busbecq, *The Turkish Letters of Ogier Ghiselin de Busbecq* (Oxford: Oxford University Press, 1968).

20. For information see Vaughan, *Europe and the Turk*, and Daniel, *Islam, Europe and Empire*.

21. Fernand Braudel, *The Mediterranean and the Mediterranean World in the Age of Philip II*, 2 vols. (New York: Harper and Row, 1973).

22. There were frequent embassies between Vienna and Istanbul. For instance, a Turkish embassy visited Vienna in 1615 and agreed to revise the Zsitva-Torok treaty of 1606 and allowed the Jesuits to build churches in the Ottoman empire. The reciprocal Jesuit embassy came to Istanbul the next year and carried banners displaying the crucified Christ, provoking a huge popular reaction.

23. See Stanford and Ezel Shaw, *History of the Ottoman Empire and Modern Turkey*, 2 vols. (Cambridge: Cambridge University Press, 1977), vol. 2, p. 134.

24. For an interesting discussion of five types of nations and nationalism in Europe, see Liah Greenfeld, *Nationalism: Five Roads to Modernity* (Cambridge, Mass.: Harvard University Press, 1992).

25. The literature on the reform movement is abundant and well known; it is also quite repetitive. For a somewhat new approach see Cyril E. Black and L. Carl Brown, eds., *Modernization in the Middle East: The Ottoman Empire and its Afro-Asian Successors* (Princeton: Darwin Press, 1992).

26. It is obvious that Canning had his history wrong. The original Ottoman state was an enterprise of free subjects whose faith was a "frontier Islam," that is, the folk religion of mystic brotherhoods which were in fact civic associations of free individuals. The popular *tarikats* preserved this characteristic throughout the duration of the Ottoman empire and were periodically persecuted and closed, with their leaders jailed—both in Ottoman and republican times—for being opposed to the government. It was the government which took control of and used religion for its own purposes. The practice continues in today's Turkey.

27. The provisions of this treaty are treated at length by Roderic Davison, *Reform in the Ottoman Empire, 1856-1876* (Princeton: Princeton University Press, 1962).

28. The well-known Ottoman historian Ahmed Cevdet Paşa provides an excellent description of this change of mind towards Europe. He even gives a personal example of this extraordinary love for everything European, noting that the high-ranking Ottoman families abandoned the three-legged, several-inches-tall traditional *sofra* and adopted French-style dining tables. The historian borrowed money to buy a table and make peace with his demanding wife. *Tezakir 1-12* (prepared by Cavid Baysun), Ankara, 1986.

29. William Langer, *European Alliances and Alignments, 1871-1890*, 2nd ed. (New York: Random, 1950) and D. Harris, *A Diplomatic History of the Balkan Crisis of 1875-1878* (Stanford: Stanford University Press, 1968).

30. Quoted by L. S. Stavrianos, *The Balkans Since 1453* (New York: Holt, Rinehart and Winston, 1958), p. 404.

31. R. Shannon, *Gladstone and the Bulgarian Agitation, 1876* (London: Nelson, 1963) and David Harris, *Britain and the Bulgarian Horrors of 1876* (Chicago: University of Chicago Press, 1939).

32. W. N. Medlicott, *The Congress of Berlin and After* (London: Methuen & Co., 1938).

33. Even the Slavophile R. W. Seton-Watson, despite his well-known dislike of the Turks, could write that "the Bulgarian atrocities became what they never ought to or need have become—a burning issue between the two great parties in the state....issues of foreign policy came to be considered not on their merits, but from the angle of party prejudice and with a passion and bias such as is almost unequalled in our history since the days of Queen Anne." Cited from *Disraeli, Gladstone and the Eastern Question: A Study in Diplomacy and Party Politics* (London: Cass, 1962), p. 57.

34. These views are found in various versions of the sultan's *Hatirat* (Memoirs).

35. Ahmed Cevdet Paşa, the great historian, could not hide his indignation that money played such a great role in European life. In one of his memoranda to Abdülhamid he wrote that the "real religion of the English was money." This negative Ottoman image of Europe as a materialistic civilization was reinforced by other historical memories. Greeks remembered that Andronikus, the Byzantine ruler who had gone to Florence in 1439 to seek unity in the name of a common Christian faith, was jailed by some merchants because of old debts. The Turks also remembered that prince Cem, the brilliant poet and son of Mehmet the Conqueror, was sent by the Knights of Rhodes, where he had sought refuge, to Rome, where he lived in captivity for a long time and was finally poisoned in order to prevent his capture—and exploitation—by the French. During his long stay in Rome, his brother, Sultan Beyazit II (1481-1512) paid 100,000 ducats annually to Cem's captors so that he would not be released and therefore able to start a revolt against his brother.

36. Oscar S. Straus, *Under Four Administrations, From Cleveland to Taft* (Boston: Houghton Mifflin, 1922), p. 46.

37. From 1820-76 a total of 3,185 books were published in the Ottoman empire. Of these, a total of 1,356 were in literature, 902 in the natural sciences, 741 in religion, and 186 in areas concerned with government matters. During Abdülhamid's 33-year reign (1876-1909), a total of 9,124 books were published; 2,950 in literature, 3,891 in the positive sciences, 1,307 in religion, and 976 on official issues. See Orhan Gologlu, *Abdülhamid Gerceği* (Istanbul, 1990), p. 406.

38. See Bernard Lewis, *Islam and the West* (Oxford: Oxford University Press, 1993).

2

Turkey and the West Since World War II

Bruce R. Kuniholm

The complicated relationship between Turkey and the West since World War II has essentially been rooted in mutual security concerns. Geopolitics determined that the United States was the key security partner for Turkey during the Cold War, hence its relationship is the central focus of this chapter. The Cold War's aftermath has modified Turkey's geopolitical imperatives, setting into motion forces which both draw Turkey to, and threaten to separate it from, the West.

Beginning of the U.S.-Turkey Relationship

At the end of World War II, Joseph Stalin's attempts to acquire the Turkish Straits, his support for Georgian and Armenian irredentism in Kars and Ardahan, and Soviet pressure to make Turkey accommodate its desires all had a profound effect on Turkish-American relations.[1] In spite of Soviet attempts to distort the record, former Soviet premier Nikita Khrushchev's memoirs give some indication of what motivated Stalin's policies toward Turkey. According to Khrushchev, Lavrentii Beria, head of Stalin's huge police network and a Georgian like Stalin, teased and goaded Stalin into demanding the return of Turkish territories that briefly (from 1878-1921) had been part of Georgia (it was Stalin who negotiated the Soviet border with Turkey in 1921). Beria argued that Turkey was weakened diplomatically by World War II and would be unable to resist such demands. As Khrushchev has acknowledged, Beria and Stalin "succeeded in frightening the Turks right into the open arms of the Americans."[2]

During the crisis over Turkey in August 1946, in what he considered his most important decision since the bombing of Hiroshima a year before, president Harry S. Truman concluded that it was vital that the Soviet Union, neither by force nor the threat of force, obtain control over Turkey. He decided, therefore, that the United States must resist, even with arms, any Soviet aggression against Turkey.[3]

This key decision resulted in the reformulation of U.S. policies not only towards Turkey but toward Iran and Greece as well.[4] It also led to the establishment of what later became the U.S. Sixth Fleet and, in the wake of Britain's withdrawal from the region, to a clear recognition by the U.S. that it had undertaken an unprecedented commitment to maintain the balance of power in the Near East. This U.S. policy was publicly articulated by the president in March 1947 (a month after the British, who had been informed of America's August 1946 position, had decided to withdraw their forces from Greece and Turkey). What was not understood at the time the Truman Doctrine was enunciated was what that commitment would mean in practice.

The Turks, in the face of a prolonged Soviet war of nerves and suffering from the enormous cost of continued mobilization, repeatedly sought unequivocal support—more substance than the rhetoric of the Truman Doctrine. The primary mission of Turkey's large standing army at that time was to deter aggression. Turkey's mobilization plan, according to General Omar Bradley, was not complicated: "Everyone turns out to fight, and that is all the plan amounts to."[5] Turkey's determination to deploy its army, if necessary, suggested that its defeat could be realized only through a costly war. This was something the Nazis and the Soviets had recognized during World War II. The early postwar years had made clear to the Turks, however, that the Soviets had means short of war by which to achieve their ends. As a result, Turkey's postwar ambassadors to the U.S. made repeated representations regarding the provision of a U.S. guarantee to Turkey's security in order that the Soviet Union not misjudge the situation.

The United States, however, confronted with competing priorities, had been forced to turn its immediate attention away from the Near East and toward Europe (via the Marshall Plan and NATO). Hence, while U.S. officials continued to regard Turkey as critical to security interests, they put it on a back burner. While they attempted to cope with the Soviet acquisition of atomic weapons and pondered over what to do about the victory of the People's Republic of China, the question that remained was how far they should go in accepting their new responsibilities in the Near East. One answer, provided by the Deputy Chiefs of Staff in January 1950, was that U.S. military and strategic interests in the area were now viewed as almost negligible in light of interests in other areas. Major

General Lyman Lemnitzer, Director of the Office of Military Assistance in the department of defense, and later Chairman of the Joint Chiefs of Staff, confirmed this trend of thinking. The importance of the area had not changed, he explained; simply put, higher priorities in other areas made it impossible to devote any substantial portion of the U.S.'s limited resources to the region.[6]

The North Korean invasion of South Korea in June 1950 raised anew the question of Turkey's strategic importance.[7] British plans in the region were to concentrate on the defense of what they called the Middle East's "inner core" or "inner ring," centered in and about the 38,000-person garrison at Suez. Available forces made defense of the "outer ring"—running from the Mediterranean coast above Silifke in Turkey, along the Taurus Mountains and the rim of the Turkish plateau to Lake Van, and along the arc of the Zagros Mountains to Bandar ʿAbbās at the Strait of Hormuz in Iran—extremely difficult. The United States, in the event of an attack on Turkey, was prepared to deploy what were referred to as "available" forces.[8] In reality the United States was not in a position to deploy much of anything. Its armed forces, numbering 12 million in 1945, had been cut to 3 million in 1946 and 1.6 million by 1947. This problem would be remedied within a year, as the U.S. defense budget, which had been reduced to thirteen billion dollars before the Korean War, shot up to fifty billion dollars.

In the interim, the Turks committed a combat brigade to the war in Korea. The Turkish combat commitment, while symbolic of Turkish support for the principle of collective security and solidarity with the United States and a clear demonstration of its potential contribution to NATO, was motivated by its desire to join NATO and receive a security guarantee from the U.S.—just as its abandonment of one-party rule in the early postwar years was motivated in part to underscore its allegiance to the West.[9] The Turks did not come begging, however. What they had to offer in exchange for a security guarantee was a strategic role in the defense of Europe the importance of which was only gradually becoming appreciated. Their plans, in the event of a Soviet attack, envisaged a delaying action in Thrace, withdrawal to Anatolia, and successive delaying actions in the mountains behind the "outer ring" to İskenderun in the southeast. The potential deterrent value to NATO of Turkey was far more significant than these preparedness measures might suggest. Their role, however, would take time to be developed.

Among the factors that increased Turkey's strategic importance to the West at this time, and indeed made it vital, was that the Middle East was supplying 75-80 percent of all European oil. The region's proven reserves—estimated in 1950 to be approximately 40 billion barrels—were equal to those of the rest of the world and almost double those of the

United States. If "probable" or "possible" reserves were taken into account, estimates approached 150 billion barrels. Denial of Middle East oil, it was recognized, would seriously jeopardize the European Recovery Program. The region was described as "vital" but the U.S. still questioned whether it could be defended.

The Turks saw themselves as being more threatened than the NATO countries and less able to protect themselves. Because they were not protected by a treaty they were concerned that the Soviets might be tempted to repeat their previous pressures.

Within the United States, there were serious differences over the value of Turkey's role in an alliance. Admiral Forrest P. Sherman, Chief of Naval Operations, saw Turkey and Greece not only as the northern flank of the Mediterranean but also as tied to the problem of western Europe as well. Previously, Sherman observed, the United States had thought of the two countries in a Middle Eastern context; the current situation required that they be regrouped as an entity. Army Chief of Staff General J. Lawton Collins, on the other hand, saw Turkey as part of the Middle East and therefore a British responsibility and wanted to encourage the Commonwealth to do more for the Middle East. The United States was kidding itself, he asserted, if it planned to put forces in the area. From the standpoint of the Turkish Army, he noted, Turkey was a part of the Middle East. In the event of trouble, it would have to pull out of European Turkey almost at once, falling back to southeastern Turkey. He acknowledged that the Turks could be of considerable help but his focus was on western Europe—"First, last, and always."[10]

When the Korean War expanded the U.S. defense budget fourfold, these difficult military choices were no longer required and categorical conceptions of Turkey's geographical locus no longer necessary. The debate would not be resolved; rather, the economic framework which constrained it—the U.S. defense budget—would be changed by the Korean War. In the final analysis it was General Dwight D. Eisenhower, in his role of Supreme Allied Commander of Europe, who would determine Turkey's role and the relationship between Turkey and the West.

A Deeper Security Relationship

While Eisenhower's conception of the relationship between Turkey and the West took time to develop, being complicated by difficult bureaucratic and political problems, his strategic conception for the defense of Europe, outlined for president Truman in January 1951, gave some indication of the role he envisaged for Turkey. Europe, Eisenhower told Truman, was shaped like a long bottleneck with Russia the wide part, western Europe the neck, and Spain the end. The West controlled the bodies of water (the North Sea and the Mediterranean) on either side of the bottle and had land on the other side of the water (England and North Africa) appropriate for placing bases. The West had to rely on land forces in the center and apply great air and sea power on both flanks. As far as the Mediterranean was concerned, this meant giving arms to Turkey and Yugoslavia and supporting them with a great fleet of air and sea power. If the Russians tried to move ahead in the center he would hit them hard from both flanks, allowing the center to hold and forcing the Russians to pull back.[11]

Up until this time Turkey had been seen as the only country in the eastern Mediterranean capable of sustained resistance to the Soviets. It constituted a deterrent to Soviet aggression and provided something of a protective screen for the region. Loss of Turkey to the Soviet Union, it was recognized, would give the Soviets a valuable strategic position in the region and threaten not only Western oil interests in the Persian Gulf but Europe's economic viability as well. What was new in Eisenhower's developing conception, which favored the perceptions of the Air Force and Navy over the Army, was the "conviction" of a mutuality of benefits in the Turkish-American relationship.

For the United States to obtain Turkey's full cooperation in international security issues, or to assure its cobelligerence in the event of an attack on Europe, a U.S. security commitment was required. If the Soviets attacked Iran and Turkey remained neutral, the Soviet right flank would be protected. If Bulgaria attacked Greece, Turkey would not oppose Bulgaria unless intervention was dictated by the requirements of a larger security framework that included the United States. A U.S. security commitment was also necessary to secure access to Turkey's valuable bases and to close the Straits. Without such a commitment, there was a concern that Turkey would drift toward neutrality, as it had in World War II and as Iran appeared to be doing under Mohammad Mosaddeq (who had become prime minister in April 1951). The result would be that the United States and western Europe would lose the assistance of a potentially useful ally.

As a member of NATO, on the other hand, Turkey would be important to the Supreme Allied Command Europe (SACEUR)—both as a deterrent to a Soviet attack on either Europe or the Middle East and by forcing the Soviet Union to commit significant forces to protect its southern flank and its vital oil fields around Baku. So, in May 1951, president Truman decided that the United States should press for the inclusion of Turkey and Greece as full members of NATO.[12] In September 1951 the NATO Council unanimously voted to extend invitations to

Turkey and Greece and in February 1952 the two countries were formally admitted to full membership.

In the early years of the postwar Turkish-American relationship one of the requirements for the United States and Turkey to become allies was a sense of reciprocity. A conviction that there were mutual benefits in such an alliance was necessary to make credible, and therefore possible, the mutual obligations that were essential if it were to endure. As president Celal Bayar told assistant secretary of state George McGhee, Turkey "wants to give a guarantee, and it would like to receive a guarantee."[13]

Stalin, Ankara knew, harbored little love for the Turks. That there was substance to Turkish concerns is evident not only in his actions in the early postwar years, but in his successors' mea culpa less than three months after his demise. In a 30 May 1953 note, the Soviets informed the Turks that the governments of Armenia and Georgia had renounced their territorial claims against Turkey and after reconsidering the question of the Straits they believed Soviet security could be assured by conditions acceptable to Turkey--an unusual public retraction and tacit admission of Stalin's past sins.[14] By then, however, Turkey was a member of NATO and Soviet attempts to alter Turkey's alliance fell on deaf ears.

The process of incorporating Turkey into the defense of Europe, though necessitated by geopolitical factors, was facilitated by Turkey's strong desire to acquire an explicit security commitment and by its willingness to reciprocate for that commitment by making an important contribution to Europe's defense. U.S. support for Turkey and for the balance of power in the Near East, to put it another way, was reciprocated by Turkish support for the balance of power in Europe. If Turkey were part of the outer "ring" of concentric circles whose locus was at Suez, it was also a part of the southern flank of a front whose center was in western Europe. The two were interconnected and Turkey was the linchpin.

Under the Eisenhower administration, assumptions that undergirded Turkey's accession to NATO were reinforced and Turkey's role in U.S. defense policy was strengthened. In 1955 Turkey joined the western sponsored Baghdad Pact which, after the fall of the Hashemite regime in Iraq in 1958, changed its name to the Central Treaty Organization (CENTO). High-altitude U-2's were stationed at Incirlik air base near Adana beginning in 1956 and electronic installations for gaining information from the Soviet Union were set up along the Black Sea. In accordance with an agreement reached in 1957 the United States stationed strike aircraft equipped with tactical nuclear weapons in Turkey. Turkey granted extensive military facilities and made it possible to extend U.S. capabilities to mount effective air strikes against the Soviet Union.[15]

Turkish bases were available for contingencies in the Middle East and were used by U.S. forces (who notified rather than consulted Turkish authorities about their plans) as a staging area for the crisis in Lebanon in 1958.[16]

During the Eisenhower administration, military assistance averaged approximately $200 million a year.[17] In 1951, when he was SACEUR, General Eisenhower had underscored Turkey's strategic value and advocated giving arms to the Turks in a briefing for president Truman and his cabinet. Four years later, as president, Eisenhower pointed out to secretary of the treasury George Humphrey that it was better and cheaper to assist the Turks' build-up of their own armed forces than to create additional U.S. divisions. Economic assistance to Turkey, he believed, was the best possible way to buttress U.S. security interests in the Near East, thoughts that were echoed by his cabinet.[18] When we go to the Hill on defense matters, secretary of state John Foster Dulles told the Turkish ambassador Feridun Erkin in 1955, "Turkey is our No. 1 exhibit."[19]

Cuban Missile Crisis

When Sputnik dramatized the Soviet long-range missile threat to the United States in October 1957, the United States pushed the NATO Heads of Government at a meeting in December (attended by the prime minister of Turkey who participated in the decision) to agree to deploy missiles and stocks of nuclear warheads on the continent to alter the perceived loss of confidence in the U.S. commitment to Europe. General Lauris Norstad, as SACEUR, determined the citing requirements—a euphemism, apparently, for finding countries that would accept the missiles. While most members of the alliance were reluctant to take on this additional burden, the Turks were not—despite strong opposition to their stand by the Soviet Union.[20]

In October 1959 the United States and Turkey reached agreement on the deployment of a squadron of Jupiter missiles, although they agreed to make no public statement. The almost two-year delay in reaching an agreement apparently was due to the complicated details involved.[21] By the end of 1959 the Turks had selected the fields for their deployment outside of İzmir and Turkish foreign minister Fetin Rüştü Zorlu, who in December expressed his appreciation to Eisenhower for the Jupiters, looked forward to getting them up as soon as possible.[22] The missiles were not installed until fall 1961, apparently became operational in spring 1962,[23] and were formally handed over to the Turks only on 22 October 1962 in the midst of the Cuban missile crisis.[24] The missiles, which were owned by Turkey, were under the operational control of SACEUR, who could use them only with the agreement of the Turkish and U.S. governments—the United States retained custody of the warheads. The delay in deployment was due to the technical complexities of the problem, the specialized training that was necessary before the Turks could operate the missiles, and the fact that the Jupiters were obsolete before they were deployed; hence, there were second thoughts by both the Eisenhower and Kennedy administrations.[25]

John McCone, then Chair of the Atomic Energy Commission, visited the Turkish bases in the fall of 1960 with a subcommittee of the Joint Committee on Atomic Energy, and recommended to president Eisenhower that the Jupiters be removed from Turkey and replaced with Polaris submarines but administration officials felt that the Turks would resist.[26] In April 1961, president John F. Kennedy asked for a review of the Jupiter deployment to Turkey.[27] In June, a response drafted by George McGhee, Chair of the Policy Planning Council and former U.S. ambassador to Turkey, concluded (with General Norstad's concurrence) that cancellation of the deployment might be seen as a sign of weakness in the aftermath of Khrushchev's hardline position at Vienna. When secretary of state Dean Rusk had discussed the matter with the Turkish foreign minister Selim Sarper at a CENTO meeting (in April 1961), McGhee observed, the latter reacted very negatively. McGhee saw any attempt to persuade the Turks to abandon the project as unlikely to succeed because General Norstad himself, in discussing the matter with Sarper, had emphasized their military importance.[28]

The Jupiter missiles were liquid-fueled (hence slow in their reaction time), "soft" in their configuration, and therefore vulnerable. As such they were obsolete relative to submarine-based Polaris missiles that were solid-fueled, mobile, and therefore relatively invulnerable. But while they have been disparaged, particularly in retrospect, by former officials such as Rusk who asserted that Turkish motorists could strike them with a BB-gun or a .22 caliber rifle and that they were so out of date that the U.S. could not be certain which way they would fly, they were thought by some at the time, including General Norstad and Rusk himself, to be a significant military asset.[29] Eighty percent of the missiles were maintained ready for deployment on short warning, Rusk observed in a memo to the president shortly after the crisis. This meant that tactical warning of a Soviet attack would permit the Turks to launch twelve of their fifteen 1.45 megaton warheads at targets inside a 1,500 mile radius within fifteen minutes. The three squadrons of Jupiters (two in Italy and one in Turkey), moreover, were targeted on over one third (45 of 129) of the Soviet medium and intermediate range ballistic missile sites facing Europe. Of significance to the rest of their NATO allies in Europe was the presumption that Turkey and Italy would divert Soviet missiles aimed at other targets in western Europe.[30]

The Turkish attraction to the missiles, U.S. ambassador to NATO Thomas Finletter observed, was that the Turks felt more assured by a weapon on their own territory and somewhat in their own hands. Even if they didn't control the warheads and the missiles were subject to a dual key arrangement, it was important from their point of view that they could participate in the process and share control. The Turks saw the Jupiters as symbols of the alliance's determination to use atomic weapons against a Soviet attack on Turkey—this, Finletter asserted, was "a fixed GOT view"—and hence they saw them as symbols of the U.S. commitment to deter such an attack.[31] As Robert Komer observed in a memo to McGeorge Bundy about their removal shortly after the crisis: "I fear that in looking at the JUPITER question we may be far too rational and logical about a problem which is really high in subjective emotional content. [Robert] McNamara knows the JUPITERs are of no military value. But the Turks, Italians, and others don't—and that's the whole point."[32] Given Turkish perceptions, and in spite of the rational arguments for not deploying Jupiters in Turkey, the missiles had already been deployed. Their removal during the Cuban missile crisis, were it necessary, presented the Kennedy administration with an even greater problem than just reversing an earlier decision—that of the conclusions that the Turks, NATO allies, and adversaries might draw. It was not enough to say that such weapons invited attack and held the U.S. hostage in major crises; that their removal would enhance national security and strengthen deterrence; that removal had been proposed earlier and would have been effected sooner or later anyway; and that it could contribute to a face-saving solution to the crisis.

As administration officials knew, it was the United States who had sold the Turks on the military value of the missiles and the Turkish parliament had only recently appropriated money for their deployment. The Soviet ambassador to Turkey had told the Turks that a nuclear war was on their doorstep.[33] Under these circumstances, to withdraw the missiles under pressure risked creating the impression that the U.S. move was a sell-out, a bargain at Turkey's expense, a weakening of Europe's defenses intended to remove a threat in the Western Hemisphere. Withdrawal could establish a precedent for other concessions and raise profound questions about the credibility of the U.S. commitment to deter Soviet adventures in Europe. At the very least, U.S. officials recognized, the Jupiters would have to be replaced by hardened land-based nuclear missiles, a seaborne nuclear force, or substantial economic and military assistance.[34]

The role of Turkey's Jupiter missiles in the Cuban missile crisis clearly was central, however limited our understanding of some aspects of the crisis may be. The Turkish missiles did become part of the discussions during the crisis between Kennedy and Khrushchev and the missiles were removed in April 1963, plans for removal having begun on 29 October 1962.[35] Even today, as two scholars have recently observed; "It is clear that the full story of the technical status of the Jupiters has yet to surface."[36] What happened—however one chooses to characterize the understanding that was reached—permitted the United States to assert that in fact there had been no deal and allowed Khrushchev not only to avoid complete humiliation but also to argue (at least within the Kremlin) that the Soviets had in fact achieved some concrete gains. Private understandings sometimes permit such felicitous interpretations. Defusing a difficult situation was imperative and while the Jupiters were important enough to deploy (at least at the time that the decision was taken) they were not so important as to stand in the way of resolving a confrontation that they were designed to deter in the first place.

Beyond technical details, the Jupiters were far less important in and of themselves than the fact that they were perceived as important by the Turks. U.S officials were less worried about their military value than their psychological value—that is, how the decision to remove them would be interpreted by allies such as Turkey, the assessments that adversaries such as the Soviets would make of that decision, and the effect of the decision on our allies's faith in the U.S. commitment to deter a Soviet attack. To the extent that the Jupiters invited attack, were obsolete by the time they were installed, and that assurances regarding their removal were consistent with strategic plans, strengthened deterrence, and in no way compromised Turkish trust in the United States, their removal appears to have been a wise decision.

In the aftermath of the Cuban missile crisis a seed of doubt about NATO commitments was planted among the Turks. They began to appreciate the fact that possession of particular weapons systems, while providing certain assurances and addressing some of their security needs, could also make them a target and render them vulnerable to decisions that were made in Washington. From now on they would be far more sensitive to the possibility that the alliance could pull them into a crisis that was of no direct concern to them. These concerns were widely discussed in the Turkish press, where assumptions about Turkish foreign policy, more freely questioned in the aftermath of the 1960 revolution, had an impact on official attitudes. With the withdrawal of the Jupiter missiles from Turkey, Ankara's importance in U.S. nuclear strategies diminished and an impediment to Turkey's better relations with Moscow was removed. Official visits were exchanged with the Soviet Union and improved Turkish-USSR relations slowly followed.[37] This does not mean that U.S.-Turkish relations immediately deteriorated. In fact, when president Kennedy was assassinated in November 1963, public places of entertainment were closed, a street was named after him, and there was a general outpouring of sympathy in Turkey.

What complicated U.S.-Turkish relations in subsequent years was not the Cuban missile crisis but the Cyprus crisis that began in late 1963, after president Kennedy's death. In Turkish eyes, the culprit was president Lyndon B. Johnson, who warned prime minister İsmet İnönü in a June 1964 letter that he should not use any U.S. supplied equipment to invade Cyprus. In that letter, Johnson called into question U.S. obligations under NATO if Turkey took a step that resulted in Soviet intervention. This so-called "Johnson letter," as it was being drafted by Dean Rusk (with the assistance of Harland Cleveland and Joseph Sisco), was described by under secretary of state George Ball as "the most brutal diplomatic note I have ever seen" and produced what he subsequently characterized as "the diplomatic equivalent of a time bomb."[38] The extent to which Rusk's willingness to draft such a harsh letter was influenced by his having been overly concerned about the Turkish reaction to the withdrawal of Jupiter missiles during the Cuban missile crisis is an interesting although unanswerable historical question. It is fair to say, however, that after the Cyprus crisis of 1963-64 U.S.-Turkish relations were clearly less tied to the axioms and enforced solidarity of the early postwar years.[39] A clear example of this shift can be found in the statements of İnönü, who as late as August 1963 could deny that any "deals" had been made on the question of Soviet missiles in Cuba but who by January 1970 was complaining that a bargain had been made and the Turks never notified.[40]

Warming Relations with the Soviet Union, Cooling with the U.S.

Historical judgements are extraordinarily complicated, since the past requires time to play out. How something turns out matters. History, moreover, has no control groups and one cannot replay it under different scenarios. It is fair to say that the Cold War reached a critical turning point with the Cuban missile crisis. From Khrushchev's point of view, the "agreement" to remove the Jupiter missiles "was primarily of moral significance....Kennedy recognized that the time had passed when you could solve conflicts with the USSR by military means."[41] Kennedy could have said much the same about Khrushchev. Common interests were more easily perceived and rapprochement between East and West became possible although it would take almost thirty years before the Cold War would end. As the Cold War turned the corner, doubts about the U.S. commitment to Turkey, first generated by the Cuban missile crisis and reinforced by the Johnson letter, however problematical at the time, did not destroy the US-Turkish alliance. Rather, they produced a Turkish response to the emerging international situation that was desirable if not inevitable: a more realistic assessment of Turkey's problems and a more independent, multifaceted conception of its options than had been possible in the early Cold War years. Such a conception was encouraged by Soviet president Nikolai Podgornyi, whose visit to Turkey in January 1965 picked up on an earlier theme sounded by Stalin's successors. This time, Soviet apologies found a far more receptive audience.

On 5 January 1965, Podgornyi told the Turkish Grand National Assembly that a shadow had been cast over Turkish-Soviet relations for some time since World War II and acknowledged that inappropriate and incorrect statements made in the Soviet Union had played a negative part. The Soviet Union, he noted, stated openly that those were incorrect statements; such events should be a thing of the past.[42] Podgornyi's comments came during the first visit to Turkey by a Soviet parliamentary delegation in more than twenty-five years. They were seen in Turkey as an indirect admission of Soviet responsibility for strains in their relations in the late 1940s and 1950s and paved the way for an improvement.

While the Turks continued to distrust the Soviets, their policies were more flexible and less structured by the earlier assumptions of a bipolar world. Better Turco-Soviet relations were marked by visits, principled agreements, and economic assistance and complemented a diminishing level of grant assistance from the United States, which was increasingly mired in the Vietnam war. Freedom from the ideological strait jacket that had characterized early postwar policies resulted in a somewhat more independent international posture, as indicated, for example, by the decision in 1965 not to participate in the U.S.-sponsored proposal for a multilateral nuclear force in Europe.

The new balance that was evident in Turkish policy could be seen by comparison with earlier events. During the war in Lebanon in 1958, for example, the United States had used Turkish bases to support its intervention. Following events of the early 1960s, the Turks were more guarded about their use of Turkish facilities for non-NATO contingencies. During the 1967 Arab-Israeli War the United States was allowed to use communications stations in Turkey but not Turkish bases for refueling or supply activities. In the 1973 Arab-Israeli War the United States was not permitted to use Turkish bases for direct combat or logistical support, although it could use communication stations in Turkey during the resupply effort. The United States also utilized Turkish bases for the evacuation of American citizens during the Jordanian civil war in 1970 and the Iranian revolution in 1979.

The Cyprus crisis in 1974, meanwhile, again tested mutual obligations and responsibilities. In July, Turkey occupied the island to protect the Turkish minority from the "Hellenic Republic of Cyprus"—led by an international terrorist, installed by a coup, backed by the military dictatorship in Athens, and bent on union with Greece. A second Turkish action in August—according to the Turks to consolidate vulnerable positions—according to the Greeks to expand their base—precipitated the U.S. congressional embargo on transfers of military equipment to Turkey (effective 5 February 1975) and resulted in a subsequent decision in Ankara to suspend U.S. operations at military installations in Turkey (as of 26 July 1975). These developments made explicit what had been implicit until then: access to facilities was directly related to decisions on military assistance and forced discussion over the merits of continuing the special relationship.

In the wake of the Cuban missile crisis (and the beginning of a new political environment following the Constitution of 1961), Turkey's economic relations with the European Community (EC) markedly improved—particularly with Germany. The "Ankara Association Agreement" of 1964 and a supplementary agreement in 1971 provided for a transitional stage toward full integration in the EC. Europe's economic growth created a demand for Turkish labor, eased unemployment in Turkey, and through remittances from Turkish workers eased foreign exchange shortages and balance of payments deficits. The number of Turkish workers in Germany, which stood at 22,054 in 1963, doubled in 1964 and again in 1965, 1969, and 1971. By 1973 there were 528,474 workers whose remittances totalled 2.5 billion German Marks.[43]

The oil crises of 1973-74 and 1978-79, however, and Turkey's lack of developed indigenous energy resources, caused Turkey's oil bill, which was only $124 million in 1972, to rise to $1.2 billion in 1977 and to $3.86 billion in 1980.[44] High oil bills and a recession in Europe (which occasioned a halt to Turkey's labor migration), led Turkey to drain its foreign exchange reserves, to rely on state economic enterprises as a short-term solution to job creation, and to borrow on the short-term credit market—policies that contributed to a vicious cycle of hyperinflation, stagnation, and huge balance of payments deficits that ultimately proved unsustainable.[45]

Relations between Ankara and Moscow, meanwhile, continued to improve. By 1978, the Soviet Union was aiding forty-four different development projects in Turkey and by the end of the decade Turkey received more Soviet economic assistance than any country in the third world except Cuba. Prime minister Bülent Ecevit declared in May 1978 that Turkey felt "no threat" from the Soviet Union.[46] However, in December 1979, after the Soviet invasion of Afghanistan, the Turks were far more worried than after the fall of the shah.

During Ronald Reagan's first administration, relations between the U.S. and Turkey improved markedly as the East-West conflict raised the specter of a new Cold War and appropriations for Turkey's defense needs correspondingly increased. Even under conservative estimates, U.S. assistance to Turkey in its various forms throughout the 1980's amounted to well over one billion dollars a year.[47] But perceptions of the international balance of power began to change during the second Reagan administration as the result of a number of factors: the accession to power of general secretary Mikhail Gorbachev; the gradual thaw in U.S.-Soviet relations; the impending Soviet withdrawal from Afghanistan; and the International Nuclear Forces agreement. Under these circumstances, appropriations for Turkey's defense needs, while significant, became less urgent to the United States; congressional committees, faced with serious budget constraints, were increasingly confronted with a lack of means to meet all their interests.

During George Bush's administration, U.S-Soviet relations continued to improve following the Soviet withdrawal from Afghanistan. Developments in eastern Europe and the Soviet Union fundamentally altered the threat previously posed NATO. In Turkey, meanwhile, anger over a congressional debate on the so-called Armenian resolution, which proposed a day of commemoration for the alleged genocide of 1.5 million Armenians by the Ottoman empire, exacerbated worsening U.S.-Turkish relations. The source of Turkish concern, aside from a belief that these judgements were best left to historians, was that the resolution, if passed by the U.S. congress, would give legitimacy to future claims by Armenians for compensation and territory in Turkey. In response, U.S. port visits and training missions were halted, restrictions were put on the modernization of facilities, and meetings on military cooperation were suspended. The cancellation of the U.S.-Turkish Defense and Economic Cooperation Agreement was threatened and the U.S.-Turkish relationship itself was called into question before the resolution was narrowly defeated in early 1990—on the eve of the Gulf War and as the Cold War was drawing to a close.

The bottom line in the U.S.-Turkish relationship during the Cold War was that when U.S.-Soviet relations were troubled (as they had been in the late 1940's and 1950's, and as they were during periodic crises), relations between the United States and Turkey generally improved. These good relations were founded on U.S. military and economic assisttance as well as a U.S. guarantee of Turkey's security—a guarantee that served as a deterrent against a Soviet attack—in exchange for the use of

Turkish facilities and bases and an important Turkish role in the defense of the West.[48] But as U.S.-Soviet relations improved, the U.S.-Turkish relationship became more troubled as both sides raised questions and challenged the other's notion of their reciprocal obligations. This development was virtually inevitable after the threat that bound the allies together began to recede.

The Cuban missile crisis, in a sense, served as a catalyst for changes already underway and signalled the beginning of the end of the Cold War. It legitimized a new generation of leaders in the United States and the Soviet Union who, learning from experience, were prepared to take steps necessary to reduce the potential for catastrophic conflict. It underscored both the challenges and opportunities provided by a more sober assessment of the new weapons systems at their disposal—an assessment that included a greater appreciation of their vulnerabilities and limitations as well as their potential for destruction.

The U.S.-Turkish relationship was central to Western security in the early Cold War years and crucial to Turkey's survival. But as changes occurred, adaptive measures were necessary and even desirable. The demise of Stalin, the advent of Khrushchev and his campaign of de-Stalinization, the acquisition of new weapons systems in the Soviet Union and the United States, and the gradual evolution of the international balance of power toward a rough parity—all contributed to a new climate of opinion. This was an atmosphere in which thoughtful voices would articulate new points of view and help pave the way for a relaxation of tensions, an opportunity for Turkey to focus on the evolution of its own internal political problems, the ascendancy of economic issues, and the more complicated international environment of the post-Cold War era. The road would not be smooth and one could argue about the milestones but the direction was clear.

Over thirty years ago, on 19 February 1963, Robert Komer, who would later become the U.S. ambassador to Turkey, wrote assistant secretary of state Phillips Talbot an insightful memo in which he noted:

> We have never really decided in our own minds whether to treat Turkey primarily as a NATO partner (whose main need was military aid for the defense of Europe) or as an underdeveloped country whose primary need was to become a going concern. As a result we have pursued both aims—and fully succeeded at neither. My own bias is well known: i.e., that the threat to US interests from bloc aggression involving Turkey is less urgent than that arising from Turkey's failure to become a going concern....
>
> Can we (and our European allies) afford to alter the proportions of our assistance sufficiently to get Turkey well on the road to self-

sufficiency (except for the major hardware) over the next decade, without incurring unacceptable military risks? This, to me, is the nub of the problem and one on which we ought to make up our minds.[49]

This observation characterized differences in official thinking about Turkey toward the end of the Eisenhower administration as well as in the Kennedy administration, and it would continue to do so among U.S. officials who were unable to make up their minds until the end of the Cold War, when Turkey could worry less about unacceptable military risks and begin to focus much more directly on the difficulties of becoming "a going concern."

Throughout this period, Turkey continued to play a crucial strategic role—albeit against what was in retrospect a diminishing threat. It helped to deter a Soviet attack on NATO's central front because its forces posed a threat to Warsaw Pact forces in the Balkans and the Transcaucasus. If deterrence failed, it was believed that the potential threat from Turkey would impede Soviet capacity to reinforce the central front. Installations in Turkey, meanwhile, made it possible to detect, intercept, and limit the projection of Soviet airpower into the eastern Mediterranean. At sea, Turkish control of the Bosporus blocked the projection of Soviet naval power into the Aegean. Outside the European theater, Turkey's land mass and its bases deterred Soviet ambitions in the Persian Gulf. In their absence, Soviet support for and accessibility to such countries as Syria and Iraq would have been much more pervasive and potentially threatening to U.S. interests and would have created serious problems for Israel. Finally, as NATO's only Muslim country, Turkey also provided a cultural bridge between Europe and the Middle East.

Post-Cold War Relations

If Turkey's security relationship with the West was solidly grounded in mutual interests, its economic relationship, while increasingly significant in terms of trade, nevertheless ran into serious obstacles as Turkey sought integration into the world economy and attempted to contribute to the restructuring of a greater Europe—of which it increasingly aspired to be a full member. The process of overcoming these obstacles began in the mid-1980s when the first of a series of broad based economic stabilization measures were introduced. Placing great reliance on market forces, subsequent Turkish governments eliminated subsidies to inefficient public-sector enterprises, curtailed imports, increased exports by devaluing the lira, cut oil consumption, introduced a tight monetary policy to limit inflation, and removed barriers to foreign investment. Over time these economic measures, while not all successful, would begin to turn around Turkey's economy. By 1987, they had tripled the export share in the GNP to 20.4 percent.[50] In the 1980's, Turkey's exports rose from $2.9 billion to $11.7 billion. Exports to the EC averaged 40 percent of total exports throughout the decade, with Germany by far the greatest recipient—importing an average of 17.5 percent. By 1991, the EC received over 50 percent of Turkish exports, of which Germany received over half, or more than 25 percent of the total.[51]

In 1987, meanwhile, Turkey applied for admission to the EC. With the decline of the Soviet Union, the EC began to give priority to economic and political concerns over NATO's military priorities and it was less responsive than it otherwise would have been to the Turks' application. With the EC's 1989 decision to postpone consideration of Turkey's application concerns were raised about Turkey's size, population, and low level of development. Purchasing power in Turkey was one-third that of the EC average, while the country suffered from high inflation rates and high unemployment. More than 50 percent of the labor force was employed in agriculture and the Community was concerned about the access of Turkish labor to the EC labor market at a time when unemployment was a problem for the twelve economies.[52] The Turks, in turn, began to look to other mechanisms—and in particular to the Black Sea Economic Cooperation initiative—to help modernize their country.

While the Turks saw the lack of support for their entry as the denial of a right that they had earned through the NATO alliance and their strong commitment to Europe, they were not surprised. The government, putting on its best face, emphasized the report's affirmation of Turkey's qualification to become a full member and its call for a customs union between Turkey and the EC by 1995. Membership in the EC, Turks believed, would guarantee their continued westernization and cement their identity in Europe. Rejection of Turkey's membership, president Özal warned, would push Turkey away from Europe and encourage the spread of religious fundamentalism throughout the region. Islamic fundamentalists had never captured more than 10 percent of the vote in Turkey before 1994 but their cause clearly would be fueled by such rejection.

On the geopolitical level, meanwhile, as reduction of the Soviet military threat to Europe diminished Turkey's importance to the NATO alliance, Turkey's foreign policy began to reflect changing realities. In Vienna in December 1989 foreign minister Mesut Yılmaz met with seventeen Turkish ambassadors to improve relations between East and West and construct a broad outline of future foreign policy. Turkey, the ministers concurred, should definitely stay in NATO but establish closer ties with the East. If it were to be accepted as a member of the EC, it would have to take greater steps toward democracy and improve its human rights record. The ministers noted that while Turkey's strategic importance was lessened by East-West detente, it was not eliminated. Its geographical location would dictate its continuing significance to the alliance. The major threat to Turkey, however, was no longer seen as coming from the north but rather from the southeast.

The Gulf War corroborated the wisdom of Turkey's latest threat assessments. It also underscored its continuing (although changing) geopolitical influence. While the decline of the Soviet Union diminished Turkey's role in NATO, it enhanced Turkey's relative influence in the Persian Gulf, where the end of the Cold War created a less stable environment. Turkey's contribution to the anti-Iraq coalition included closing the Iraqi pipeline, permitting the allied coalition access to its military bases from which Iraqi targets were bombed, and deploying the Turkish Army along the Iraqi border. This forced Iraq to deploy its troops to the north and raised the prospect of a two-front war. The crisis underscored the value of its Turkish alliance to the United States and corroborated estimates within both governments of Turkey's continuing—albeit, changing—geopolitical importance.

What Lies Ahead?

With the end of the Cold War, both Turkey and the West continue to feel their way in the international environment that has emerged in its wake. Where notions of the balance of power after World War II were little changed from those which preceded it, the post-Cold War era already looks very different. The Soviet Union's demise has ended the stabilizing effect of a bipolar balance of power and unleashed numerous regional and ethnic conflicts. The world that evolved after World War II underscored the threat posed to Turkey by the Soviet Union and required that it undertake a mutual security arrangement with the West. The end of the Cold War, on the other hand, has diminished the threat posed by Russia, whose territory no longer borders Turkey, and has unleashed wars among Turkey's neighbors—in the Balkans, in the Caucasus, and in Iraq—none of which would have been likely during the Cold War and each of which has the potential to draw Turkey into bloody conflicts.[53]

One of the best historians of the Cold War, John Gaddis, has noted that the rivalries of the Cold War have given way to a new contest: that between the forces of integration and fragmentation in the international environment.[54] On the one hand, political, economic, technological, and cultural forces are breaking down barriers that have historically separated nations and peoples; the logic of these forces, undergirded by support for the open market, suggests economic integration. Integration is compelling to Turkey, which has actively sought to be part of the Western European Union, the European Community, the Black Sea Economic Cooperation Region (which the Turks initiated), and the Economic Cooperation Organization, to name a few. Whether for security, economic prosperity, or management of common environmental problems, such organizations promise to improve Turkey's lot.

On the other hand, forces such as religion, self-determination, and nationalism are exacerbating old frictions and creating new barriers—in some cases where none existed before. These forces suggest political fragmentation and are gnawing at Turkey, threatening to undermine not only Turkey's aspirations for integration with the international economic community but its very national identity. It is Gaddis' belief that the end of the Cold War has resulted not in an end to threats but in the diffusion of them; that the problems nations will confront are more likely to arise not from the kinds of competing ideologies that existed during the Cold War but from the competition between the forces of integration and fragmentation.[55] The contradiction between abandoning control of our economic lives (suggested by market theory) and taking control of our political lives (suggested by democratic theory) is profound; according to Gaddis, the fault line between the forces of integration and fragmentation may be "as long, as deep, and as dangerous...[as] the one between democratic and authoritarian government that preoccupied us through so much of the twentieth century."[56]

Whether or not Gaddis is right, it is clear that the new international environment that Turkey confronts is much more complicated than that which it faced during the Cold War era, when the legacy of Mustafa Kemal Atatürk reigned supreme. From the very beginning of modern Turkey, eliminating ethnic differences by fiat was a means to an end: creating the cohesion necessary for the modern Turkish state. Such cohesion, fostered through both persuasion and repression, helped to create a national identity that enabled Turkey to withstand threats to its territorial integrity and sovereignty in the years following the Lausanne conference and throughout the Cold War.[57]

In recent years Turkey has come into its own as a regional power. More secure about its identity, it has begun to address some of the existential problems that were submerged in the process of nation-building and to reconcile itself with its past. Where the immediate threat to Turkey's existence during the Cold War was geopolitical, those most prominent in the post-Cold War era are fundamentally different: cross-cutting forces that can be construed as either integrating or fragmen-

ting—Pan-Islamism, Pan-Turkism, and Kurdish separatism and nationalism in its many manifestations.[58]

Selim Deringil has argued that since the disappearance of the Ottoman
empire Turkey has had a recurring "identity crisis" that emerges in times
of economic, social, and political strife and recedes when Turkish elites
feel sure of themselves and their future.[59] If that is the case, it is
reasonable to assume that among the problems that Turkey currently
confronts the Kurdish problem will be the cause for a profound identity
crisis. Even under the best of circumstances it would take a lot of self-
confidence to deal constructively with such an enormous problem. The
very act of addressing it will not only raise profound questions about
Turkish identity; it will also severely challenge the Turks' self-confidence.
It is already causing serious differences between Turkey and its allies.

In coping with the forces of integration and fragmentation—and we
should be clear that the terms are no more than heuristic attempts to
capture a number of complex trends that defy simplification—caution is
clearly warranted. Jumping to conclusions that either one or the other is
desirable, Gaddis argues, could be a mistake. Many might assume that
any force for integration—the EC, for example—is a good thing. But
forces for integration (the international markets in oil and armaments)
were also what made the threat posed by Saddam Hussein possible. The
logical consequence of a fully integrated world, to cite another example,
could be the loss of national sovereignty and identity, submerging state
autonomy within a larger economic order. The consequence of a fragmented world, on the other hand—and the Kurdish question if badly
managed could go in this direction—could be virtual anarchy, shattering
state authority. It is Gaddis' conclusion that instead of balancing states
and ideologies, what must now be balanced are processes that tend
toward integrationist and fragmentationist extremes; nations must weigh
the advantages and disadvantages of these processes.[60]

The conflict between these two processes—and the object of their
struggle is no less than the sovereignty and territorial integrity of the
nation-state—constitutes a fundamental challenge to the international
state system. It means that individual countries must reassess their
identity, the assumptions upon which they were founded, and the
mechanisms by which their citizens have organized themselves. In
Europe and the United States, debates over the Maastricht treaty and the
North American Free Trade Agreement (NAFTA) have raised precisely
these questions. In the Soviet Union and Yugoslavia, movements for self-
determination have led to the dissolution of those states, while the new
"states" they have spawned must work out the question of whether or
not, and if so the extent to which, they, too, must be further divided.

Such questions are not always so apocalyptic for every country. Nonetheless, the questions posed are very difficult and have no simple answers. In the United States, the question of secession and the decision of the North to oppose it led to a civil war—a war which, even 130 years later, has not totally resolved some of the fundamental problems that contributed to it. The debate in the United States over NAFTA, as noted, has gone to the very heart of how the U.S. thinks of itself as a nation, the responsibilities and obligations of leadership, and the relationships between the nation and the larger economic and political international order. Nation-building isn't easy. Nation-saving isn't either.

For Turkey, the problem of balancing processes that tend toward integrationist and fragmentationist extremes means supporting those that advance its general interests; opposing, modifying, or accommodating those that threaten its sovereignty or territorial integrity; and, where action is necessary, doing what has to be done to restore its equilibrium and make it possible to meet the challenges of the post-Cold War era. If in the past the basis for its relationship with the West was geopolitical, with common values being important but of secondary concern, the basis for the future will increasingly reverse the priority of these two factors.[61] While the Turks have begun to explore their ties to the East with much greater energy and dynamism, their strategic and economic ties, and ultimately their common values with the West, will remain fundamental.

Notes

1. For greater detail see Bruce R. Kuniholm, *The Origins of the Cold War in the Near East: Great Power Conflict and Diplomacy in Iran, Turkey, and Greece*, 2nd ed. (Princeton: Princeton University Press, 1994).

2. Strobe Talbott, ed., *Khrushchev Remembers: The Last Testament* (Boston: Little Brown, 1974), pp. 295-296.

3. *Foreign Relations of the United States, 1946*, vol. VII (Washington, D.C.: United States Government Printing Office), pp. 840-842. (Hereinafter cited as FRUS).

4. For the policy statements on Greece, Turkey, and Iran, see *FRUS, 1946*, VII, pp. 240-245, 894-897, 529-536.

5. *FRUS, 1951*, V, p. 31. Parts of the following discussion draw on Bruce R. Kuniholm, "U.S. Policy in the Near East: The Triumphs and Tribulations of the Truman Administration," in Michael Lacey, ed., *The Truman Presidency* (Cambridge: Cambridge University Press, 1989), pp. 299-338 and Bruce R. Kuniholm, "Rings and Flanks: The Defense of the Middle East in the Early Cold War," in Keith Neilsen and Ronald Haycock, eds., *The Cold War and Defense* (New York: Praeger, 1990), pp. 111-135.

6. *FRUS, 1950*, V, pp. 122-123.

7. For new light on the origins of this war see the discussion in *Cold War International History Project Bulletin* 3(Fall 1993).

8. See, for example, *FRUS, 1950*, I, p. 387. For the problem of assessing "vital" interests see *FRUS, 1950*, III, p. 1693, and *FRUS, 1951*, V, pp. 10-11.

9. In the course of the Korean War almost 30,000 Turks served in Korea, where approximately 10 percent suffered casualties. Their actions led General Douglas MacArthur to characterize them as "the bravest of the brave."

10. *FRUS, 1951*, V, pp. 27-42.

11. *FRUS, 1951*, III, p. 454.

12. The relative strategic importance assigned to Turkey over Greece is indicated by NSC 109 (on Turkey) and NSC 103/1 (on Greece), which shows that in February U.S. policy toward Greece did not include support for Greek membership in NATO. This policy was amended in May in light of the decision to press for Turkish membership in NATO.

13. *FRUS, 1951*, V, p. 470.

14. Ferenc Vali, *Bridge Across the Bosporus: The Foreign Policy of Turkey* (Baltimore: Johns Hopkins University Press, 1971), pp. 174-175. In the manuscript of his forthcoming book devoted to Stalin's foreign policy during the postwar years, Vojtech Mastny suggests that Soviet foreign minister Viacheslav Molotov was interested in improving relations in order to weaken the recently-concluded Balkan Pact.

15. Francis Powers, *Operation Overflight* (New York: Tower, 1970), p. 41; George Harris, "Turkey and the United States," in Kemal Karpat et al., *Turkey's Foreign Policy in Transition: 1950-1974* (Leiden: E.J Brill, 1975), p. 56; NSC 5708/2, 29 June 1957; *FRUS, 1955-1957*, XXIV, pp. 720-721; and NSC 6015/1, "U.S. Policy Toward Turkey," 5 October 1960.

16. George Harris, *Troubled Alliance: Turkish-American Problems in Historical Perspective, 1945-1971* (Washington, D.C.: American Enterprise Institute, 1972), p. 67.

17. Financial Appendix to NSC 6015/1, "U.S. Policy Toward Turkey," 5 October 1960.

18. *FRUS*, III, part 1, 31 January 1951, p. 454 and *FRUS*, XXIV, 5 January 1955, p. 608.

19. *FRUS, 1955-1957*, XXIV, p. 643.

20. Memorandum from William Brubeck (Department of State) to McGeorge Bundy (The White House), "Jupiters in Italy and Turkey," 22 October 1962, John F. Kennedy Library; State Department memorandum from William R. Tyler to Secretary Rusk, "Turkish and Jupiter IRBM's," 9 November 1962; and memorandum from Secretary Rusk to President Kennedy, "Political and Military Considerations Bearing on Turkish and Italian IRBM's," 9 November 1962, Lyndon B. Johnson Library.

21. Ibid.; Department of State Telegram 1085 to American Embassy, Ankara, 7 October 1959, Dwight D. Eisenhower Library. Much of this section is drawn from the paper "Turkey's Jupiter Missiles and their Affect on U.S.-Turkish relations," presented by the author at a conference sponsored by the European University Institute in Fiesole, Italy in October 1992.

22. Memorandum of Conference with the President, 6 December 1959, Dwight D. Eisenhower Library.

23. Barton J. Bernstein, "The Cuban Missile Crisis: Trading the Jupiters in Turkey?" *Political Science Quarterly* 95, no. 1(Spring 1980): 100. Bernstein's revision of the essay, cited in n. 35, now argues for March or April 1962 instead of July 1962.

24. Raymond L. Garthoff, *Reflections on the Cuban Missile Crisis* (Washington, D.C.: Brookings, 1987), p. 37.

25. Harris, *Troubled Alliance*, p. 92.

26. *Executive Sessions of the Senate Foreign Relations Committee* (Historical Series), Volume XV, Eighty-eighth Congress, First Session, 1963 (Washington, D.C.: United States Government Publishing Office, 1987), p. 104.

27. National Security Action Memorandum No. 35, "Deployment of IRBM's to Turkey," 6 April 1961.

28. Memorandum for McGeorge Bundy from George McGhee, "The Turkish IRBM's," 22 June 1961, John F. Kennedy Library. See also Raymond Hare, Oral History Interview, 19 September 1969, p. 22, John F. Kennedy Library.

29. David Welch and James G. Blight, "The Eleventh Hour of the Cuban Missile Crisis: An Introduction to the ExComm Transcripts," *International Security* (Winter 1987/88): 17 and Michael R. Beschloss, *The Crisis Years: Kennedy and Khrushchev, 1960-1963* (New York: Edward Burlingame Books, 1991), p. 439.

30. See the Rusk memorandum, cited in note 20. See also the memo from William Tyler to Secretary Rusk, "Turkish and Italian IRBM's," 9 November 1962, John F. Kennedy Library. As Welch and Blight observe: "It is clear that the full story of the technical status of the Jupiters has yet to surface." Welch and Blight, "The Eleventh Hour of the Cuban Missile Crisis," p. 18.

31. See State Department telegrams from Secretary Rusk to Thomas Finletter in Paris (2345) and Raymond Hare in Ankara (445), 24 October 1962, and from Finletter to Secretary Rusk (Polto 506), 25 October 1962, John F. Kennedy Library.

32. See memo from Robert Komer to McGeorge Bundy, 12 November 1962, John F. Kennedy Library.

33. Vali, *Bridge Across the Bosporus*, p. 129.

34. See, for example, the memorandum from Roger Hilsman, Director of the Bureau of Intelligence and Research, to Secretary Rusk, 27 October 1962, John F. Kennedy Library and the memorandum from Walt Rostow to McGeorge Bundy, "Turkish IRBM's," 30 October 1962, John F. Kennedy Library.

35. McGeorge Bundy, *Danger and Survival: Choices about the Bomb in the First Fifty Years* (New York: Random House, 1988), pp. 404-407, 428-439. For further discussion on Khrushchev's Turkish missile trade proposal, or to examine the negotiating strategies that the Kennedy administration considered, see Bruce J. Allyn, James Blight, and David Welch, "Essence of Revision: Moscow, Havana, and the Cuban Missile Crisis," *International Security* 14 (Winter, 1989/90): 157-159, 163-165. See also "Cuban Missile Crisis Meetings, 27 October 1962," *Presidential Recordings*, President's Office Files, John F. Kennedy Library; and Barton J. Bernstein, "Reconsidering the Missile Crisis: Dealing with the Problem of the American Jupiters in Turkey," in James A. Nathan, ed., *The Cuban Missile Crisis Reconsidered* (New York: St. Martin's Press, 1992), pp. 55-129. Bernstein is

particularly critical of the manner in which access to crucial documents has been controlled.

36. Welch and Blight, "The Eleventh Hour of the Cuban Missile Crisis," p. 18.

37. Harris, *Troubled Alliance*, pp. 93-95 and Karpat et al., *Turkey's Foreign Policy in Transition*, pp. 58-59.

38. George W. Ball, *The Past has Another Pattern: Memoirs* (New York: W.W. Norton & Co., 1982), p. 350.

39. Much of the section that follows is drawn from Bruce R. Kuniholm, "Turkey and NATO: Past, Present, and Future," *Orbis* (Summer 1983): 421-445.

40. Harris, *Troubled Alliance*, p. 93, n. 19.

41. Jerrold L. Schecter and Vyacheslav V. Luchkov, eds., *Khrushchev Remembers: The Glasnost Tapes* (Boston: Little, Brown and Co., 1990), p. 179.

42. See the *Foreign Broadcast Information Service Daily-Report*, 6 January 1965, pp. M1-3, 7 January 1965, pp. M1-5, and 11 January 1965, pp. M1-4.

43. Z.Y Hershlag, *The Contemporary Turkish Economy* (London: Routledge, 1988), p. 86; Tosun Arıcanlı and Dani Rodrik, *The Political Economy of Turkey: Debt, Adjustment and Sustainability* (New York: St. Martin's Press, 1990), pp. 231-232; and Nermin Abadan-Unat, *Turkish Workers in Europe, 1960-1975: A Socio-Economic Appraisal* (Leiden: E.J. Brill, 1976), pp. 387-389.

44. Kuniholm, "Turkey and NATO: Past, Present, and Future," p. 430.

45. Arıcanlı and Rodrik, *The Political Economy of Turkey*, pp. 234-235 and Bent Hansen, *Egypt and Turkey: The Political Economy of Poverty, Equity, and Growth* (Oxford: Oxford University Press, 1991), p. 383.

46. See Bülent Ecevit's address to the International Institute of Strategic Studies of 15 May 1978, in *Survival* 20, no. 5(1978): 203-208.

47. See Bruce R. Kuniholm, "Rhetoric or Reality in the Aegean: U.S. Policy Options toward Greece and Turkey," *SAIS Review* 6, no. 1(1986): 137-157, and especially the discussion on pp. 155-156.

48. For a detailed discussion of Turkey's strategic role in the defense of the West in the 1980's see Kuniholm, "Rhetoric or Reality in the Aegean," pp. 137-157 and Bruce R. Kuniholm, "CDI in NATO, the Southern Flank, and Alliance Defense," in Steve Szabo, ed., *The Future of Conventional Defense Improvements in NATO* (Washington, D.C.: National Defense University Press, 1989), pp. 263-286.

49. Memorandum for Phillips Talbot from Robert Komer, 19 February 1963, John F. Kennedy Library.

50. Kuniholm, "Turkey and NATO: Past, Present, and Future," p. 431 and Anne O. Krueger and Okan H. Aktan, *Swimming Against the Tide: Turkish Trade Reform in the 1980s* (San Francisco: ICS Press, 1992), pp. 148-149.

51. These figures are extrapolated from various OECD Economic Surveys.

52. Portions of this section are drawn from Bruce R. Kuniholm, "Turkey and the West," *Foreign Affairs* 70, no. 2(Spring 1991): 34-48 and "After the Gulf War: Turkey and the East," in Herbert H. Blumberg and Christopher C. French, eds., *The Persian Gulf War: Views from the Social and Behavioral Sciences* (Lanham, MD: University Press, 1993), pp. 453-467.

53. Much of the discussion that follows is drawn from Bruce R. Kuniholm, "The Lausanne Conference and the Post-Cold War Era," a paper presented at a conference sponsored by the İnönü Foundation in Istanbul in October 1993.

54. John Lewis Gaddis, "Toward the Post-Cold War World," *Foreign Affairs* 70, no. 2(Spring 1991): 103-122.

55. Ibid. See the discussion of some of these themes in president William Clinton's address to the United Nations, 27 September 1993.

56. John Gaddis, "The Tragedy of Cold War History," *Diplomatic History* 17, no. 1(1993): 1-16.

57. Eric Rouleau, "The Challenges to Turkey," *Foreign Affairs* 72, no. 5(November/December 1993): 110-126.

58. For a discussion of these issues see Bruce R. Kuniholm, "The Lausanne Conference and the Post-Cold War Era."

59. Selim Deringil, "Turkish Foreign Policy Since Atatürk," in *Turkish Foreign Policy: New Prospects* (Cambridgeshire: The Eothon Press, 1992) pp. 1-8.

60. Gaddis, "Toward the Post-Cold War World."

61. See Monteagle Stearns, *Entangled Allies: U.S. Policy Toward Greece, Turkey, and Cyprus* (New York: Council on Foreign Relations Press, 1992), pp. 22-23, 41, 79.

3

Turkey in the New Security Environment in the Balkan and Black Sea Region

Duygu Bazoğlu Sezer

Eurasia has been a fulcrum of the developments generated by the radical changes in the international system since 1989. In geographical, political, and cultural terms, Turkey rests along an axis where two worlds blend. Given its central location, the challenges of adaptation to the post-Cold War era have been both promising and demanding. The challenges have been promising essentially because the traditional Soviet threat has disappeared. The post-communist world in the Balkans and the post-Soviet world in Eurasia seemed to offer new space for mutually beneficial multilateral cooperation, with numerous newly independent states joining the international system.

On the other hand, the ethnic, national, and irredentist upheavals that have erupted in the Balkan and Black Sea regions in the wake of the Cold War have brought many of the most severe and disturbing ramifications of the geostrategic transition to the post-Cold War era up to Turkey's doorstep. These conflicts have created great instability and insecurity in the region. Given the persistence of dynamic forces pressing for a reordering of traditional political, economic, and military hierarchies, uncertainty seems likely to remain the hallmark of the international politics of Eurasia for some time to come.

Turkey's New Security Environment

The strategic withdrawal of Soviet power has led not only to the end of the Cold War but also to the collapse of communism in eastern Europe and the disintegration of Moscow's centuries-old empire. The global power configuration and dominant patterns of state behavior that have prevailed since the October revolution in 1917, and those that have existed since the end of the Second World War, have been radically altered as a result.

Turkey has been directly and immediately affected by this geostrategic change for several reasons. It is geographically contiguous to the regions where change has been most marked and it has powerful historical, cultural, and ethnic bonds with the peoples in many of the lands that have suddenly found themselves freed from communism and both Soviet and Russian hegemony. Furthermore, the centuries-old common Turkish-Russian border has ceased to exist, a development of historic significance for Turkish security policy.

The fragmentation of power in the region surrounding Turkey is linked with the strategic withdrawal of the Soviets. The monolithic power of Moscow on the northern and eastern shores of the Black Sea is gone and the littoral is now divided among Ukraine (with the largest part), Georgia, and Russia. An independent Ukraine has claimed its own maritime role in the Black Sea. How the naval balance between Ukraine and Russia evolves will have a direct bearing on Turkey beyond an exclusive concern for the military balance. The Montreux Convention of 1936 will be affected by the evolving situation, possibly raising the difficult question of the treaty's revision. Indeed, the relevance of the Convention was already the subject of debate in the West after the Soviet Union began transporting Kiev-class helicopter carriers through the Straits in 1976.[1]

The viability of the Montreux treaty in the post-Cold War era is likely to acquire greater salience in the near future in the context of anticipated increases in the volume of merchant shipping through the Straits. The Black Sea, and therefore the Turkish Straits, are among the alternative routes that are under consideration by international businesses engaged in negotiations with the government of Azerbaijan for the transport of Azeri oil to western markets.[2]

In the southern Caucasus, Soviet sovereignty has been replaced by three relatively small independent states: Georgia, Armenia, and Azerbaijan. Further to the east, Turkic-speaking republics in Central Asia have been freed from 150 years of Russian rule. Except for Armenia, all the newly independent former Soviet republics in the south share several common attributes with Turkey including ethnicity, language, culture, and history. Together they could represent a dynamic unified force, and perhaps a united political community.[3]

In the Balkans, too, liberation from communism and the phasing out of the Warsaw Pact and the Council for Mutual Economic Assistance

(CMEA) meant the emergence of an entirely new regional political and military landscape. In the Balkans, as in the northeast, the signing of the Conventional Forces in Europe (CFE) treaty had already generated hopes for an improved security environment. As had been the case with the West in the first wave of post-Cold War euphoria, Turkey looked forward to a mutually beneficial liberalization of political, cultural, and economic relations.

Most important perhaps, as Graham E. Fuller reminds us, geopolitical change in the post-Cold War era has involved other elements besides such tangible considerations as military power, geographic assets, and possession of raw materials.[4] The "neo-geopolitics," in Fuller's terminology, has activated psychological and cultural dynamics among nations. It has thus aroused sentiments, perceptions, and aspirations concerning group identity and lifestyle, as well as memories of cross-national and cross-cultural experiences. Fuller fully captures the spirit of the new geopolitics in remarking: "Without history and psychology...the Balkans is meaningless. It is language and myth, not rivers, mountains, or raw materials that link the Turkish shores of the Mediterranean to the shores of Lake Baikal over the rivers of Western China—in the real political sense."[5]

The new geopolitical undercurrents have indeed mobilized mutual awareness and sympathy among the Turks of Turkey, their ethnic and linguistic kin in the Caucasus and Central Asia, and the Balkan peoples of Muslim heritage who look to Turkey as a source of moral and material support in the formidable task of transition to post-communist societies. In this spirit, leaders of the Turkic-speaking republics in Central Asia and Azerbaijan in the east, and of Bosnia-Herzegovina and Albania in the Balkans, rushed to Ankara in 1991 and 1992 in order to tap the power of the newly energized emotional bonding for their respective political and economic needs.

Turkish enthusiasm for these peoples was in many respects startling.[6] In the past, especially within the dominant political elite, Turkish awareness about the Turkic-speaking world outside its borders was very low. Behind this taboo was the wish not to jeopardize relations with Moscow. Mustafa Kemal Atatürk's vision of Turkey portrayed Pan-Turkism and Pan-Islamism as dangerous and unrealistic ideologies. In succeeding decades they were stigmatized as politically and socially incorrect. Only among ultra-nationalists did references to "captive Turks" assert an ideological contact with the Turkic world in the former Soviet Union and China. By and large, the mainstream political elite viewed the Turkic-speaking population in the Soviet Union "as good Soviet citizens [who] would probably be gradually Russianized."[7]

A similar revival of mutual enthusiasm took place between Bosnian Muslims and Albanians. In this case, the common bond of Islam, a sense of shared history, and concern with the challenge to the Balkan balance of power by Serbian irredentism formed the forces of mutual attraction.

The new geopolitics of the Balkan and Black Sea regions has also been instrumental in creating a new domestic force in Turkey, namely the formation of foreign policy constituencies and lobbies representing different ethno-cultural communities and interest groups within the population. Several million people in Turkey are descendants of north Caucasians and Abkhazians who fled Russian conquest in the late 1850s and 1860s and were followed by later arrivals, including Chechens, Kabardans, Karachays, Nogays, Kumyks, Lezgins, Avars, and Azeris.[8] Among the descendants of Balkan people who migrated to Turkey during the Ottoman era, Turks of Albanian and Bosnian origin are estimated to number two to three million. By and large, these different ethnic groups have successfully assimilated into Turkish life. Now, when their kin in the Caucasus or the Balkans are caught up in conflicts, as the Georgians, Abkhazians, and Bosnian Muslims have been and as the Albanians of Kosovo might be, Ankara finds itself under pressure to take a position in support of their rights and interests. In the case of the separatist war in Georgia, former prime minister Süleyman Demirel's own party found itself caught between the cross-pressures exerted simultaneously by two groups of deputies, one Georgian and the other Abkhazian.

The disappearance of the Soviet threat has had enormous adverse repercussions on an entirely different front: cohesion in the western world. For Ankara, this has meant less confidence in the willingness and ability of major NATO allies to continue business as usual with Turkey. It has also contributed to the exclusion of Turkey from the process of European integration. The Turkish bid for admission to the European Community was already rejected in December 1989. Developments in the east had outpaced whatever meager prospects Turkey might have enjoyed in western European eyes. The rebirth of "a Europe free and whole" pushed "Turkey the step child" to the bottom of the list of strategic priorities for western Europe. Hence, the year when the Berlin Wall came down was a very lonely one for Turkey. As one observer of Mediterranean security affairs has put it: "Turkey, as a full participant in neither the EC or the Western European Union (WEU), and whose prospects for full membership in both remain poor, is increasingly isolated from the process of Europeanization affecting the rest of NATO's southern region."[9]

In sum, the changing geopolitical environment in the early post-Cold-War era presented Turkey with many new challenges. These included a fragmentation of power along its northern and northeastern borders following upon the strategic withdrawal of Soviet/Russian power, the entry into the international community of numerous political entities in Asia and Europe—some old, some new—sharing common attributes with Turkey including ethnicity, language, religion, culture, and history; the simultaneous emergence of local conflicts with the potential to escalate into larger regional conflicts; and the general diminution of western solidarity occasioned by the disappearance of the Soviet threat, further isolating Turkey from mainstream European political and economic developments and movements.

The Context of the Turkish View of the Outside World

Three basic assumptions have exerted a profound and sustained influence on Turkish foreign and security policy choices throughout the republican period.[10] Undoubtedly, specific priorities have been subject to change over the years. Succeeding regional and global phases in world politics necessitated different policies and positions and the exact balance of priorities has shifted over time in response to domestic and external circumstances. Nevertheless, one can detect several continuities in how interests and goals have been conceptualized. The strategies of how to preserve the values and rationales embodied in these basic assumptions have changed but the decisive weight of the assumptions themselves has remained intact.

The following influences have determined the broad parameters of policy: an acute awareness of the geostrategic importance of Turkey's location, especially in relation to the distribution of regional and global power; the inherent fragility of Turkey's relations with its neighbors given the legacy of history (most were under Ottoman rule); and the relative vulnerability of its ideology of westernization, modernization, and commitment to a liberal political regime faced with a deeply-rooted hostility to subservience to the West.

Only in times of deep structural change in the world system has Turkey's strategy been redefined. For the most part, between 1923 and the end of the Second World War circumstances dictated an isolationist and neutral orientation. The end of the Second World War changed that drastically. Turkey came out of its shell to join the western alliance in order to protect itself against the Soviet threat and to safeguard and further consolidate its westernizing, modernizing domestic regime. At this stage regional insecurities were not a result of the Ottoman legacy but rather a function of Soviet influence in the Balkans and the northern Middle East. Today, because the international system has been subjected to another structural transformation of historic proportions, Turkish strategy has again been redefined, this time in the direction of greater activism and involvement in regard to the issues and political affairs of surrounding regions.

Geostrategic Considerations

The first assumption which defines the Turkish elite's approach to the outside world is almost invariably cast in geostrategic terms. Turkey's location at the crossroads of Europe and Asia, occupying, in the east, a commanding position over the northern Middle East and the Gulf and, in the west, over lines of communication from the Black Sea through the Mediterranean to Gibraltar, has instilled a strong awareness of the country's potential strengths and weaknesses in influencing regional and possibly global power balances.

The specific military and political implications of Turkey's geostrategic attributes are dynamic, taking on new meaning in response to structural changes in the international and regional systems, as well as to the changing implications of militarily relevant technologies. The most powerful foundation for geostrategic assumptions, however, are what are perceived to be the lessons of history.

One of the historical constants in Turkey's geostrategic position has always been the Russian factor. The strategic importance of any given geographical location is enriched above all else by its proximity to centers of power. In the Turkish case, geostrategic significance has been related to its proximity to Soviet/Russian power and to the oil-rich Gulf region. With this location, Turkey has potentially been capable of influencing Soviet/Russian interests as well as global power concerns in and around the Gulf. History also provides formative experiences, and since the time of Peter the Great Turkish-Russian history consisted of a seemingly unending series of wars of Russian expansion into the Ottoman lands of the northern Black Sea region, the Caucasus, and the Balkans. It is common knowledge that the Straits were regarded by czarist diplomats as "the 'key' to the Russian house which properly belonged in the Russian pocket."[11]

In the post-Cold War era, the precise nature and scope of Turkey's geostrategic significance has once again been subjected to a reassessment in light of the profound alteration in global and regional power balances. Despite the uncertainties of this era of transition, however, Turkey's potential ability to influence the course of developments in several of the world's most troubled regions to its north, east, and west continues to assign it considerable importance. This was reaffirmed most powerfully during the Gulf crisis in 1990-91.

The Gulf War crystallized the tendency to view Turkey's strategic significance in the post-Cold War era overwhelmingly within the context of the Middle East and Gulf region. The collapse of the Soviet Union has further reinforced this perception. In the meantime, the security of the Mediterranean in general and of NATO's southern flank in particular has turned into one of the central concerns of European security. The growing importance of the Black Sea given anticipated increases in the foreign trade turnover of the riparian states, projects to use the sea to transport Azerbaijani oil to western markets, the unsettled nature of the security relationship between Ukraine and the Russian Federation, and the general instability of the Balkans since the breakup of former Yugoslavia all warn against the simplistic notion that the strategic relevance of the Turkish Straits in particular, and the Black Sea-Mediterranean system in general, may be declining in the post-Cold War era.

Historical Considerations

The legacy of Turkish-Ottoman rule in the regions neighboring Turkey has an impact on perceptions and policy. Except for Iran, all of Turkey's current neighbors were either fully or partly under Turkish-Ottoman rule for long periods. The resentment, on various levels of intensity, felt by these countries as a result of this historical experience, as well as the territorial, ethnic, and property questions inherited from the past have not been conducive to the establishment of mutual trust. An unarticulated but almost constantly present apprehension in Turkish security policy conceptualization is the specter of anti-Turkish coalitions among its former Ottoman neighbors such as occurred in the First Balkan War. Nevertheless, modern Turkish diplomacy has generally succeeded in achieving and sustaining stability in its relations with the former Near East, with the exception of Greece in recent decades.

Today, however, when the Balkans, the southern Caucasus, and the Middle East are undergoing a painful transition and regional power balances are being reordered, historical passions and legacies of mistrust have been revived and once again influence national positions and policies. For example, speculation about Turkey's alleged neo-Ottomanist and Pan-Turkist aspirations have been heard in Moscow, Athens, Belgrade, and even Teheran, reflecting dynamic forces that have brought back collective memories filled with images from the past. Assertions made largely for domestic consumption by high-level Turkish officials and opposition leaders in the wake of the break-up of the Soviet Union about "the rebirth of the Turkic World from the Adriatic to China" have also heightened perceptions of Turkey's supposed neo-Ottomanism.[12] A new intellectual and political interest in Ottoman history on the part of many Turks did manifest itself in the first years of the post-Cold War era but the nature and scope of that interest hardly equates to the emergence of Turkish irredentism and expansionism.[13]

The policy corollary to Turkey's trepidation about possible revanchism, and especially a revanchism coordinated among several of Turkey's former Ottoman territories, has been its own repudiation of irredentist aspirations. The National Pact (1920) defined the boundaries of the new Turkey on behalf of which the nationalist forces under Mustafa Kemal's leadership conducted the war of independence. Together with the Lausanne treaty of 1923, which confirmed the birth of the new Turkey and hence marked the end of the Ottoman state, it forms the basis for a consensus in favor of an anti-revisionist, status-quo foreign policy. However, Turkey's detractors do not always agree. Domestic opponents argue that Mosul in northern Iraq and the Dodecanese islands in the southeastern Aegean should not have been surrendered. Greece, Turkey's major foreign detractor, argues that the accession of Hatay to Turkey and Turkish policies in Cyprus are obvious examples of Turkish irredentism.

Ideological Considerations

Turkey's political elite felt the need to protect the domestic order predicated on western ideas and models of socio-political organization against internal turbulence, or worse yet from direct challenges from the outside. Founded and forcefully led until 1938 by Atatürk, an enlightened professional soldier, the Turkish Republic's domestic political order and international role were defined in radically different terms than those that had characterized state and society in the Ottoman empire which it replaced. The narrowly defined priorities of Turkey's external orientation were primarily a function of domestic exigencies. Its isolationist foreign policy represented pragmatism at its best, for Turkey needed to devote its energies to internal development. It was their mutual isolation from the West that largely helped foster Soviet-Turkish cooperation. Yet Turkey was always careful to confine its relationship with Russia to interstate issues, foreclosing the possibility of ideological interaction.

A thorough transformation of an essentially Islamic society on the model of the West was a formidable task. From the very beginning the new regime had to cope with the inherent tension between the westernizers/modernists and the traditionalists/Islamists. However, under the direction of a one-party government the reforms ultimately prevailed, paving the way for the political and social modernization of Turkey at a steady pace.

A discussion of Turkey's philosophical-ideological world view as a factor in its security decisions is of critical importance because of the close interrelationship between the sustainability of the socio-political order and the nature of the changing external environment. The Turkish case of a traditional Muslim society which has chosen to modernize on the western model through aggressive political and social engineering was unprecedented in its time and to this day remains unique in its scope and comprehensiveness.

Turkey's uniqueness was however inherently precarious. It required an hospitable external environment to sustain and reinforce domestic change. It bred international vulnerabilities by depriving Turkey of a clearly defined socio-cultural identity that could be drawn upon as a source of strength in resisting potentially adverse influences and that could serve as a basis for solidarity and affiliation with others. Since Turkey was neither a fully westernized nor an orthodox Islamic society, its pro-western domestic regime was anathema to its neighbors. This in turn made the task of safeguarding the domestic order against external challenges more difficult.

Turkey's domestic socio-political order has been tested severely by external forces. The first test came from Moscow, whose goal of exporting communism was a major threat to the Turkish domestic order throughout the seventy years of Soviet foreign policy until its transformation by Mikhail Gorbachev beginning in 1987. The geographic expansion and increasing political weight of Islamic radicalism, and in particular the anti-western domestic and foreign policies of neighboring Iran under the mullahs since 1979, comprise a new source of strain on the systemic vulnerability of the Turkish domestic regime.

Accordingly, the preservation of Turkey's unique domestic order and socio-political identity as a modernizing "European" country but with an Islamic cultural mold has comprised a fundamental element of Turkish foreign and security policy thinking. This ideological imperative has been almost invariably present in the process of decision-making, promoting, restraining, or constraining Turkey's relations with other actors, especially within the region. Turkey's inward-looking posture during the interwar years was intended to focus the country's energies on the consolidation of the domestic transformation. Later, the initial Turkish decision to join the western alliance in the post-World War II period was driven as much by this ideological preoccupation as it was by the military dimension of the Soviet threat. Turkey endured the criticisms and resentments that emerged from many quarters in the largely anti-western Muslim and Asian worlds. In the 1950s, 1960s, and 1970s it confronted the ideological challenge of the non-aligned world as well.

The same impulse has been at work more recently, when Turkey has approached the newly independent republics in the southern Caucasus and Central Asia as well as some of the post-communist states in the Balkans, but in a thoroughly altered international context. Today, Turkey's effort to safeguard its domestic values based on the western ideas of secularism, democracy, and market economics by "exporting" them to the newly liberated republics in the Balkans, the Caucasus, and Central Asia is generally encouraged in western circles—much to the resentment of radical Islamic forces. The potential of Turkey to act as a role model, especially in the Turkic/Muslim world in the East, has been portrayed as a factor serving the broader interests of world peace and stability.[14] Yet while western ideals, regimes, and systems seem to have prevailed over communism, and the Second and Third Worlds appear to have embraced them in principle, most political analysts agree that the road ahead for their firm emplacement in these societies is beset by formidable unknowns, if not impassable roadblocks.

These three fundamental assumptions of Turkey's approach to the outside world have recently undergone a substantial refocusing and strategic redirection. No longer do they dictate a narrow, inner-directed focus and strategic perspective. They reject isolation from the international community as the best insurance against foreign interference and meddling. Of equal significance, they no longer confine foreign and security policy thinking to political-military matters but reach out to include a variety of economic and communication dimensions. Political, social, and economic change within Turkey as well as the dynamics of the new geopolitical environment have allowed the Turkish leaders who were at the helm when the Cold War ended, particularly former prime ministers Turgut Özal and Süleyman Demirel, to reinterpret the vitality of the formative concepts underlying Turkish foreign and security policy in larger, international terms.

In externalizing the spirit of these concepts, Turkey has not turned toward irredentism or expansionism. It has merely assumed a greater willingness to play the role of regional arbiter, intermediary, and role model, while simultaneously attempting to take advantage of new opportunities which promise to expand Turkish political and economic influence. Turkish leaders have often talked about influence but have repeatedly rejected notions of political and territorial hegemony.[15]

Potentially the most important initiative that Turkey has taken in the post-Cold War era, indicating its resolve to act as a positive force for regional peace and stability in the long-term, has been its leadership in forming the Black Sea Economic Cooperation project among eleven countries (including Greece, Albania, Moldova, Armenia, and Azerbaijan, which are not Black Sea riparians). It has likewise participated in various international conflict resolution efforts—in the Minsk Group under the auspices of the Conference on Security and Cooperation in Europe (CSCE) to help find a negotiated solution to the Armenian-Azerbaijani conflict over Nagorno-Karabakh and in the difficult UN-sanctioned NATO operation to enforce the no-fly-zone over Bosnia-Herzegovina. These are clear indications of Turkey's greater responsibility for regional stability in the areas surrounding it.

The Balkans

Turkey is a Balkan country geographically, historically, and culturally. This sense of belonging to the Balkan complex allows Turkey to recognize its legitimate interests and concerns, especially during times of change in the nature of political regimes and the distribution of power in the region.

The Balkans are a strategic link between Turkey and western Europe and a major factor in the range of political, economic, security, and cultural bonds that Turkey has formed with the outside world. Two and a half million Turkish citizens live in western Europe and more than half of Turkish foreign trade is conducted with that region. A reordering of political boundaries and associations in the Balkans that would enhance the dominant position of a single country such as Serbia, or create a *de facto* regional hegemony on the part of an entente between Serbia and Greece, would place Turkish security interests at risk as well as reducing its freedom to cultivate traditional and new interests and relationships.

There is a powerful sense of affinity between the Turks of Turkey and ethnic Turkish and Muslim minorities throughout the Balkans. Bosnian Muslims, Albanians, and others have managed to remain quite friendly towards Turkey, contrary to the general trend of negative collective memories concerning Turkish-Ottoman rule in the region.[16]

This affinity has been inspired by emotionally charged perceptions of common cultural and historical bonds. These pro-Turkey leanings have the potential to complicate and even forestall the implementation of anti-Turkish coalitions and policies in the Balkans launched on the pretext of avenging the legacy of Turkish/Ottoman rule.

Turkish Policies

Although Turkey was satisfied with the broad outlines of the political status quo in the Balkans, it was relieved at the dissolution of communist systems and the Soviet-led Warsaw Pact. Turkey originally adopted a conservative position on the simmering Yugoslav crisis, hoping that the

Yugoslav federation could be maintained through internal negotiations and compromise. Ankara did not wish to see the former Yugoslavia's dismemberment. From the Turkish perspective, former Yugoslavia had been a moderating force in the Balkan balance and had ruled over its relatively small ethnic Turkish and large Muslim populations benignly. Viewed through the lens of a state-as-rational-actor paradigm, the fragmentation of former Yugoslavia would serve neither broader regional nor specific Turkish national interests.

Once disintegration ensued and the Bosnian Muslim population of the internationally recognized republic of Bosnia-Herzegovina became the victims of the project to create a "Greater Serbia," Turkey's position changed. New policies were designed to serve three immediate and interrelated objectives: to end the bloodshed in Bosnia-Herzegovina; to preserve that republic's independence and territorial integrity; and to prevent the engulfment of Kosovo, Albania, Macedonia, the Sanjak, and Vojvodina in a larger Balkan war with the potential to drag in other powers with their own interests in the regional politico-military balance. The threat of a wider Balkan war loomed heavily in Turkish perceptions.

Turkish policies have essentially sought to contain Serbian aggression. According to Turkey, the government in Belgrade was the prime force behind Bosnian Serbian aggression against the Bosnian Muslims and its brutal manifestations in policies such as ethnic cleansing. On 7 August 1992, Turkey elaborated the details of an Action Plan to be implemented by the United Nations Security Council. In the face of persistent Serbian aggression and the ineffectiveness of UN sanctions, Turkey called for a selective lifting of the arms embargo to allow the Bosnian Muslims to procure weapons and equipment for their self-defense and for a limited military engagement by the international community to enforce the UN sanctions.

On the other hand, Turkey has consistently shunned the option of a unilateral use of force—despite pressure by the domestic opposition in favor of such an option.[17] The speculation outside Turkey that it intended to exploit the Bosnian conflict through a show or use of force apparently failed to take account of the domestic situation in Turkey. The Turkish government would not risk unilateral military involvement in Bosnia-Herzegovina, especially knowing that geographical and logistical constraints would seriously complicate a sustained operation. Turkey engaged in an active diplomatic campaign to mobilize the international community to take a more resolute stand against Serbian aggression. In April 1993, it joined the NATO operation for enforcement of the seven-month old no-fly zone over Bosnia-Herzegovina.

Turkey's policies have failed to bring about its objectives in Bosnia-Herzegovina because of a complex set of factors whose impact has for the moment allowed the Serbian dreams of a Greater Serbia to be achieved at the expense of the Bosnian Muslims and possibly the Croats. The international community has allowed Serbian aggression to be rewarded. It is possible that the "Muslim" identity of the Bosnian Muslims has been at the heart of the major European powers' unwillingness to lift the arms embargo that unfairly deprived the Muslims of weapons of self-defense against a disproportionally armed "Christian" Serbian adversary. The example has been a poor one, and the problem will not go away. The next serious challenge facing the international community in the Balkans is likely to be the question of Kosovo.

Turkey's bilateral relations with several other Balkan countries have flourished. Two consecutive agreements on confidence-building measures between Bulgaria and Turkey in 1991 and 1992 and the restoration of the rights of the ethnic Turkish minority by Sofia have had an enormous positive impact, moving Turkish-Bulgarian relations decisively away from mutual distrust.

Albania has received priority attention and assistance in its drive to consolidate the post-communist transition. Turkey was the first state to recognize Macedonia, in January 1992 at the same time that Croatia, Slovenia, and Bosnia-Herzegovina were recognized. Macedonian leaders have appealed to Turkey, as did those of the Bosnian Muslims and Albanians, to defend their cause in international fora and for direct assistance. Turkey has been rendering economic, technical, and humanitarian assistance to all of these countries, as well as to Bulgaria.

The Role of the Greek-Turkish Conflict

The Yugoslav conflict is a product of intra-Yugoslav dynamics and tensions. On the other hand, external factors have affected its course, scope, and regional impact. One of these factors has been the adversarial and deeply competitive nature of Greek-Turkish relations.

The past behavior of Greece and Turkey on regional issues indicates that even as allies they tended to approach proposals for cooperation— such as Balkan denuclearization in the Cold War era, projects for economic cooperation, and the question of minorities—primarily with the "other side" in mind. Both states have developed their respective strategies on the basis of zero-sum calculations. The Yugoslav crisis has offered them the most recent and dramatic occasion around which to structure their mutual competition so as maximize their national interests.

Research findings indicate that the pro-Serbian policies of Athens during the Yugoslav crisis have been based to a large extent on Greece's perception of how the evolving situation might or might not work to

Turkey's advantage.[18] Above all else, Greece was uncomfortable with the idea of a new Muslim state almost next door. The possibility of such an entity encouraged worst-case scenarios because of the Greeks' foregone conclusion that a Muslim state, with positive roots in Ottoman history, would be friendly to Turkey. Accordingly, Serbia and the Bosnian Serbs were granted the full support of Greece in their struggle against what the Bosnian Muslims were seen to symbolize both politically and culturally. Greece was initially the key force supporting Serbia and the Bosnian Serbs in the international arena; strong Russian backing came later.

The Greeks' pro-Serbian position complicated the development of a coherent western strategy to protect the republic of Bosnia-Herzegovina against Serbian aggression. Greater Serbia owes its present position to a large extent to Greek diplomacy, whose central concern was to deny Turkey opportunities for attracting new friends and potential allies in the Balkans. The destruction of Bosnia-Herzegovina in the form in which it was recognized by the international community in spring 1992 and the informal Greek-Serbian entente, together with the evocations by both Greek and Bosnian Serb leaders of the common bond of Orthodoxy as the emotional basis of their cooperation, have reinforced Turkish concerns that the Balkans might become dominated by a strong anti-Turkish and anti-Muslim coalition in which Greece would play a decisive role.

The Yugoslav crisis might have evolved differently had Greece and Turkey chosen to cooperate rather than compete in the evolving geopolitical environment in the Balkans. They might not have been capable of preventing the breakup of Yugoslavia but they could perhaps have contained the conflict and prevented it from radicalizing and polarizing Balkan politics to the extent that it has. Therefore, one of the key elements of Balkan security in the post-Cold War era should be a radical reconceptualization of Greek-Turkish relations.

The Southern Caucasus and Central Asia

"Turkic" Diplomacy Begins

As with former Yugoslavia, Turkish thinking about the future of the Soviet Union did not envision its final disintegration until it had nearly occurred. The tradition of assigning the highest priority to relations with Moscow and of abstaining from relations with the Soviet Turkic peoples was sustained almost until the end of the existence of the USSR.

Following the decision to change its policy in the fall of 1991, however, Turkey moved quickly. In September 1991, teams of Turkish diplomats visited the capitals of each Soviet republic and upon return recommended granting formal recognition and the establishment of diplomatic relations. "By the end of 1991, Turkey had totally abandoned its Moscow-centered stance and embarked on a program of active relations with the Soviet successor states."[19]

Turkey became the first country to recognize Azerbaijan and the Central Asian republics. In fall 1991 and spring 1992, the presidents of Uzbekistan, Turkmenistan, Kyrgyzstan, and Kazakhstan paid visits to Turkey upon the invitation of then president Turgut Özal. Özal had stopped in Alma Ata (Almaty) during his visit to the Soviet Union in March 1991. Former prime minister Süleyman Demirel crowned the budding relationship at its early stages with a high-powered visit to the four Central Asian republics on 27 April-4 May 1992 where he pledged financial assistance to the tune of $1.2 billion.[20] His scheduled visit to Dushanbe was canceled at the last minute due to the sudden escalation of the crisis in Tajikstan. On 4-15 April 1993 president Özal went on an official tour, stopping in Uzbekistan, Kyrgyzstan, Kazakhstan, Turkmenistan, and Azerbaijan.

A series of inter-governmental meetings were held between Turkey and the Turkic countries throughout 1992-93, culminating in numerous cooperation agreements. The summit meeting held on 30-31 October 1993 in Ankara among the heads of state of Azerbaijan, Kazakhstan, Kyrgyzstan, Uzbekistan, Turkmenistan, and Turkey committed the six countries to the institutionalization of their contacts at all levels, including the summit, and to the establishment of joint working groups in several fields. The Ankara Declaration issued at the end of the summit meeting constituted the most important expression up to that point of a will to work together. Another significant development, offering substance to the so-far vague concept of the "Turkic World" has been the agreement reached on 10 March 1993 among the six on the creation of a common Turkish alphabet based on the Latin alphabet. The conference held in Ankara on 6-7 May 1993 to found the "Eurasian Chamber of Commerce and Industry" is another milestone. In 1992 Turkey pledged to admit 10,000 students from former Soviet republics into Turkish universities.

Turkey also hosted the second summit meeting of the Economic Cooperation Organization (ECO) in Istanbul on 6-7 July 1993. The ECO, originally composed of Pakistan, Iran, and Turkey, was enlarged in 1992 by the admission of the Muslim republics of the former Soviet Union and Afghanistan. The ECO is generally perceived to be the major forum within which Turkish and Iranian philosophies of political and social organization subtly compete. Former prime minister Demirel refused to define the ECO as a "Muslim Common Market," insisting that it had only an economic cooperation dimension, not a political one.[21]

Turkish Objectives

On the basis of hindsight gained from two years experience, today one might be better able to answer the following critical questions. What were and are the fundamental Turkish objectives in the southern Caucasus and Central Asia? To what extent have they been fulfilled?

Turkey had hoped for the democratic transition and increasing interdependence of the former southern Soviet republics, which would serve two interlocking purposes simultaneously: it would contribute to peace and stability in Eurasia and it would allow Turkey to deepen its relations with a region that was anticipated to be inherently friendly and responsive as well as profitable.

Did Turkey entertain hegemonic aspirations? Was it motivated by Pan-Turkic and Pan-Turanian dreams? The answer is a resounding "No!" There is no question that "the historical embrace of the Turkic world," as prime minister Süleyman Demirel described it upon his return from visiting the Central Asian republics, was accompanied by a heavy dose of sentimentality on both sides. Behind initial exuberance, high-ranking Turkish officials were aware that the newly evolving relationship needed to be defined as one among equals. Prime minister Demirel underlined this point repeatedly, saying; "Our cooperation with those republics does not mean we will put our mortgage in their economic and political policies. If we do that, they would move further away from us. Respect for their identity should be the main principle of Turkey."[22]

On the other hand, it is in the nature of the international system that states compete for political and economic influence and advantage. Such competitive behavior is an accepted norm so long as it is carried out peacefully and with respect for sovereignty, independence, and equality. The very fact that these states were young and weak—however rich in natural resources—made them appear vulnerable to the political domination of external powers determined to exploit such weaknesses. The record so far indicates that Turkey was not motivated by an intention to dominate the "Turkic World"; nor did it have such capability even if it wished to do so. Besides, leaders in each of the new republics appeared sufficiently competent, nationalistic, and independent from the very beginning as not to have aroused such illusions in external powers interested in the region—with the possible exception of the Russian Federation. In fact, if one takes a narrow, short-term perspective, the relationship until now has been on the debit side for Turkey. Turkey has not only allocated greater resources to the domestic development of the new republics than it has received in actual economic links with Turkic countries, it has also striven hard to facilitate their incorporation into the network of international diplomacy, and especially the powerful and prestigious western community.

Pan-Turkism or Pan-Turanianism enjoys neither official nor broad popular support in Turkey.[23] The National Action Party (MAP) of Alpaslan Türkeş represents the major organized political movement identified with ultra-nationalism. Even within this party, the territorial dimensions of the "Turkic World" remain unclear. The MAP had 13 deputies in the 450-member Turkish Grand National Assembly and its vote potential in 1993 was presumed to be around 3 percent of the electorate. There are extreme nationalist groups inside the two major center-right parties; the True Path Party currently in power and the Motherland Party founded by Turgut Özal. But the Great Unity Party, a splinter party from the MAP, had only six deputies in parliament.

In short, ultra-nationalism has persistently been a marginal force in the legitimate Turkish political-ideological spectrum. Yet, the inherent power of nationalism to mobilize people for expansionist or irredentist causes cannot be underestimated, especially in the post-Cold War era. Ultra-nationalism might find recruits in Turkey but it would be less in response to the appeal of the so-called "Turkic World" than because of mass frustration with rising terror by the Kurdistan Workers' Party (the PKK or *Partiye Karkeran Kuridistan*), anti-Turkish Kurdish nationalism, Armenian advances in Azerbaijan, and the plight of the Bosnian Muslims. Coupled with mounting economic stress at home, these issues may even facilitate the merger of Turkish nationalism with Islamic radicalism, as appears to be already occurring.

Turkey's specific goals in approaching the former Soviet republics have been to "export" its own ideology and regime based on western ideas and ideals and to cultivate cultural and economic relations. The first objective is very much in line with Turkey's constant sensitivity to its position as the single and most advanced westernizing state in the entire Islamic world. Given the deteriorating regional climate over the last decade, the adoption of the "Turkish model" by the former southern Soviet republics would offer Turkey security by expanding the liberal, democratic, and secular belt to the border of China. Turkish anticipation in this regard was reinforced, and possibly took cues from, the encouragement of influential western circles.

Expanded relations with these countries seemed simultaneously to offer new possibilities for cultural and economic development, especially at a time when Turkey's position in Europe was faltering. The post-Cold War era brought to the surface the inner tensions between Turkey and its western allies. Its "European" identity was questioned as Europe and the U.S. began to redefine their historical responsibilities. Turkey needed to develop new ties and relationships in an era of geostrategic change that threatened to leave it isolated. While the new geopolitical space to the east could not offer a real strategic option to Turkey in the foreseeable future, at least it could help cushion the impact of a seemingly inevitable exclusion from an evolving united Europe.

The Special Position of Azerbaijan

Azerbaijan has enjoyed special importance in Turkish perceptions and policies.[24] Historically, culturally, linguistically, and geographically the Azerbaijanis have been the closest among the Turkic peoples to the Turks of Turkey. Former nationalist leader president Abulfaz Elçibey's admiration for the Turkish model, which he reiterated in strong terms in an address before the Turkish Grand National Assembly during an official visit to Turkey in June 1992, complemented the Turkish vision of a rising new liberal, secular, and democratic geopolitical area to the east.

Though the small autonomous enclave of Nakhichevan directly borders on Turkey, as well as Armenia and Iran, Azerbaijan's potential natural wealth, including most importantly oil, is a great source of interest for Turkey, which is a net importer of fossil fuels. The richness of the common heritage and the importance attached to relations with Azerbaijan recently led foreign minister Hikmet Çetin to describe the essence of the relationship as one between "one nation but two states."[25]

Azerbaijan's post-Soviet domestic development has traced a turbulent course primarily under the strain of the conflict with Armenia over Nagorno-Karabakh, which in turn has put a great deal of stress on Turkey's regional diplomacy and bilateral relations with Azerbaijan. While giving political support to Baku's position that Nagorno-Karabakh is Azerbaijani territory, Turkey has urged a negotiated settlement. It has desisted from providing direct military assistance to Azerbaijan—a source of deep frustration to Turkish nationalists—of the sort that would alter the balance of power between the belligerents.

The difficulty of maintaining a balance between Turkish sympathies for Azerbaijan and the desire not to get involved directly in a conflict with larger regional implications has ultimately satisfied no one. The defeat of Azerbaijani forces and the occupation of over 20 percent of the country by Armenia led to the downfall of Elçibey, its first elected president, at the hands of a military leader who chose Gaidar Aliev, an ex-KGB and Politburo official under Leonid Brezhnev, as his replacement.

The venue for a negotiated settlement has been the eleven-nation Minsk Conference (which includes the United States, Germany, Russia, Turkey, Armenia, and Azerbaijan) mandated by the CSCE's Council of Ministers on 24 March 1993. Pending the convening of the conference, its member have been meeting as the Minsk Group since June 1993, parallel with the advances by Armenian forces deep into Azerbaijan. Turkey has undertaken an active role in this first conflict-resolution mission by the CSCE in one of the most troubled regions of the former Soviet Union. It has appealed for a special dialogue with Moscow on the basis of their mutual interest in and responsibility for peace and stability in the region. However, there were basic differences in their approach concerning the first steps. While Turkey insisted on both a cease-fire and the withdrawal of Armenian forces from occupied territories, Russia only demanded the former.

Regional Rivalry in the Southern Caucasus

The effect of the armed conflicts in the southern Caucasus on Turkey's interests and policies in this region has been extremely unfavorable. The initial Turkish goal of acting as a positive force by assuming a responsible leadership role in the difficult transition period has been frustrated. Scenarios that might have fostered regional peace and stability through economic and commercial cooperation have been scaled down, perhaps indefinitely. In earlier and more promising times, Paul B. Henze, a close Turkey watcher, anticipated that Turkish mediation efforts could be a responsible and effective force for regional peace.[26] The role of Russia in the southern Caucasus and Central Asia, however, has frustrated the effectiveness of Turkish initiatives and policies.

At the bilateral level, the prospects for normalization of Turkish-Armenian relations received a major setback. Despite the heavy legacy of history, Turkey had looked forward to a new stage in Turkish-Armenian relations and in that spirit extended recognition. The moderate tone of Armenian president Levon Ter-Petrossian encouraged Turkey to forgo its initial demand that Armenia formally and publicly renounce irredentist claims on Turkish territory as a precondition for recognition. Turkey also invited Armenia to join the Black Sea Economic Cooperation zone.[27] It extended humanitarian assistance in the form of wheat deliveries in fall 1992 while at the same time allowing the transport of international humanitarian aid across its territory. Bilateral talks were held in winter 1992-93 for the supply of electric energy, which failed to materialize largely due to the project's adverse impact on Turkish-Azerbaijani relations.[28] The course of the Armenian-Azerbaijani conflict through 1993 reversed the momentum achieved in Turkish-Armenian relations. The Armenian refusal to agree to a cease-fire and withdrawal from the occupied Azerbaijani territory remains an extremely serious challenge to regional peace and Turkish security interests.

The civil war in Georgia became another source of frustration for the Turkish vision of regional peace and stability through cooperation. The demographic fabric of Turkish society, including many Turks of Georgian and Abkhazian origin, as well as the friendly attitude of Georgian leader Eduard Shevardnadze, had fostered a positive image in Turkey about Georgia in general, reconfirmed by prime minister Demirel's visit to Tbilisi on 30 July 1992. There were no conflicts between the two countries except the indirect implications of the civil war on Turkey's regional diplomacy. Turks of Abkhazian origin also have a positive link with the separatists, creating a delicate situation for Turkey not only in its diplomacy but in its overall approach to ethnic separatism. The head of state of Abkhazia visited Turkey in late July 1992 seeking recognition of the Abkhaz parliament's declaration of independence.[29]

The impact of the conflicts in the southern Caucasus has perhaps taken its biggest toll on Turkish-Russian, and to a lesser extent on Turkish-Iranian, relations. Turkey's interest in post-Soviet Azerbaijan and the Turkic countries of Central Asia appears to have triggered apprehension in Moscow and Teheran about presumed Turkish intentions to create a monolithic Turkic world centered around Ankara. Conversely, Turks tend to see Russia more in the role of an actual party to the local conflicts than as an arbiter. Iran is perceived as the major force behind the increased penetration of fundamentalism in Central Asia.[30]

The importance attached by Moscow to the "south" within its "near abroad," the dominant voice of the Russian military on the issue of security in the near abroad, and overt and covert pressure on former Soviet republics to join the Commonwealth of Independent States (CIS) are clear indications that Russia is not resigned to the loss of its empire. Russia does see Turkey and Iran as its most important regional rivals. Clearly, Russia has important interests in the former Soviet republics, including the welfare of twenty-five million ethnic Russians and the security of its borders in areas of local conflicts. On the other hand, these conflicts have offered Moscow the opportunity gradually to re-establish political and economic control along its periphery. Recent developments in Georgia and Azerbaijan support this assessment. After having openly charged Moscow throughout 1993 with direct military involvement on the side of the Abkhaz separatists, president Shevardnardze finally joined the CIS in September 1993 in a move to elicit Russian support for his cause.

The forced removal of president Elçibey, a strong nationalist and a vocal anti-Russian, and his successor Aliev's decision to reorient Azerbaijan towards Moscow are indications of the resumption of a predominant influence by the Russian Federation in the region. The change of government in Baku in early summer 1993 saw the *de facto* suspension of the preliminary Turkish-Azerbaijani agreement signed on

13 March 1993 for a pipeline to transport Azeri oil from Baku through Turkey to the Ceyhan terminal on the Mediterranean. The state-owned Turkish Petroleum Company holds a 1-7 percent share in the international consortium. Turkish authorities argue that the Baku-Ceyhan route would be the most cost-efficient among the alternatives.[31] The Turan news agency in Baku has reported that according to the most recent Russian-Azerbaijani agreement, Azeri, Kazakh, and Turkmen oil would be transported to western markets through Russia.[32]

The armed conflicts in the southern Caucasus have also strained Turkish-Russian relations because of their repercussions on the CFE treaty negotiated in 1990. They have allowed Moscow to claim that the flank limits established by the CFE treaty no longer correspond to its security needs in these new circumstances. Turkey rejects the Russian arguments, maintaining that tampering with the CFE treaty would pave the way for its ultimate collapse.[33]

Conclusions

Formidable challenges lie ahead for the principal foreign policy objectives of Turkey in the early years of the post-Cold War era with regard to the Balkan and Black Sea region. Restoration of peace and stability is needed so that the plethora of ethnic, national, and territorial conflicts and wars that have seized the region will not spiral into a regional war. The radicalization and polarization that have distinguished Balkan and southern Caucasian politics since the break-up of the Yugoslav and Soviet federations threaten such a war.

A most worrisome aspect of the developments in the region from the perspective of Turkish foreign and security policy interests has been the revival of the Muslim-Christian dichotomy in the Balkans and to a lesser extent—at least for the moment—in the southern Caucasus. Religious militancy against "the other" has become an important element of Balkan politics. The Serbian nationalist leaders, joined by Greece, have invoked the traditional image of "the Muslims" in order to sustain their irredentist war. Moreover, one can detect the beginnings of an anti-Muslim Orthodox coalition between Athens, Belgrade, and Moscow. While the trend seems to have more subtle manifestations in the southern Caucasus, there is no question that pro-Armenian sympathies on the part of the Russians are shaped to an important degree by a sense of a shared Christian identity and culture.

The intensification of these trends and developments would be especially detrimental to long-term Turkish interests. This could eventually mobilize a more powerful movement in the spirit of "the

Crusades" against Turkey, the only major Muslim country in the Balkans, in a region which has not yet come to terms with its Ottoman past. And it could further penetrate Turkey's domestic politics, strengthening the power base of radical Islamic politics and supporting movements for a stronger Muslim identity among the Turkish population.

Developments in Central Asia do not look promising either. Instability within the Central Asian region, as well as the scale of problems within each individual republic, present very fundamental obstacles to the development of meaningful, long-term relationships. Not least, Turkey's overall resource base is too limited to allow it to act alone as a major force for change.

In contrast, Russia seems well-positioned to regain its pre-eminent influence in this region. For one thing, powerful patterns of economic dependence inherited from the Soviet era demand the return of Russian influence. Second, the West seems to have little interest in the long-term independence of the Central Asian republics if that would mean deterioration of relations with Russia. The West seems in effect to have conceded to Moscow's claim to be the sole peacekeeper in the so-called near abroad, especially in its "southern" section. Encouraged by western ambivalence, Russia has increasingly assumed an assertive, if not intimidating, posture in its approach to Turkey in connection with the "south" of the near abroad.

Iran is likely to be the major outside influence next to Russia. Russia seems less apprehensive about the long-term implications of Iran's growing role in Central Asia than about the revival of the concept of the Turkic world. Also, Iran's contiguity and oil wealth place it at an inherently advantageous position. In the two years since independence, the southern Soviet republics' options in developing in a westwardly direction have considerably narrowed. Turkey might have been the fundamental force to help lay the domestic and external basis of that orientation. But its own inherent limitations and vulnerabilities, the scope of the region's needs and problems, and the pre-eminence of Russian influence have greatly constrained Turkey's potential to serve as a role model for a liberal, democratic, and secular reconstruction of the states and societies in the former southern Soviet republics.

Notes

1. For a representative view see Ted Greenwood, "Soviet Intimidation of the West: The Violation of the Montreux Convention," *Global Affairs* III, no. 4(Fall 1988): 50-71.

2. The Turkish Oil Pipeline Company (BOTAŞ), a state enterprise, represents Turkey in the International Oil Consortium founded in 1992 to negotiate a deal with Azerbaijan for the right to develop its oil field. For estimates of possible increases in tanker traffic if Azerbaijan oil were to be transported through the Straits see BOTAŞ, "Note on the Passage of Tankers Through the Straits," mimeographed manuscript (Ankara, 1993).

3. For a description of the five major groups of Turkic languages see Türkkaya Ataöv, "The Language Bond: The Turkic-Speaking People of the Former USSR," *NATO's Sixteen Nations* (Special Issue) 38, no. 4(1993): 67-79.

4. Graham E. Fuller, "The New Mediterranean Security Environment: Turkey, the Gulf, and Central Asia," in Ian Lesser and Robert Levine, eds., *The RAND Institute Conference on the New Mediterranean Security Environment: Conference Proceedings* (Santa Monica, CA: RAND, 1993), p. 45.

5. Ibid.

6. Nearly all major newspapers ran informative serials on the Balkan Muslims and Turkic people in southern Caucasus and Central Asia in the first wave of curiosity about these little known "kin" and "brothers." See Bilal N. Şimşir, "Asya Türk Cumhuriyetleri ve Türkiye" [The Asian Turkish Republics and Turkey], *Milliyet*, 28 December 1991; Fatih Yılmaz, "The Turkic Republics in the Former Soviet Union: Central Asia Awakens," *Cumhuriyet*, 15 December 1992; and Abdurrahman Yıldırım and Bülent Kızonlık, "Turkish Capital on the Silk Road," *Cumhuriyet*, 19 May 1992.

7. Paul B. Henze, *Turkey: Toward the Twenty-First Century* (Santa Monica, CA: RAND, 1992), p. 31.

8. Ibid., p. 29.

9. Ian O. Lesser, *Bridge or Barrier: Turkey and the West After the Cold War* (Santa Monica, CA: RAND, 1992), pp. 88-89.

10. This conceptual framework has been developed primarily on the basis of data obtained from records of statements by high-ranking public officials. One of the most important primary sources for this are the official records of the Turkish Grand National Assembly (TGNA) published in the *Tutanak Dergisi* [The Journal of Minutes—TGNA-JM]. For this study the TGNA-JM has been reviewed every three years for the period 1930-1990 and every year for 1990-1993.

11. Ivo. J. Lederer, "Russia and the Balkans," in Ivo J. Lederer, ed., *Russian Foreign Policy: Essays in Russian Foreign Policy* (New Haven: Yale University Press, 1962), p. 420.

12. For examples of such statements by Turkish officials see Turgut Özal, "21. Asır Türkiye'nin ve Türklerin Asri Olacak," [21st Century Turkey Will Belong to Turkey and the Turks], speech at Çelik Palas, Bursa, 22 May 1991; "The New Year Message," Ankara, 1 January 1992; opening statement at the International Symposium on Turkey's Strategic Priorities [Türkiye'nin Stratejik Öncelikleri], Marmara Hotel, Istanbul, 5 November 1991.

13. For a similar assessment see Graham E. Fuller, *Turkey Faces East: New Orientations Toward the Middle East and the Old Soviet Union* (Santa Monica, CA: RAND, 1992), p. 39. For a feature story on how some intellectuals and politicians see Turkish influence in a neo-Ottomanist light see "The Neo-Ottomans," *Aktuel Weekly Journal*, 20 June 1992, pp. 7-12.

14. For samples of editorials and opinions in the western media in support of Turkey's potential to act as a role model, with special emphasis on its unique position in the Islamic world, see "The Importance of Being Turkey," *The Economist*, 24 August 1991; "Star of Islam," *The Economist*, 14 December 1991; "The Sick Man Recovers," *The Times*, 28 January 1992; "The Turkish Model on Display," *Newsweek*, 3 February 1993; and "A Gathering of Ideas: Special Report," *Newsweek*, 3 February 1992.

15. Süleyman Demirel, *Başbakan Süleyman Demirel'in Türki Cumhuriyetler Gezisi ile İlgili Olarak TBMM Genel Kurulunda ve DYP TBMM Grup Toplantısında Yaptığı Konuşmalar* [Prime Minister Süleyman Demirel's speeches at the TGNA General Assembly and the TPP's Assembly meeting], Ankara, May 1992, pp. 11-13 and *Cumhurbaşkanı Süleyman Demirel'in TBMM'nin 19. uncu Dönem, 3 üncü Yasama Yılının Açılışında Yaptıkları Konuşma* [Prime Minister Süleyman Demirel's speech for the inauguration of the TGNA's 19th session, 3rd legislative year], Ankara, 1 September 1993, pp. 11-12.

16. For official descriptions of Turkish interests and policy see Statement by Deputy Prime Minister Erdal İnönü on Cyprus and Bosnia-Herzegovina, *TGNA-JA*, Period 19, Legislative Year 1, Vol. 16, 18 August 1992, pp. 23-113; Statement by Foreign Minister Hikmet Çetin at the 47th Session of the United Nations General Assembly, 25 September 1992, New York; Statement by Ambassador Mustafa Akşin (Permanent Representative of Turkey to the United Nations) at the United Nations Security Council, 13 November 1992, New York; and Prime Minister Süleyman Demirel, *Hersey Türkiye için* [Everything For Turkey]: A Report on the Performance of the 49th Government), Ankara, 24 August 1992, p. 37.

17. On the opposition's demands for more coercive diplomacy towards Armenia see *TGNA-JM*, Period 19, Legislative Year 1, Vol. 16, 18 August 1992.

18. For a detailed discussion of this argument see Duygu Bazoğlu Sezer, "Turkish Security in the Balkans," in Costa Tsipis, ed., *Balkan Security* (forthcoming).

19. Henze, *Turkey: Toward the Twenty-First Century*, p. 29.

20. For the specifics of the credits allocated to each republic and types of humanitarian assistance delivered see Demirel, *Everything for Turkey*, p. 52.

21. Demirel, *VII.Basın Toplantısında Yaptıkları Konuşma*, [Statement at the Seventh Press Conference], 21 July 1993, p. 21.

22. Cited from the *Turkish Daily News*, 8 May 1992.

23. On 1 July 1992, *Milliyet*, a major national newspaper, reported that the Danıştay, the High Administrative Court, rejected the appeal by the nationalist Aydınlar Ocağı to be classified as a public-service association. In its negative opinion, objected to by one member, the High Court determined that in a democratic regime the state could not fund an association dedicated to the promotion of Turkish nationalism.

24. For official positions and opposition views on Turkey's relations with Azerbaijan see the records of the general debate in the parliament in the wake of the Armenians' 1993 spring offensive into Azerbaijan: *TGNA-JM*, 90th Session, Period 19, Legislative Year 2, vol. 34, 13 April 1993, pp. 13-17, 61-86.

25. Dışişleri Bakanlığı, Dışişleri Bakanı Hikmet Çetin Tarafından Dışişleri Bakanlığı 1994 Mali Yılı Bütçe Tasarısının TBMM Plan ve Bütçe Komisyonu'nda Görüşülmesi Vesilesi ile Yapılacak Konuşma, [Statement by Foreign Minister Hikmet Çetin before the TGNA's Commission on the Plan and the Budget, Meeting on the Budget for Fiscal Year 1994), 17 November 1993, p. 23.

26. Henze, *Turkey: Toward the Twenty-First Century*, p. 31.

27. The president of the Gagauz republic in Moldova expressed his county's wish to join the Black Sea Economic Cooperation zone (apparently frustrated by Moldova which is itself a member) in "The Gagauz want to join the BSECZ," *Milliyet*, 2 February 1992. The Republic of Macedonia has also sought to join, but to date without success.

28. For the parliamentary opposition to assistance to Armenia see *TGNA-JM*, 74th Session, Period 19, Legislative year 2, Vol. 30, 25 February 1993, pp. 342-346.

29. "We Want Friendship, not War," *Cumhuriyet*, 27 July 1992.

30. The Office of the Secretary General of the National Security Council (MGK), the highest decision-making body in the Turkish system of internal and external security, has recently issued a publication, MGK Genel Sekreterliği, *Neden Hedef Turkiye?* [Why is Turkey the Target] (Ankara: Kiyap Yayın Dağıtım, 1993), detailing the activities of various religious sects in Turkey as well as those in Iran in an attempt to export its regime.

31. BOTAŞ, *Rapor* (Ankara, 1993).

32. "Azeri Oil Will Flow Through Russia," *Cumhuriyet*, 26 November 1993.

33. For Turkish views see "Russia Objects to CFE Treaty," *Cumhuriyet*, 23 September 1993; "Warning from Russia," *Sabah*, 25 September 1993; and "Signals to U.S.A. on CFE Treaty," *Milliyet*, 27 September 1993.

4

The Turkic and Other Muslim Peoples of Central Asia, the Caucasus, and the Balkans

R. Craig Nation

The Central Asian, Caucasus, and Balkan regions are distant geographically and distinct culturally. They are nonetheless related by shared historical legacies and by common contemporary problems. These regions form part of the great arc of Islamic civilization stretching from Africa and Europe across the heart of Asia. All experienced communist rule and all have been victimized by considerable instability following the collapse of the Soviet and Yugoslav federations. The civil or inter-state wars in Tajikistan and Georgia, between Armenia and Azerbaijan over the Nagorno-Karabakh enclave, in Chechnya, and in former Yugoslavia have claimed tens of thousands of lives over the past several years and in several cases show no sign of abating. Though the term "arc of crisis" that is sometimes used to describe the areas in question may be misleadingly broad, it is certainly not without foundation.

The geographical and civilization hub of these strife-torn regions is Turkey. In some cases the links are historical, derived from centuries of common governance within the Ottoman empire. In some cases they are ethnic, resting upon the presence of indigenous Turkish minorities. In other cases they are linguistic and cultural, shaped by a common Turkic identity or by the context of Islam. Geopolitical concerns also attach Turkey to what are in most cases contiguous areas of considerable strategic importance. The Kemalist tradition demanded a pro-western orientation in international policy and discouraged involvement in regions defined as peripheral to the European and American focus of modern Turkey's aspirations. But events associated with or accompanying the end of the Cold War have enhanced Turkey's status as a regional power, complicated its policy agenda, and called many of the long-standing dogmas of Kemalist foreign policy into question. In Central Asia, the Caucasus, and the Balkans Turkey has discernable interests at stake and would seem to be well-positioned to pursue them.

The factors encouraging a more active Turkish foreign policy are balanced by a number of important cautions. In no instance may Turkey's interests in the Central Asian, Caucasian, or Balkan regions be described as truly vital. The attraction of Central Asia or the Caucasus as a field for Turkish engagement must be weighed against a prudent concern for maintaining stable relations with the Russian Federation, with whom Turkey has important commercial ties. The Balkan region is caught up in a frightful chaos, intimidating to any outside actor contemplating involvement. Here too, Ankara must balance its priorities with the sometimes conflicting agendas of its American and European allies. Turkey's economic performance over the past decade has been impressive, but it is still a developing nation whose achievements remain fragile—economic and technological limitations place significant constraints upon aspirations to a more dynamic regional role. Turkey's international agenda is also extremely demanding. The major challenges are still the familiar dilemmas of relating to Europe, managing friction with regional neighbors, overcoming the pattern of confrontation with Greece including the unresolved Cyprus problem, and most of all handling the escalating rebellion in Kurdistan, the attempted suppression of which is presently estimated to absorb about 30 percent of Turkish military assets.[1]

In the long-term the most significant barrier to an expanded role for any external actor in Central Asia, the Caucasus, and the Balkans may prove to be the complex realities of the regions themselves. Widely separated geographically, ethnically and culturally diverse, possessed of considerable economic potential, and located at sensitive geostrategic crossroads, these regions are not without indigenous resources, the potential to attract diverse external sponsorship, and the capacity to play off contenders for influence against each other.

Central Asia and the Caucasus

Central Asia has always been a crossroad of cultures, home to a succession of distinctive civilizations over several millennia prior to its absorption by the Russian empire from the 1860s onward. Geographically, the region is divided between a belt of steppe and grassland in the north including the great lakes of Aral, Issykkul, Balkash, and Baikal; a rim of oases and fertile valleys further south in Central Asia proper; and the imposing mountain chains of the Pamir knot. Sixty percent of the region is desert and the struggle with aridity has been constant throughout its history. Traditionally economic activity was divided between the steppe customs of nomadry and transhumance, sedentary agriculture in the oases and river valleys, and a commercial culture thriving in the great cities of the "Silk Road," the key commercial link between Asia, Europe, and the Middle East from classical times through the early modern period. A first critical turning point in the history of the region came with the arrival of the conquering Arabs bearing the banner of Islam in the eighth century. Thereafter Central Asia was drawn inexorably into the orbit of Islamic civilization. The Mongol conquests initiated by Chingis Khan in the thirteenth century attached Central Asia to a succession of Mongol khanates, stretching at their height from China to central Europe, but the ruling Mongols soon adapted to the dominant Turkic and Persian cultures. Under Timur lenk (Tamerlane) (1336-1405) the region was brought under central control and during his reign and that of his successors the Timurids (1405-1507) a classical Central Asian civilization with its centers at Samarkand and Herat reached its pinnacle. The fall of Herat to the Uzbeks in 1507 was accompanied by a phase of cultural regression that continued into the twentieth century.

The decline of Central Asia is usually associated with the gradual loss of importance of the silk road following Vasco de Gama's successful pioneering of a naval route to India via the Cape of Good Hope in 1498. Economic decline was accompanied by social stagnation, sometimes explained with reference to the influence of Islam itself or to the persistence of traditional clan and extended family social structures. Chronic political fragmentation may also be cited—the Uzbeks and their successors failed to overcome the gap between nomads and sedentarists around which much of the region's history revolves and no new central- izer of the stature of Tamerlane was to appear.

By the eighteenth century the Kazakh Small, Middle, and Great Hordes served as a shield between Russia and the backward Central Asian emirates of Khiva, Bukhara, and Kokand. From the reign of Peter the Great (1689-1725) onward Russia probed into the steppe, building fortresses and striking transitory alliances with local rulers. From 1822 to 1848 the Kazakh Hordes were conquered and the steppe belt absorbed into the Russian empire. Then directly confronted by an expanding Russia and with very few internal resources, between 1865 and 1884 the Central Asian emirates were brought into the empire as well.

Perhaps more important in the long term than the conquest of the region was the linkage with Russia that developed in its wake. Ties were originally military and administrative. Beginning in 1865 new governor generalships of "Turkestan" in the south with its capital at Tashkent and of "the Steppe" in the north including the territories of the modern republics of Kazakhstan and Kyrgyzstan were created and placed under direct Russian military administration. Demographic ties followed on the basis of a policy of Russian settlement on promising agricultural lands and an expanding commercial and administrative presence. The growth in the Russian population was accompanied and accelerated by economic relations, especially those born of the movement toward intensive cotton cultivation that followed the American Civil War and the Baku oil boom across the Caspian sea from the 1870s onward. Closer economic ties led in turn to the creation of a transportation infrastructure tying Central Asia to the Russian north, keyed to the construction of great rail lines. The iron roads that bound Central Asia to the north, writes S. A. M. Adshead, "put Russia in a position to dominate the economy of its share of Central Asia and, for a time, its demography too. A considerable inflow of Russians and Russian industry followed, particularly to Kazakhstan and Tashkent."[2]

By the dawn of the twentieth century railroad construction and industrial expansion had created a unified, regionally specialized national economy spanning the entire territory of imperial Russia, including export-oriented agriculture in Ukraine, oil industry in the Baku area, mining and metallurgy in southern Ukraine, and textile industries in Moscow, St. Petersburg, and Łódź that already received more than a third of their raw materials from the Central Asian provinces. Central Asia also served Russia as a geostrategic buffer with the British Raj in southern Asia. The "Great Game" for influence that accompanied Russian penetration of the region was resolved by the Anglo-Russian entente of 1907, an arrangement creating spheres of influence with an essentially strategic logic based upon a partition of Persia that reinforced the importance of Russian dominance in the Caucasus and Central Asia proper.[3]

Resistance to Russian rule among the Muslim peoples of the empire was concentrated intellectually within the more open Tatar communities of the Volga region and the Crimea. The Kazan Tatar Shihabeddin Mardjani (1818-1889) forwarded a modernist (Jadist) movement influenced by reform currents within the Ottoman empire that sought identity within a larger community of Turkic speaking peoples. The Crimean Tatar publicist İsmail Bey Gasprinskii (Gasprali) (1851-1914) looked to the emergence of a confederation in which a Muslim-Turkist state and a Russian state would coexist. "Russians and Turks," he wrote in 1905, "are bound together in a huge common plain extending from the foothills of the Altai and Pamirs to the swamps of the Baltic Sea....Such it was in the past, and in the future these peoples will understand that they must work hand in hand in order to find the way of life they both need."[4] The

Volga Tatar Rizaeddin Fahreddin (1858-1936) argued for a Pan-Islamic community inspired by the social ideals of the Persian intellectual Jamal al-Din al-Afghani (1839-1897). Such currents cannot be said to have struck deep popular roots prior to 1914. The Russian Revolutions of 1917 were preceded in the summer of 1916 by a Kazakh uprising but it was provoked almost exclusively by worsening living conditions and military conscription and was put down unceremoniously by czarist troops.[5]

The years of revolution and civil war extracted a terrible toll in Central Asia due to systematic resistance to Soviet power and concomitant repression as well as to famine and epidemic disease. For most of Central Asia, however, the White armies and Russian imperial tradition that they embodied did not offer a positive alternative to Soviet power. Organized resistance took the form of the *Basmachi* rebellion (the term literally means "outlaw" with the connotation of "freedom fighter") in the Fergana valley, launched in 1918 and continuing sporadically through the 1920s. The death of the former Young Turk leader and Pan-Turkist Enver Paşa while fighting with the Basmachi in a local engagement during August 1922 indicates some general sentiment within the movement on behalf of a larger regional identity but it remained essentially confined to Fergana. By the mid-1920s the Basmachi had been contained and the way cleared for the Sovietization of Turkestan.

What exactly Sovietization would entail was at first not altogether clear. The Bolsheviks came to power with a liberal nationalities policy based upon a critique of Russian imperialism that included a promised right of succession but these pledges were not consistently respected. The Bolshevik activist and Volga Tatar Mir Said Sultangaliev (1892-1940) aspired to a united Turkestan within a Soviet federation and espoused a variant of Islamic socialism but his ideas were condemned in 1923 and in 1940 he was executed by Stalin.[6] During the 1920s the official policy of *korenizatsiia* (nativization) encouraged cultural self-assertion linked to the emergence of an indigenous administrative and intellectual elite but drew the line at national separatism. In 1926 the Latin alphabet was adopted in place of the traditional Arabic script but between 1935-1939 it was in turn replaced by the Cyrillic script. The effective Russian dominance that was a much resented legacy of the imperial period seemed to have returned almost unaltered.

In 1922 Turkestan was associated with the Soviet Union as one of its four founding republics. The year 1925 saw the first in a series of administrative restructurings that would eventually result in the division of the region into the five union republics of Kazakhstan, Turkmenistan, Uzbekistan, Kyrgyzstan, and Tajikistan. The decision to create smaller administrative units is often described as a classic example of "divide and rule" imperial logic, though it may also be regarded as a sincere effort to find a reasonable pattern of administrative sub-division corresponding to actual existing patterns of identification.[7] No apportionment could have been satisfactory to all and the legacy of Soviet administration in Central Asia has left numerous unresolved problems in place.[8]

The Soviet impact upon Central Asia included a dynamic of modernization that brought impressively higher educational and public health standards in its train.[9] Soviet power also provided a context for rapid population growth (the population of Central Asia has tripled since 1913), encompassing both an expansion of indigenous village populations and an increase of the Slavic populations in cities and industrial areas. Economic development was real but also quite unbalanced. The colonial pattern of cotton monoculture in Uzbekistan and adjacent areas was maintained and extended and almost all modern sectors and urban conglomerates tended to be dominated by Russians. At the end of the Brezhnev period the four Central Asian republics except Kazakhstan, which contained 11.4 percent of the Soviet population, produced only 6 percent of the Soviet gross social product. With a poverty line fixed at seventy-five rubles of income per month (in 1988 rubles), thirty-six million Soviet citizens lived below the poverty line of whom seventeen million were Central Asians, that is 43 percent of the total. Azerbaijan, Kyrgyzstan, Turkmenistan, Tajikistan, and Uzbekistan occupied the last five places among Soviet republics for educational outlays, public health, and social services per capita and the infant mortality rate in the region was approximately double the very high Soviet average. Nor were the severe regional imbalances characteristic of the Soviet economy being corrected. Between 1965 and 1987 Central Asia's share of Soviet gross social product remained stagnant.

By the 1980s Central Asia was caught up in the long-term structural problems that were to some degree also those of the Soviet Union as a whole. Its cotton monoculture, based upon widespread use of chemical fertilizers and intensive irrigation, had contributed to an ecological disaster of immense proportions, including the poisoning of ground water due to runoff from improperly built and maintained canals and the progressive desiccation of the Aral sea.[10] Its expanding population confronted shrinking economic opportunity within the region but felt ⸱ strong, culturally based disinclination to seek employment outside it. Population growth without a corresponding increase in water resources posed a long-term dilemma with no reasonable solution in sight. Lack of employment opportunities had created a tendency toward flight from the cities, making Central Asia one of the few world regions where the relative proportion of the urban population was stable or diminishing.[11] The area's entrenched elites, represented by bastions of the Soviet establishment such as Sharif Rashidov (first secretary of the Uzbek

Communist party from 1959-1983) and Dinmukhamed Kunaev (Kazakh party boss from 1959-1986), presided over rigid and corrupt patronage systems. Despite the achievements of the Soviet period Central Asia, like the Soviet Union of which it was a part, appeared to cry out for change.

Perestroika provoked new tensions in Central Asia, including outbreaks of communal rioting in the densely populated Fergana valley. In May/June 1989 clashes between the indigenous Uzbek population and Meskhetian Turks deported to the region after World War II left 112 dead and over 15,000 displaced. Disputes over land and water rights between Uzbeks and Kyrgyz provoked even more destructive rioting in Kyrgyzstan's Osh province during June/July 1990, with a death toll of 320. Popular mobilizations also accompanied the replacement of Brezhnev era leaders such as Kunaev, who portrayed themselves as champions of local rights against overbearing control from the "center." The "Uzbek Cotton Affair," a series of legal processes between 1983 and 1987 attempting to expose endemic corruption in high places, which led to the replacement of forty of the sixty-five Uzbek communist party secretaries, was deeply resented within Uzbekistan as a form of external meddling. Kunaev's retirement in December 1986 (and initial replacement by a Russian) sparked street fighting in the Kazakh capital of Almaty, with up to two hundred reported injured.

Though destructive, these tensions were not particularly destabilizing, and they were not accompanied by a substantial movement for national independence. The first variant of the Commonwealth of Independent States (CIS), set up hastily during a meeting at Belovezhskaia Pushka near Brest in December 1991 and including only the Slavic republics of Belarus, Russia, and Ukraine literally left the Central Asian republics out in the cold. Led by Nursultan Nazarbaev of Kazakhstan, the Central Asian republics were able to insist upon their inclusion in the new variant of the CIS created one week later at Almaty. The entire clumsy episode did not speak well, however, for the future of a long-term association between the peoples of Central Asia and their former Russian patrons.

The situation which the republics of Central Asia confronted upon achieving nominal independence was unenviable. More than a century of Russian domination had left all the marks of colonial oppression in its train. Under Soviet power Central Asia modernized rapidly but as an appendage of the Soviet economy and in a context of pervasive discrimination. Though blessed with certain inherent assets, including a young and skilled work force, a significant degree of industrialization, important petroleum and mineral resources, a well-developed public transportation system, and its situation as a *carrefour géopolitique*, the region was totally unprepared to stand on its own.[12]

First reactions to the prospect of independence tended to emphasize the dynamics of decolonization and regional integration. The cultural and civilizational divide between Russia and Central Asia was wide and enduring. Russian imperial rule had undermined economic self-sufficiency, enforced political domination from an external metropole, and practiced systematic discrimination against local nationals. Under the circumstances it was not surprising that for many independence meant first of all the challenge of "beginning the process of decolonization and nation-building" including rapid movement toward full national autonomy, the consolidation of new sovereignties, and eventually, perhaps, the elimination of artificial internal boundaries on behalf of a larger regional entity.[13]

The image of an integrated Central Asia with a dominant Islamic and Turkophone character, capable of playing an independent role on the stage of world affairs, is an appealing one. For the foreseeable future, however, it has revealed itself to be a chimera. Though the idea of Turkestan is ancient, the only modern experience of unified governance in the region occurred under Russian and Soviet domination. Post-Soviet elites in power have demonstrated little interest in surrendering the prerogatives of leadership to some kind of federative entity and several generations of shared political experience appear to have created a certain national affiliation among their varied citizenries. On the sub-national level, extended family, clan, and regional affiliations are also strong and potentially divisive among a population 80 percent of which still lives in rural districts.[14] Moreover, any project for integration would risk becoming a recipe for control by the demographically dominant Uzbek community and would be resisted as such by others. Not least, dependence upon Russia in the economic, political, and security areas would make any kind of sharp rupture highly unpalatable. James Critchlow concludes that "the establishment of a united Turkestan would be possible only through a cataclysmic political upheaval."[15]

Turkey's Role in the Region

In view of the incapacity of Central Asian polities to move decisively toward full sovereignty or meaningful federation and given the "geopolitical vacuum" left behind by the decline of Russian/Soviet power, some analysts have suggested that a modern variant of the "Great Game," a rivalry for influence between regional powers, is about to take hold in the region.[16] Of the various regional actors perceived as candidates for influence Turkey is usually considered to be the best placed. The region's predominantly Turkic character creates an obvious cultural link. For many Turks, disappointed with Europe's decision to adjourn discussion of their country's application for membership in the European Community in 1989, the opportunity to assert a leadership role in a major world region which was also the birthplace of the Turkish nation seemed irresistible. Turkey's special relationship with the U.S. and membership in NATO were likewise posed as sources of major advantage. Analysts troubled by the potential for an expanding Iranian presence, or with a presumed threat of Russian neo-imperialism, presented a "Turkish Model" of secular democracy, market economics, and a pro-western geostrategic orientation as a positive alternative. In search of leverage since the collapse of the Soviet Union reduced its value to the West as a strategic partner, Turkey itself sought to emphasize its capacity to play the role of bridge between East and West. Indeed, in the wake of the Soviet collapse enthusiasm for Turkey's "bold bid for leadership and influence in the region" often seemed to know no bounds.[17]

Turkey has undertaken several positive initiatives in post-Soviet Central Asia. It has signed over 160 protocols and cooperative agreements with the six former Soviet republics of Muslim heritage, pledged more than $886 million in Eximbank credits to the region (about one-third of which has been used), and worked to build infrastructural ties in transport and telecommunications, to extend financial and business contacts, and to reinforce cultural relations by developing scholarship and student exchange programs. Nonetheless, the original exaggerated enthusiasm for Turkey's role in the region has already been replaced by what might fairly be called an equally exaggerated disillusionment.

Turkey's economic weaknesses place constraints upon its ability to provide economic aid and assistance. Its initiatives have therefore of necessity been concentrated in its areas of special interest. The most important interactions have been with Azerbaijan, with whom Turkey shares a small common border (a twelve kilometer border with the Azeri enclave of Nakhichevan), close linguistic and cultural affinity, and important economic interests (50 percent of Turkey's trade with the six former Soviet republics of Muslim heritage in 1992 was with Azerbaijan). The natural gas and hydrocarbon reserves of Uzbekistan, Turkmenistan, and Kazakhstan are also attractive but the lack of a common border with Central Asia proper makes Ankara to some extent dependent upon regional partners in developing infrastructural ties. For their own part, the Central Asian republics may be expected to remain cautious about reducing their leverage by embracing external sponsorship too one-sidedly. Philip Robins is correct in concluding that "hard decisions based on interests rather than fanciful notions of ethnic solidarity are informing decisions on both sides."[18]

Turkey also confronts competitors for influence. Iran's common border with Azerbaijan and Turkmenistan enables it to offer access to the Indian Ocean to landlocked Central Asia, as well as overland transit via Turkey to Europe. It too has ethnic and linguistic ties, with the Persophone Tajik community and with the predominantly Shiia Azeris, and motives for engagement, both as a means for overcoming international isolation and to preempt potential threats to its territorial integrity. For these very reasons Teheran's policies have not, by and large, been geared to the export of Islamic radicalism but rather to the pursuit of pragmatically defined state interests.[19] China's Xinjiang province is a geographical extension of Central Asia, it constitutes one-sixth of the territory of the People's Republic, and 60 percent of its fifteen million residents are Turkic Muslims. Beijing must to some extent be concerned with geopolitical stability in the region and its cautiously assertive policies, according to one commentator, have the potential to create "long-term conflict with its two traditional regional rivals, Turkey and Russia."[20] Pakistan, India, Saudi Arabia, and other powers have also sought in various ways to assert a regional role.[21]

Rivalry for influence in post-Soviet Central Asia need not take the form of sharp geopolitical competition. The original "Great Game" of the late nineteenth century was a projection of the European balance of power system into colonial domains and was importantly conditioned by Central Asia's weakness and passivity. These conditions no longer apply. The newly independent states of Central Asia have much greater autonomy than their nineteenth century predecessors and their interests are best served by diverse patterns of regional interaction. These interests help to explain the proliferation of regional organizations to which the Central Asian states have become attached, including the Turkish-sponsored Black Sea Economic Cooperation project (which includes Azerbaijan but not the republics of Central Asia); the Teheran-inspired Caspian Sea Council (Azerbaijan, Iran, Kazakhstan, Russia, Turkmenistan); the Russia-led CIS; a revived Economic Cooperation Organization (with Afghanistan, Azerbaijan, Kazakhstan, Kyrgyzstan, Tajikistan, Turkmenistan, and Uzbekistan joining charter members Iran, Pakistan, and Turkey); and the North Atlantic Cooperation Council (linking NATO and former Warsaw Pact members with the Soviet successor states in a loose framework for security cooperation). The Economic Cooperation Organization has been described by one observer as "a first step towards a potential common market of three hundred million people."[22] For the moment, however, almost all of the new multilateral organizations within which Central Asia is attempting to assert its identity are relatively weak.

Russian Influence in Central Asia and the Caucasus

The only regional power in a position to dominate Central Asia and the Caucasus remains Russia. A more pessimistic and increasingly more prevalent view of the region's future has come to accept the conclusion that some kind of "reattachment" to Russia in the context of the CIS is unavoidable. There is much to be said for this conclusion from the point of view of both the Russian Federation and the individual Central Asian republics. Economic links are strong and in many cases Russia is able to offer the region advantages that it cannot obtain elsewhere, notably guarantees of internal and external security.

Amidst the disarray that followed the destruction of the Soviet state, Central Asia was to some extent ignored by a new generation of Russian policy makers anxious to prioritize relations with the U.S.A. and Europe. Subsequent disillusion with the West, political resistance to the liberal policies originally pursued by Boris Yeltsin and his foreign minister Andrei Kozyrev, and institutional resistance from the "power ministries" responsible for national security affairs have contributed to an important change of priorities. One may speak of a new Russian engagement in Central Asia and the Caucasus, revealed by the role played by Russian forces in shaping the outcome of the civil war in Tajikistan during 1992 and in contributing to the collapse of the pro-Turkish government of Abulfaz Elçibey in Azerbaijan in the summer of 1993 as well as by Moscow's military intervention in Chechnya.

Tajikistan's first post-Soviet presidential election in November 1991 was won by Rakhmon Nabiev, a conservative leader of the Tajikistan Communist Party. Urban unrest in March-May 1992 led to the creation of a coalition government in which the opposition Popular Front (combining nationalist, democratic, and Islamic parties) obtained eight of twenty-four portfolios. The compromise satisfied no one and by the summer a full-fledged civil war between contending factions was under-way. The outcome was determined by the Russian 201st Motor Rifle Division stationed in Dushanbe which intervened at the decisive moment against opposition forces. After a protracted conflict that may have cost up to 50,000 lives, in November a new, pro-Russian government took power under the leadership of Imomali Rakhmonov. From its base in Khodjent, Rakhmonov's movement had already signed a bilateral Friendship treaty with Russia in May 1993 that envisioned close military cooperation. In power, it suppressed the organized opposition, appointed the Russian general Aleksandr Shishliannikov as defense minister, and proceeded to rebuild Tajik armed forces under Russian and Uzbek tutelage.[23] Resistance continues, staged from base areas in Afghanistan where an indigenous Tajik population of over eight million was originally joined by more than a hundred thousand embittered refugees (since reduced to about half that size due to repatriation). Moscow has worked to encourage a negotiated solution to the Tajik conflict but the regime in Dushanbe is likely to remain dependent upon Russian backing for some time to come.

Russian intervention in the Tajik conflict served to bolster the authority of a sympathetic government challenged by domestic opposition. In Azerbaijan, Russia's involvement contributed to the ouster of a leader whose priorities sharply contrasted with its own. Indeed, Russia's meddling in Azerbaijan was only the latest in a long series of interventions that have characterized its relations with the Caucasus since the subjugation of the region in the first decades of the nineteenth century. The czarist presence in the Caucasus dates from victories in the two Russian-Iranian wars of 1804-1813 and 1826-1828. The treaty of Gulistan of 1813 fixed the Russian-Iranian border at the Araz river, thereby dividing the area's Azeri population between the two states, and the treaty of Turkmanchai of 1828 extended Russian territories to include the Erivan and Nakhichevan khanates. From 1840, Azerbaijan was subject to direct military rule during Russia's campaigns to subdue the rebellious north Caucasian tribes. Between May 1918 and April 1920, against the background of the Russian civil war, an Azerbaijani Democratic Republic asserted a tentative right to independence but it could not hold out against the consolidation of Soviet power. From 1922-1936 Azerbaijan was associated with the Soviet federation as part of a Transcaucasus republic including Armenia and Georgia. In 1936 it became a republic in its own right but its subordination to the Kremlin remained intact. In the Caucasus as in Central Asia the essentially colonial relationship born under the czarist autocracy was in important ways reasserted in the context of the USSR.

The breakup of the USSR seemed to renew the promise of Azeri independence but, preoccupied by its ongoing conflict with Armenia over the Nagorno-Karabakh enclave, Baku has not been in a position to consolidate new state structures. In January 1990, the pro-independence Azeri Popular Front was suppressed by Soviet armed forces in the midst of pogrom-like anti-Armenian rioting in the streets of Baku. Following the demise of the USSR, the Front returned to seize power in a bloodless coup of May 1992, ousting Ayaz Mutalibov, a representative of the old Soviet establishment whose government had been discredited by military defeats. The new government of Abulfaz Elçibey moved to assert a pro-Turkish and Pan-Turkist orientation, accused Russia of abetting the Armenian side in the Karabakh conflict, and in October 1992 refused Azerbaijani membership in the CIS. Within a year, however, Elçibey's movement had exhausted its political capital and in June 1993 he was overthrown in turn by the rebel warlord Suret Huseinov. In a surprising turn of fortunes, after occupying the capital, Huseinov issued an invitation to Gaidar Aliev, first secretary of the Azerbaijani Communist Party from 1969 to 1987, to return to power as president. Aliev pledged his government to uphold Azeri independence but also asserted the need for close relations with Moscow. In the space of six years of war and turmoil Azerbaijan seemed to have moved full circle.

Elçibey's defeat was to some extent of his own making. His government proved to be as prone to corruption and administrative incompetence as its predecessors. The failure to hold promised elections alienated a good part of the democratic intelligentsia, originally an important source of support. Meanwhile continuing economic decline, which struck hardest at the urban poor and Karabakh refugees, undermined the government's social base. Decisive, however, was the failure to reverse the course of events on the Karabakh front. When, after another series of defeats between February and May 1993, Huseinov sent his private army on the march toward Baku in June, he encountered almost no serious resistance.

Elçibey envisioned Azerbaijan as a part of an emerging Turkish sphere of influence in the Caucasus but in the end Ankara could or would do nothing to reverse the course of events that led to his fall. In contrast, quiet support by Moscow for the Armenian campaign in Karabakh helped to subvert the Popular Front and the Russian military command in Azerbaijan clearly sided with Huseinov during the power struggle. The Aliev government, solicitous of Russian interests, has brought Azerbaijan back into the fold of the CIS. News of Elçibey's fall was greeted by protests in Turkey but in September 1993 prime minister Tansu Çiller paid a conciliatory visit to Moscow and Azerbaijan-Turkish relations remained stable.

The outcome of the Azeri crisis was a disappointment for Turkish diplomacy though perhaps not an irremediable defeat. Aliev has been anxious to ensure Ankara that its vital interests will not be threatened, Turkey has an obvious interest in avoiding open confrontations with the Russian Federation, and Baku and Ankara would both be well-served by a more even-handed Russian policy toward the Karabakh conflict. "In resuming its role as dominant power in the region," notes Stéphane Yerasimos, "Russia must also reestablish a certain equilibrium."[24] Moreover, the Aliev government has striven to maintain at least some degree of independence. Azerbaijan is the only CIS-member state without Russian forces stationed on its national territory.

On 20 September 1994 Baku signed an eight-billion dollar agreement with a consortium of western oil-companies allowing for the exploration and extraction of its off-shore oil. Though originally party to the agreement (the Russian state-owned oil company *Lukoil* secured a 10 percent share) Moscow subsequently raised numerous objections and has resorted to political and economic pressure to force Azeri compliance.[25] Meanwhile, Aliev has hinted that he may prefer Turkey's proposal for a Baku-Yumurtalık pipeline (possibly transiting Iran) to transport Caspian Sea oil to the Russian-sponsored project with the terminal at the Black Sea port of Novorossiisk (and possible connections to the Mediterranean, bypassing the Bosporus, through a new pipeline traversing Bulgaria and Greece).[26]

In the Tajik and Azeri cases, as well as in other armed conflicts on the periphery of the former Soviet Union, a pattern of manipulative engagement based upon policies of destabilization, selective intervention by military forces in place, and the establishment of spheres of influence or *de facto* Russian hegemony has emerged.[27] These initiatives seem to reflect an emerging consensus within the political establishment concerning Russian interests in the near abroad that may be summarized with regard to Central Asia in three issue areas.

The first area is ethnic solidarity with the large Russian populations of Central Asia—a significant part of the twenty-five million strong Russian diaspora now living outside the confines of the Russian Federation. Approximately 27 percent of the total population of the five Central Asian republics, or 13 million citizens, are non-Muslims, including 9.5 million Russians. Russians constitute 8 percent of the population in Tajikistan, 10 percent in Uzbekistan, 12 percent in Turkmenistan, 24 percent in Kyrgyzstan, and 38 percent in Kazakhstan. This is essentially an urban-based, skilled work force that plays an important economic role. The tendency toward flight from the region that has seen up to 10 percent of the Russian population depart over the past two years is disturbing to Russian and Central Asian leaders alike. Russia has repeatedly asserted its right to defend the interests of Russian residents outside the boundaries of the Russian Federation and in so doing has created a permanent pretext for interference in the affairs of its neighbors. Kazakhstan, whose large Russian population is concentrated in the north and which has been described by one well-placed commentator as "an area of vital Russian interests for ethnic, economic, and security reasons" is particularly exposed to Russian pressure.[28]

A second issue area is concern for the Islamic factor, manifest as a desire "to prevent Islamic radicals from coming to power in the Central Asian republics and to quell the rise of Islamic feelings among the Muslims in Russia itself."[29] There is an Islamic revival in progress in Central Asia, though it may be argued that it is primarily cultural in content and really no more than a normal reaction to several generations of Soviet-inspired official atheism. A politicized Islamic movement with an ideology broadly comparable to fundamentalist currents elsewhere in the Islamic world has also emerged but it remains fragmented and weak.[30] The Islamic Renaissance Party, originally created as a region-wide organization with a Pan-Islamic ideology, had by 1992 splintered into autonomous national sub-units.[31]

Russian concern for the dynamic of Islamic fundamentalism in Central Asia and the Caucasus has an objective foundation nonetheless.[32] The worsening material situation of the Central Asian republics is bound to create social tensions and, as elsewhere in the Islamic world, one channel for the expression of these tensions will be a divisive, politicized Islam.[33] The widespread perception that fundamentalism menaces the Russian population and encourages migration puts pressure on the authorities in the Kremlin to keep the problem under control.[34] Islamic movements represent a significant part of the organized political opposition to Central Asian leaders in power—in almost every case former communists recast as nationalists whose authority rests upon more or less severe authoritarian controls. There is also the potential for a spillover effect within Russia itself. The large Muslim community of the Russian Federation is very well represented in major cities as well as in a number of autonomous national units that form something like a belt reaching from the north Caucasus along the Volga to Tatarstan and Bashkiria in the Russian heartland. Though the resort to armed force to crush the secessionist movement in the north Caucasus republic of Chechnya launched by Moscow during December 1994 may not have been moti-vated primarily by the Islamic factor, concern for the potential role of Islam as a source of political instability was clearly perceived to be part of the problem.[35] Since the days of şeyh Shamil the northern Caucasus has been a focus for resistance to Russian domination as well as of Islamic consciousness. The Muslim peoples of the northern Caucasus have been politically organized since November 1991 in a Confederation of the Peoples of the Caucasus and Islamic or ethno-national extremism may well be stimulated as a consequence of the grim fighting in Chechnya.[36] Tatarstan, spanning the central Volga at Kazan and the only Russian autonomous republic where the indigenous population forms a relative majority (48 percent of the population is Tatar against 43 percent Russian) conducted a referendum on sovereignty on 21 March 1992 which carried by 61.4 percent and has used the threat of secession to negotiate special privileges. The oil-rich republic of Bashkiria beyond the Volga in the Urals, where Muslim Bashkirs constitute 22 percent of the population and Tatars 28.4 percent, has likewise used the threat of secession as the basis for a demand for concessions.

A final area of concern for Moscow relates to its broader geostrategic interests in inner Asia. The difficult legacy of Soviet engagement in

Afghanistan has made this a sensitive problem but the motives that led the leadership of Leonid Brezhnev to intervene in Kabul in December 1979 have not lost all their cogency. It is not in Moscow's interests to permit an important external penetration of the region, nor to allow Central Asia to devolve into "a new arena for external rivalry and intervention" outside of its effective control.[37] Central Asia is a seismic zone in international relations where the interests of major powers including Russia, Turkey, Iran, India, Pakistan, and China have the potential to conflict and overlap. The Russian Federation's emerging security doctrine makes a priority of maintaining a *droit de regard* upon the affairs of the near abroad and this is likely to be reflected in Central Asia and the Caucasus by the maintenance of Russian armed forces in place, by a strengthening of cooperative security mechanisms on a bilateral level and within the context of the CIS, and by strong reactions to real or suspected external sponsorship of anti-government forces such as seems to be occurring in Tajikistan.[38] Geopolitical balances in Eurasia's "Islamic crescent" have been severely disrupted by the Iranian revolution, the continuing civil war in Afghanistan, and the breakup of the USSR. Viewed from Moscow, the need to reassert some kind of regional security system capable of containing unrest appears self-evident.[39]

Russia has sufficient motivation to reassert itself in the politics of Central Asia and the Caucasus but perhaps not always sufficient means. Though Turkey has not swept into Turkestan as the successor of a receding Russian empire, it remains engaged in a long-term rivalry for influence that has the potential to become more acrimonious. The second summit of Turkic states held in Istanbul during September 1994 (bringing together Turkey, Azerbaijan, Kazakhstan, Kyrgyzstan, Turkmenistan, and Uzbekistan), though it strove to avoid direct challenges to Moscow, revealed ongoing tensions. A spokesperson for the Russian foreign ministry expressed concern over "an effort to establish a closed bloc within the Turkic world" and Turkish president Süleyman Demirel responded sharply, asserting that as "independent states" the Turkic republics "don't need anyone's permission to meet together."[40] Russian-Turkish rivalry in the Caucasus and Central Asia, it appeared, would remain a central theme in regional politics for some time to come.[41]

The Balkans

The Muslim peoples of the Balkans, until the collapse of Ottoman rule at the end of the First World War, were the privileged residents of a theocratic empire. The troops of the Osmanlı dynasty first crossed the

Bosporus in 1345. Under sultan Murad I (1359-1389) Ottoman armies marched through the valley of the Maritsa into the Balkans, reaching the Vardar in 1372, Sofia in 1385, Niš in 1386, and defeating the armies of the Serbian czar Lazar at the mythic battle of Kosovo Polje near Priština in 1389. Murad I died on the battlefield of Kosovo Polje but his conquests brought Ottoman authority into the heart of the Balkans, where it would remain for the next five centuries. The fall of Constantinople to sultan Mehmet II "the Conqueror" in 1453 made the Ottomans the heirs of Byzantium and reinforced what would become the empire's essential historic character: a loosely-bound imperial state spanning Asia Minor, Europe, and northern Africa. Waves of Ottoman conquests broke against the walls of Vienna in 1527 and 1683. It was not until a series of defeats culminating with the treaty of Karlowitz in 1698 had forced the Ottomans back from the marches of Hungary that pressure against Europe was finally reversed.

The Ottoman empire was divided territorially into the Asian and European regions of Anatolia and Rumeli, each administered by a governor general. These were in turn sub-divided into districts (*sanjaks*) controlled by military governors. The peoples of the empire were distinguished, not on the basis of ethnicity or language, but rather confession. Non-Muslim minorities were designated as *rayas* (flocks) and organized into *millets* (nations) on the basis of religious affiliation. Alongside the Muslim *ulema* in Constantinople sat the Greek Orthodox Patriarch, the Armenian Patriarch, the Jewish Chief Rabbi, and other religious leaders, each representing a particular confessional group.

Compared with the Christian civilizations of early modern Europe the Ottoman empire practiced broad religious tolerance. Non-Muslim minorities were nonetheless subjected to various kinds of discrimination sufficient to create a sense of disadvantage. Over centuries of interaction in a common political framework a certain portion of the Christian population of the Balkans opted for conversion to Islam. Conversions notably involved a majority of the Albanian peoples and the *Bogomil* (*Pataren*) Christian communities concentrated in northern Herzegovina, whose Manichaean convictions were condemned and repressed as heresy by the Orthodox church. Ottoman patterns of administration and control, including the refusal of a policy of assimilation, combined with the tortured geography of the Balkan peninsula to encourage fragmentation and localism. The Ottomans remained the masters, however, and their overlordship inevitably generated resentment which, often exaggerated in popular memory, continues to poison relations among the region's peoples to this day. "The Turk," wrote the Bosnian novelist and Nobel Prize winner Ivo Andrić in a passage fairly reflective of these resentments, "could bring no cultural content or sense of higher historic mission, even to those South Slavs who accepted Islam; for their Christian subjects, their hegemony brutalized custom and meant a step to the rear in every respect."[42]

During the course of the nineteenth century three dynamics helped to create the context for the dilemmas of contemporary Balkan politics. The first was the failure of reform efforts within the Ottoman empire, which were never successful in reversing the empire's long decline. Simultaneously, the rise in national consciousness of the Christian peoples of the Balkans, in part under the influence of the French Revolution and in part as a reaction to increasing fiscal pressures exerted by the Ottoman authorities, created a climate of general instability. Serbian uprisings in 1804 and 1815 initiated a period of national agitation that would continue unabated up to and beyond the creation of the autonomous Balkan nation states. Accompanying the rise of Balkan nationalism was the increasing intervention of the great European powers, concerned for the implications of Ottoman weakness on the balance of power. The waning of Ottoman authority, constant national agitation, and chronic great power interference combined to create the "Eastern Question" and to produce the spark that would set off the Great War.

The collapse of the Ottoman empire left the Balkan Muslims on their own. The new Turkish Republic resolved a part of its minority problem with Greece by carrying out a reciprocal forced transfer of populations following the latter's expulsion from Asia Minor in 1922 but a substantial Muslim presence remained throughout the Balkan region. The treaty of Lausanne of July 1923 which concluded Turkey's War of Independence left ethnic Turkish settlements in place in Thrace and on certain Aegean islands and larger, compact Muslim communities existed in Albania, Bosnia-Herzegovina, and Bulgaria.[43] In Sarajevo, a Yugoslav Muslim Organization led by Mehmed Spaho sought to defend the cultural and spiritual interests of the Bosnian Muslims in the radically changed postwar environment. In the difficult circumstances of king Alexander's Yugoslavia it looked increasingly to the Croatian national movement for support against Serbian domination.[44] When the German occupation of the Balkans during the Second World War brought the fascist puppet state of Ante Pavelić and his *Ustaša* movement to power in Zagreb it promptly absorbed Bosnia-Herzegovina, declared Bosnian Muslims to be citizens of the Independent State of Croatia, and proceeded to organize the massacre of hundreds of thousands of Serbians, Jews, and Roms (Gypsies). Reprisals by the Serbian-nationalist Chetniks rivaled the Ustaša atrocities in ferocity if not in extent. The Bosnian Muslim community did not initiate these events and was divided in its reactions to them, though several leading figures in the Yugoslav Muslim Organization associated themselves with the Pavelić government and some Muslim extremists joined the ranks of the Ustaša militia. These were extravagant horrors and their disastrous and enduring legacy can hardly be exaggerated.

Immediately after the Second World War, official hostility on the part of the new communist authorities caused a certain amount of emigration of Muslim peoples from Bosnia and the Sanjak district of southern Serbia and a students' self-defense organization entitled Young Muslims (one of whose members was Alija Izetbegović) was repressed by the Yugoslav federal authorities in 1949-1950. Josef Broz Tito's Yugoslavia nonetheless resurrected a sovereign Bosnia-Herzegovina and worked to integrate the Muslim peoples into a Yugoslav family of nations. Muslims were granted their own religious administrations and publications, offered constitutional pledges of freedom of religion, and beginning with the 1971 census recognized as an official "nation of Yugoslavia." Fundamentalism or Islamic radicalism hinting at the need for some kind of exclusionary Islamic republic was however severely repressed. In 1983 thirteen Muslim leaders, with Izetbegović as prime defendant, were tried in Sarajevo on charges of propagating Muslim nationalism and sentenced to long prison terms.

On the eve of the collapse of Soviet communism and the disintegration of Yugoslavia, the situation of the Muslim peoples of the region was in some ways comparable to what it had been in the wake of the Ottoman collapse. For the most part minorities surrounded by latent hostility, subject to a wide range of inherited prejudices but with potentially potent sources of external sponsorship, the Balkan Muslims were a volatile element in the region's confrontational politics. The breakdown of the Balkan state system posed the question of their status anew and J. F. Brown was correct in asserting that in a recasting of Balkan order the role of the Balkan Muslims was "likely to be divisive and could be decisive."[45]

Bulgaria

Bulgaria was geographically proximal to the seat of the Sublime Porte at Istanbul and it continues to contain the Balkan's largest relative Muslim minority. Bulgaria's population of 8,500,000 includes nearly 822,000 ethnic Turks (9.7 percent of the total population) and 150,000 Bulgarian Muslims, often referred to with the mildly derogatory term *Pomak*. There is also a Rom minority of 288,000, 40 percent of which is estimated to be affiliated with Islam. Altogether about 13 percent of Bulgaria's population is Muslim.[46]

Ethnic Turks began to settle in Bulgaria after the Ottoman conquests of the fourteenth century and they have been permanent residents ever since. The majority live in distinct areas of settlement in the tobacco growing areas around Kurdzhali in the southwest and the wheat producing zones of the Dobrudzha, though there are also areas of Turkish settlement in the Stara Planina (Balkan) mountains of central Bulgaria and in the Rhodope mountains in the south. The traditional homes of the Pomaks are isolated communities in the valleys of the Rhodope and Pirin mountain ranges.[47]

The large Muslim minority has been a constant source of concern for Bulgarian authorities. As is the case with many of the Christian cultures of the Balkans, a part of Bulgaria's national identity is built around the myth of resistance to Turkish domination, a theme that is vividly reflected in Bulgaria's national novel, Ivan Vazov's *Under the Yoke*, which portrays the national uprising of 1876-1877 and its brutal suppression. Since 1990, Bulgaria as a whole has had a negative birth rate but the growth rate for ethnic Turks, Pomaks, and Roms is considerably higher than that of the ethnic Bulgarian population. The Muslim population also has a more youthful profile and its share of the population is increasing both absolutely and as a proportion of the active work force. The predominantly ethnic Turkish areas of the southwest are immediately adjacent to the Turkish border and concern for the possible emergence of separatist movements with encouragement from Ankara, often invoked with reference to the Turkish military occupation of northern Cyprus or to the calls for the creation of a greater Albania that have accompanied the Kosovo crisis in Yugoslavia, is commonly aired.[48]

These kinds of fears have led to periodic campaigns of intimidation and repression against Muslim minorities. A culmination of sorts arrived with the "name-changing campaign" of 1984-1985, during the first phase of which all ethnic Turks of Bulgaria were required on pain of prosecution to adopt Bulgarian names. Follow up measures included official propagation of the argument that the Turks of Bulgaria were not Turks at all but rather converted Slavs; the use of force to block access to mosques; the introduction of administrative measures designed to discourage the circumcision of male children; bans on the speaking of Turkish in public places; and forceful repression of popular resistance. By the summer of 1989 such measures had provoked a mass flight of ethnic Turks across the border to Turkey. Accompanied by the forced expulsions carried out by the Bulgarian authorities, over 300,000 ethnic Turks are estimated to have left Bulgaria.

The fall of the communist regime of Todor Zhivkov in November 1989 made it possible for a new, democratically chosen Bulgarian government to put these painful episodes behind it. Since 1989, procedures have been developed for the restoration of names, overt forms of discrimination have been eliminated, and some restitution has been provided for victims.

The "Turkish question" in Bulgarian politics is far from having disappeared however. Politically organized since 1990 as the Movement for Rights and Freedoms (MRF) under the leadership of Ahmet Doğan, Bulgaria's ethnic Turkish minority came to play a central role in the post-communist political system. Parliamentary elections of October 1991 gave the former communists, rebaptized as the Bulgarian Socialist Party (BSP), 106 of 240 mandates, while the opposition Union of Democratic Forces (UDF) won 110 mandates. As the third largest Bulgarian party (the MRF is designated as a "movement" in order to avoid a constitutional ban on ethnically-based political parties), with 7.6 percent of the popular vote and twenty-four parliamentary mandates, support from the MRF was critical to the creation of any kind of stable government. During 1991 and 1992 the MRF lent support to the UDF minority government of Filip Dimitrov but relations soured as the impact of the UDF's reform program proved to be particularly damaging to the economic interests of Bulgaria's ethnic Turks. At the end of October 1992 the MRF brought down the Dimitrov government by supporting a no confidence vote and thereafter backed a non-partisan "government of experts" headed by Ljuben Berov.[49]

The MRF presented itself as a "democratic social organization of Bulgarian citizens whose goals include support for the unity of the Bulgarian peoples, prevention of all forms of discrimination, and the full and unconditional recognition of the rights and freedoms of all ethnic, religious, and cultural groups in Bulgaria."[50] Its leaders went out of their way to emphasize the organization's multi-ethnic character, commitment to the integrity of Bulgaria, and rejection of any special relationship with Turkey.[51] Given Bulgaria's poor human rights record concerning the Turkish minority there is clearly a place for such an organization. Though it cannot be attributed entirely to the influence of the MRF, Bulgaria has made progress in stabilizing relations with Turkey over the past several years, including expanded economic ties and the conclusion of a military cooperation agreement. The Muslim minority within Bulgaria is often evoked by Bulgarians as a potential source of problems but it may also serve as a positive link between them and their eastern neighbors.

General disillusionment with governing authorities has not spared the MRF, which lost ground in the parliamentary elections of December 1994 and has since experienced an internal schism.[52] The BSP emerged from these elections with an absolute majority, thus denying the MRF its former status as the key to the creation of a viable governing coalition, and the authority of its charismatic leader Doğan has been to some extent damaged by personal scandals. The MRF was clearly drained by the exercise of power, however, and if the electoral setback allows the movement to concentrate upon representing the interests of its natural constituency some distancing from the responsibility of governing may work in its long-term best interests. Regardless of the fortunes of the MRF, the Muslim minority is certain to remain a significant factor in Bulgarian politics.

Albania

At the end of the Second World War approximately 70 percent of Albania's population was Muslim. Of the remainder, 20 percent were Orthodox Christian, including an ethnic Greek minority in the southern region around Gjirokastër and 10 percent were Roman Catholic Albanians concentrated in the north in Skhodër and its environs. The bizarre dictatorship of Enver Hoxha from 1945-1985 hermetically sealed off the country from the world around it. In 1967, Albania was officially declared an atheist state and all forms of religious observance were banned and in the constitution of 1976 religion itself was formally outlawed. Since the fall of Albanian communism in 1991 these measures have been rescinded and a religious revival is in progress. Modern Albania's population of over three million is still approximately 70 percent Muslim, 20 percent Orthodox, and 10 percent Roman Catholic. What these formal designations actually mean in terms of social and cultural identity and how much weight, under the circumstances, Albania's Muslim heritage should be presumed to carry are of necessity open questions.

With a per capita GDP of $350, approximately equal to that of Sri Lanka or Indonesia, Albania has the most severe poverty and the highest birth rate in Europe. Under the government of Sali Berisha and his Democratic Party of Albania, in power since March 1992, it has struggled with the dilemmas of post-communist transition, experiencing severe declines in agricultural and industrial production and unemployment of over 35 percent. In dire need, Albania has sought fraternal aid from the Muslim world and has increased its cooperation with Turkey on all levels.[53] Its single most important external sponsor, however, is the European Union, whose assistance package includes implementation of the PHARE program, balance of payments assistance, and humanitarian and food aid.[54] Albania will continue to develop its Islamic ties but its severe underdevelopment and economic dependence upon Europe places limits upon the extent to which it can hope to pursue independent policies. In the long-term, however, Albanian's relationship with the Albanian peoples inhabiting contiguous territories within four neighboring states will become a critical issue for the region as a whole.

The Former Yugoslav Republics

Between two and three million Albanians live outside the boundaries of modern Albania in the republics of former Yugoslavia. The combined population makes the Albanians the sixth largest (and fastest growing) Balkan nationality. Small communities of ethnic Turks are scattered throughout the region and Serbia, Montenegro, Macedonia, and Bosnia-Herzegovina also contain large Slavic Muslim populations.

Montenegro's population of about 600,000 is 14.6 percent Slavic Muslim and 6.6 percent Albanian. The population of Macedonia, just over two million, is 4.8 percent ethnic Turkish, 21.1 percent Albanian, and 2.5 percent Slavic Muslim. Serbia's population of ten million is 17.2 percent Albanian (including about 100,000 Albanians resident in Serbia proper) and 2.4 percent Slavic Muslim. Finally Bosnia-Herzegovina, with a population of 4.3 million prior to the civil war, had a population divided between Slavic Muslims (43.7 percent) (the 1.6 million Bosnian Muslims made up 80 percent of the Muslim population of former Yugoslavia), Serbs (31.4 percent), and Croatians (17.3 percent). Economic hardships, the collapse of political order, the unrestrained fighting in Bosnia-Herzegovina, the frightful legacy of atrocities and ethnic cleansing, and the continual reinforcement of intolerant integral nationalism have combined to make the status of the Muslim peoples of former Yugoslavia one of the most critical issues in European politics.

Heartland of the medieval Serbian kingdom, site of the great defeat at Kosovo Polje and setting for the powerful Kosovo legend that lies at the foundation of Serbia's national identity, home to magnificent monasteries that are the glory of south Slavic culture, Kosovo has understandably held a special place in Serbian self-perception. Slobodan Milošević consolidated power in Belgrade during 1988 and 1989 by promising to defend the Serbian minority in Kosovo and he has made good on his word by suspending the region's autonomy and subjecting Kosovar Albanians to harsh military repression. The Kosovar opposition, operating from the underground, conducted a referendum on independence in October 1991 and in a secretive election in May 1992 the Democratic League of Kosova and its chair Ibrahim Rugova won large majorities. Aware of his community's isolation and exposure, Rugova has crafted a strategy of passive resistance, seeking to build up an infrastructure of governance within Kosovo and to internationalize the conflict as much as possible in search of leverage against Belgrade.[55] Rugova has been quite successful in using traditional clan structures and family allegiances to enforce discipline and maintain control at home. Kosovar Albanians have successfully boycotted Belgrade-sponsored institutions and elections and avoided provocative armed challenges. Hopes to encourage international action on behalf of the Kosovo have to date led to little of consequence. The Berisha government in Tirana has attacked Belgrade rhetorically but its weak domestic position and international exposure (with disputed regions adjacent to Kosovo, and in the northern Epirus region along the Greek border) do not make the option of aggressive engagement particularly attractive. Berisha's cautious policies have been attacked by more aggressive national groups with a Greater Albania ideology but to date the government has succeeded in neutralizing them. The Kosovo problem is far from resolved, however, and is certain to continue to provoke instability.[56]

Serbia also confronts potential instability with an Islamic dimension in its southwestern province of Sanjak. Well-known to students of diplomatic history as the Sanjak of Novi Pazar, Sanjak was garrisoned militarily by Austria-Hungary after the Congress of Berlin in 1878 as a means of blocking Serbian access to the sea. Today this small and isolated region retains considerable strategic importance. Of its 440,000 residents at least sixty percent are Muslims. The Muslim majority in Sanjak has been tempted by scenarios for autonomy or even separation but its territory blocks the major communication routes between Serbia and Montenegro, that is the two component parts of the new Federal Republic of Yugoslavia, and its retention must therefore be considered a vital interest by Belgrade. Moreover, like Kosovo, Sanjak contains important Serbian cultural sites (the Mileševo and Sopočani cloisters).

Bosnia-Herzegovina

The tragedy of contemporary Bosnia-Herzegovina has attracted a great deal of international attention to its once-neglected Muslim community. Its capital at Sarajevo, in addition to its much-touted multinational character, may be described as the cultural focus of the Muslim presence in Europe.[57] Yugoslav Muslims were highly secularized, with only 17 percent describing themselves as believers in polls conducted during the 1980s.[58] The importance of Islam as a source of cultural identity has nonetheless proved to be considerable.

In May 1990 Alija Izetbegović founded the Party of Democratic Action (PDA) as a political forum for Bosnian Muslims with a secular program but also a clear Islamic orientation. Izetbegović was tried and convicted by the Yugoslav regime in 1983 for the dissemination of a fifty page Islamic Declaration, an appeal for a resurrected Islamic identity, and was only released from prison in 1988.[59] His party split in September 1990 as a rival Muslim Bosniak Organization led by the émigré entrepreneur Adil Zulfikarpašić broke away in protest against the extent of Islamic influence within the Izetbegović faction. But in the elections of December

1990 Izetbegović's movement swept the Muslim vote. The outcome, with the three main national communities voting on strictly confessional lines, did not bode well for Bosnia-Herzegovina's viability. The PDA carried 86 of 240 seats in the new bicameral assembly, the Serbian Democratic Party linked to Milošević in Serbia carried 72 seats, and the Croatian Democratic Community with an allegiance to the government of Franjo Tudjman in Zagreb carried 44 seats, representations closely approximating the relative size of the Muslim, Serbian, and Croatian components of the electorate. By the summer of 1992, granted recognition by the international community but denied the kind of effective support that would have been necessary to maintain national integrity, Bosnia-Herzegovina was pulled into the maelstrom of the Yugoslav civil war.

The question of the identity of Bosnia's Muslims lies at the heart of the present restructuring in the Balkans. Izetbegović's embattled government has insisted upon its commitment to a multinational, multicultural, multiconfessional, and integral Bosnia-Herzegovina resting upon a distinctive Bosnian national identity. It has also actively sought international sponsorship in Muslim forums and when convenient has echoed Muslim portrayals of its cause as that of an embattled Islam pitted against an indifferent or hostile West. "What is occurring in Bosnia is not only a question for the Bosnians," writes the Bosnian spiritual leader Mustafa Effendi Ćerić; "The war in Bosnia is a global conspiracy against Muslims, this is something that all Muslims should know. What is occurring is not only the suffering of the Muslims of Bosnia, but humiliation for all the Muslims of the world."[60] Convictions such as this have become more widespread as both suffering and humiliation have intensified and Islamic influence upon Izetbegović and his entourage has clearly grown stronger.[61]

Though the idea of a "Muslim axis" in the Balkans, from Istanbul through Sarajevo to Tirana, is a bit far-fetched, by 1995 there had clearly come to be an important civilizational component to the fighting in Bosnia. Sarajevo clung to the goal of a resurrected, multicultural Bosnia-Herzegovina as a war aim but the realities of ethnic cleansing and the hatreds born of war made the Izetbegović government more exclusively based upon the Muslim population and prone to the influence of Islamic ideologies. The determination of the Izetbegović government to continue the fight rested upon the conviction that it could count on the physical and moral support of the Muslim world at large as well as a guarantee of survival from the United States. The Americans, it was presumed, solicitous toward Turkey and their Middle Eastern allies, would not allow the imposition of a Carthaginian peace at the Bosnian Muslims' expense. The Clinton administration's policy toward the Yugoslav conflict seemed to encourage such conclusions. For all of its hesitancies, it was firm in assigning primary responsibility to the Serbian side and in keeping U.S. initiatives broadly aligned with those of Turkey and other Muslim states.[62]

The Muslim world has been vociferous in its defense of the cause of the Bosnian Muslims, though somewhat more chary with material support.[63] The Turkish ambassador to Bosnia-Herzegovina, Şükrü Tufan, did not mince words in promising Sarajevo that "we stand behind you, we support you," and in condemning the purported double standard employed by the West in its dealing with Muslim nations.[64] Turkey's support for an integral Bosnia-Herzegovina conflicts with its preference for an approach based upon community rights in Cyprus but in both cases support for the rights of beleaguered Muslim peoples confronting hostile Christian majorities defines the substance of policy. Albania, with an eye to pressuring Serbia on the Kosovo question, has also aligned itself with Sarajevo, signing a military cooperation agreement with Ankara and offering the Americans access to military facilities in close proximity to the conflict zones.

The other side of the coin is represented by the community of interests that has been established between the Federal Republic of Yugoslavia, Greece, and the Russian Federation, all countries with Orthodox Christian cultures, important historical associations, and shared regional priorities. Even in their phases of greatest compliance with western counsel the Soviet and Russian governments of Mikhail Gorbachev and Boris Yeltsin refused to abandon the role of lobbyist for Russia's "historic ally" Serbia. Despite the absurdity of its haggling over the name of the Former Yugoslav Republic of Macedonia, Greece has important differences with Albania over frontier issues and is concerned about what it perceives as the potential for expanding Turkish influence in the Balkans.[65] These concerns are to some extent shared by the Slavic peoples of former Yugoslavia and belligerent extremists have not failed to give vent to them. The Bosnian Serb commander General Ratko Mladić is on record warning of an "infernal plot" between Muslims and the West "to disunite and destroy the Orthodox world, with the next target Russia" and Russia's Vladimir Zhirinovskii, speaking at the symbolic site of Vukovar in January 1994, refuted the legitimacy of any kind of Bosnian entity and growled that "an attack on Serbia is an attack on Russia."[66] Unfortunately, this kind of rhetoric could not be laughed away.

Ultimately, resolving these animosities will demand a sweeping geopolitical reconfiguration in the entire Balkan area. The Belgrade-Athens and Istanbul-Sarajevo axes cross in Macedonia and Ankara has hinted that should the Yugoslavia conflict extend into this region it would be difficult for Turkey not to become involved.[67] Such assertions may be taken with a grain of salt. The potential for the war in Yugoslavia to escalate into a general regional conflagration, with completely unforeseeable consequences, was nonetheless only too real.

A logical third party to the Balkan conflict should have been Europe itself. Both Slovenia and Croatia went to great lengths to emphasize their Catholic and European heritage, and status as bastions of western civilization "on the edge of the Orthodox and Muslim abyss."[68] Germany was commonly viewed as a kind of patron for the western republics.[69] But Europe as a whole was badly divided over options for Yugoslavia and the results of its diplomatic efforts have been modest. Through 1995 the European Union essentially cooperated with the United Nations to keep negotiating forums alive and supplied armed contingents to carry out peacekeeping and humanitarian assistance responsibilities. These were important but also limited initiatives that aimed at containing the conflict rather than grappling with the key issue of who would win.

By the spring of 1994 the "Contact Group" (France, Germany, Russia, the United Kingdom, and the U.S.) charged with facilitating peacemaking seemed to have reached the conclusion that some kind of de facto partition for Bosnia-Herzegovina, at least as the basis for a ceasefire and interim settlement, was unavoidable. But the defiance of the UN-sponsored partition-plan by the Bosnian Serbian leadership of Radovan Karadžić, symbolized by the successful counteroffensive launched against the Bihać pocket in the autumn of 1994, frustrated hopes to impose a "bad peace" that was minimally acceptable to Sarajevo. In the wake of the failure, Turkey and the Islamic world grew ever more vociferous in their vocal denunciations of the West's willingness to tolerate a genocide against Muslim peoples in the heart of Europe and Russia moved to take the Milošević government under its wing. The nightmarish logic of a "clash of civilizations" in the Balkans with Europe, Turkey, and Russia lined up on opposing sides almost seemed to have been realized.

There were a number of counter-trends that made worst-case scenarios less than likely. The Muslim factor in Balkan politics was not so evolved as to present a decisive source of cohesion among Muslim communities with their own internal divisions. Nor were the Balkan Muslims, if they were ever asked, likely to prefer to stand in permanent opposition to the Christian and Slavic cultures surrounding them. "Dreams of integration with Greater Europe," writes H. T. Norris, "are shared by Muslim Bosnians as well as Albanians, who see no inherent conflict between this wish and their own Muslim identity."[70] There was no indication that Russian support for Serbia was (or ever had been) anything other than instrumental, useful as a source of leverage in Europe but not so important as to motivate significant risks. Germany's priorities were still those of national unification and European integration, not foreign policy adventurism in an area of secondary concern.

Although Europe struggled with the Yugoslav problem it did not break apart, and in the end its search for a formula for peace seemed to lead to an approximate accord. A younger and more self-confident Turkish leadership, less preoccupied with the illusive goal of joining Europe, less dependent upon NATO as a security anchor absent a clear and present Soviet danger, and of necessity sensitive to the increased salience of Islamic consciousness in domestic politics as well as the political weight of the large communities inside Turkey of Albanian and Bosnian heritage, had good reason for positioning itself as an ally of the Muslim peoples of the Balkans. To leap from this conclusion to the assertion that some kind of neo-Ottomanism had become a decisive influence in Turkish foreign policy was completely unjustified.

Regardless of how it is resolved, the Bosnian conflict will leave deep traces. In addition to the heavy cost in lives and damage wrought, it has poisoned relations between the neighboring peoples of Bosnia-Herzegovina, peoples who have lived in harmony for generations and who will eventually have to turn back to the challenge of coexistence under much more difficult circumstances. Disputes over the proper diplomatic responses have aggravated ill-feeling and mistrust between the major European powers and set back the process of European unification. European-American relations have been affected and relations between the West and an unstable Russian Federation in the midst of its own open-ended crisis have also been tested. The war in Bosnia-Herzegovina has likewise widened an unfortunate and unnecessary rift between the Islamic and Christian civilizations of the Mediterranean and Balkan area. The greatest tragedy is that this has occurred precisely in the region that might once have seemed to be best placed to serve as a model for the harmonious intermingling and coexistence of cultures.

Turkey and the New Eurasia

The Muslim peoples of Central Asia, the Caucasus, and the Balkans all confront the challenge of redefining themselves culturally against a background of painful economic decline and severe political disorder. The breakdown of the Soviet and Yugoslav communist federations has set a process in the works that is no doubt irreversible but that is also historically unique and will require a good deal of time to complete. It is a great mistake to presume that such complex transitions can somehow move forward in a linear fashion toward predestined ends. There are no models for changes on so vast a scale and those who would seek to impose them are no doubt doomed to frustration.

Turkey is at the hub of these complicated transitions and has much to contribute to their success. It also has much at risk. Modern Turkey is a developing country with a complicated international agenda and pressing social problems. Ankara's initial enthusiasm for the challenge of engagement in adjacent regions whose populations are in some measure struggling to refind a common cultural heritage requires no justification. But commitment also brings the danger of costly entangling engagements, neglect of more pressing responsibilities elsewhere, and increased tension with other aspiring regional influentials.

The long historical associations and powerful interdependencies that still bind the peoples of Central Asia and the Caucasus to the Russian north, and the Muslims of the Balkans to their Christian neighbors, cannot and should not simply be abandoned overnight. This is so even in the catastrophic circumstances that exist at present in Bosnia-Herzegovina (where in 1991 27 percent of all marriages were mixed). The changes underway in these regions are chaotic and unpredictable and have the potential to generate almost unlimited violence. Forums for regional cooperation such as the Economic Cooperation Organization or Black Sea Economic Cooperation can help generate a climate of positive interaction and should be carefully cultivated. Emotion-laden rhetoric invoking the destinies of entire peoples and cultures has already wreaked considerable havoc and should be avoided at all costs. A minimum of order is a prerequisite for eventual geopolitical reorientations and the best way to encourage order will be through policies that make a priority of patient, non-dogmatic, pragmatic cooperation.

In the end new regional orders and patterns of affiliation in Central Asia, the Caucasus, and the Balkans will rest upon the expanded self-confidence and increased self-sufficiency of the region's peoples themselves. Turkey, along with other influential regional actors, can contribute to those ends by emphasizing positive interactions and by avoiding the trap of a confrontational conflict of interests where narrowly defined state interests are substituted for larger commitments to multilateral cooperation and peace.

Notes

1. Morton I. Abramowitz, "Dateline Ankara: Turkey after Ozal," *Foreign Policy* 91(Summer 1993): 165.

2. S. A. M. Adshead, *Central Asia in World History* (New York: St. Martin's Press, 1993), p. 218 and the discussion on pp. 217-219.

3. See the classic evaluation by A. J. P. Taylor, *The Struggle for Mastery in Europe 1848-1918* (Oxford: Oxford University Press, 1954), pp. 442-446 and Peter Hopkirk, *The Great Game: The Struggle for Empire in Central Asia* (New York: Kodansha International, 1992).

4. Cited in Serge A. Zenkovsky, *Pan-Turkism and Islam in Russia* (Cambridge, Mass.: Harvard University Press, 1960), p. 33.

5. See the account in Martha Brill Olcott, *The Kazakhs* (Stanford: Hoover Press, 1987), pp. 118-126.

6. The enduring appeal of these ideas is evoked in Alexandre Bennigsen and Chantal Quelquejay, *Les Mouvements nationaux chez les musulmans de Russie: Le 'Sultangalievisme' au Tatarstan* (Paris: Mouton, 1960).

7. Robin Wright, "Islam, Democracy and the West," *Foreign Affairs* (Summer 1993): 139 gives the traditional interpretation emphasizing the divide and rule logic of Soviet administration.

8. On the problematic legacy of Soviet-drawn borders see I. Rotar', "Izderki sovetskoi kartografii (mina zamedlennogo deistviia dlia Srednei Azii)," *Nezavisimaia gazeta*, 25 February 1992, p. 4.

9. Michael Rywkin asserts that the "Soviet educational record in Central Asia is as good as humanly possible given the objective circumstances and the low starting point." Michael Rywkin, *Moscow's Muslim Challenge: Soviet Central Asia* (London: Hurst, 1982), p. 105.

10. See the special issue of *Post-Soviet Geography* 5(May 1992) devoted to the Aral Sea crisis, *Aralskii krizis (istoriko-geograficheskaia retrospektiva)* (Moscow, 1991) and Keith Martin, "Central Asia's Forgotten Tragedy," *RFE/RL Research Report*, no. 30, 29 July 1994, pp. 35-48.

11. Between 1979 and 1989 the urban population fell from 33 percent to 31 percent in Tajikistan, from 48 percent to 45 percent in Turkmenistan, and from 39 percent to 38 percent in Kyrgyzstan. In Uzbekistan it remained stable at 41 percent. Alain Gresh, "Lendemains indécis en Asie centrale," *Le Monde diplomatique* (January 1992): 6.

12. Shafiqul Islam, "Capitalism on the Silk Route?" *Current History* (April 1994): 145-149 emphasizes the region's economic assets.

13. Citation from James Rupert, "Dateline Tashkent: Post-Soviet Central Asia," *Foreign Policy* (Summer 1992): 176. For an enthusiastic evocation of Turkey's new role as "une plaque tournante pour la métamorphose de la région" see Nicole Pope, "Ankara souhaite mettre à profit l'éclatement de l'URSS pour jouer son rôle de puissance régionale," *Le Monde*, 5 February 1992, p. 4.

14. According to the Soviet census of 1989, 60.3 percent of the population of central Asia lived in rural districts, including 80 percent of the indigenous population. *Naselenie SSSR, 1988: Statisticheskii ezhegodnik* (Moscow, 1989), pp. 24-26.

15. James Critchlow, "Will There Be a Turkestan?" *RFE/RL Research Report* no. 28, 10 July 1992, p. 50.

16. Boris Z. Rumer, "The Gathering Storm in Central Asia," *Orbis* (Winter 1993): 89.

17. Graham E. Fuller, "Turkey's New Eastern Orientation," in Graham E. Fuller and Ian O. Lesser, eds., *Turkey's New Geopolitics: From the Balkans to Western China* (Boulder: Westview, 1993), p. 68 and the entire discussion on pp. 66-76. Fuller has since tempered his enthusiasm. "Over the longer run," he wrote in 1994, "Turkish influence will probably increase rather than decrease, even though Turkey's initial expectations from its 'Central Asian brothers' have been disappointed." Graham E. Fuller, "Central Asia: The Quest for Identity," *Current History* (April 1994): 148.

18. Philip Robins, "Between Sentiment and Self-Interest: Turkey's Policy toward Azerbaijan and the Central Asian States," *The Middle East Journal* 4(Autumn 1993): 610. Eric Rouleau, "The Challenges to Turkey," *Foreign Affairs* (November/December 1993): 112 and 126 speaks of "the limits of the romance with Central Asia," and of "more sober assessments and a determination to move forward with a more solid, rational approach" replacing "pie-in-the-sky hopes."

19. On Iran's motives see Shireen T. Hunter, "The Muslim Republics of the Former Soviet Union: Policy Challenges for the United States," *The Washington Quarterly* (Summer 1992): 65-67.

20. Lilian Craig Harris, "Xinjiang, Central Asia and the Implications of China's Policy in the Islamic World," *The China Quarterly* (1993): 125. See also J. Richard Walsh, "China and the New Geopolitics of Central Asia," *Asian Survey* 3(March 1993): 272-284.

21. See A. Dastarac and M. Levent, "Islamabad regarde vers l'Asia centrale," *Le Monde diplomatique* (December 1991): 26; J. Mahan Malik, "India Copes with the Kremlin's Fall," *Orbis* (Winter 1993): 69-87; and Rasul Bakhsh Rais, "Afghanistan and the Regional Powers," *Asian Survey* 3(March 1993): 272-284.

22. Anthony Hyman, "Moving out of Moscow's Orbit: The Outlook for Central Asia," *International Affairs* 2(1993): 298.

23. On February 1993 Russian defense minister Pavel Grachev visited Dushanbe and agreed to help rebuild the Tajik army, to send a battalion of border guards to seal the border with Afghanistan, and to restore Russian anti-aircraft defenses along the frontier. Serge Schmemann, "War Bleeds Ex-Soviet Land at Central Asia's Heart," *The New York Times*, 21 February 1993, p. 12. Keith Martin, "Tajikistan: Civil War Without End?," *RFE/RL Research Report* no. 33, 20 August 1993, pp. 18-29 gives a detailed account of these events. A significant behind the scenes role was played by Uzbekistan's Islam Karimov. See Arkady Dubnov, "The Tajikistan Catastrophe," *New Times* (June 1993): 10-13.

24. Stéphane Yerasimos, "Caucase: Le retour de la Russie," *Politique étrangère* 1(1994): 82.

25. "Moscow Bares its Teeth on Azerbaijan," *Turkish Probe*, 21 October 1994, p. 12.

26. El'mar Guseinov, "Kaspiiskuiu neft' uveli iz-pod rossiiskogo nosa," *Izvestiia*, 5 October 1994, p. 3. Aliev's independence may have inspired the abortive attempt to overthrow him during October 1994.

27. Thomas Goltz, "Letter from Eurasia: The Hidden Russian Hand," *Foreign Policy* 92(Fall 1993): 92-166 and William C. Bodie, "The Threat to America from the Former USSR," *Orbis* (Fall 1993): 509-525 both criticize these policies in strong terms. Elizabeth Kridl Valkenier, "Russian Policies in Central Asia: Change or Continuity," *SAIS Review* 2(Summer-Fall 1994): 15-28 suggests by way of contrast

that it would be "unreasonable or naive" not to expect Russia to seek a "dominant position" in Central Asia, and argues that this need not lend credence to an "imperial drive theory" concerning Russian motives.

28. Alexei G. Arbatov, "Russia's Foreign Policy Alternatives," *International Security* 2(Fall 1993): 35.

29. Konstantin E. Sorokin, "Redefining Moscow's Security Policy in the Mediterranean," *Mediterranean Quarterly* 2(Spring 1993): 34.

30. For an account of the ideological orientation of Islamic leaders see "Pod zelenym znamenem: Sushchestvuet li ugroza islamskogo fundamentalizma?" *Izvestiia*, 8 January 1991, p. 4.

31. Daniil Mikul'skij, "Die Islamische Partei der Wiedergeburt: Eine Studie über Islamismus in der GUS," *Berichte des Bundesinstituts für Ostwissenschaftliche und Internationale Studien* no. 22 (1993).

32. It is obvious that the concerns are strongly felt. The Russian ambassador to the United States Vladimir Lukin, in a brief article surveying Russian security concerns, mentions the threat of Islamic fundamentalism no less than four times. Vladimir Lukin, "Our Security Predicament," *Foreign Policy* (Fall 1992): 62-65.

33. See the excellent analysis by R. G. Landa, "Islamskii Fundamentalizm," *Voprosy istorii* 1(1993): 32-41, where the social foundation of the Islamic movement in the former Soviet republics is emphasized. Bernard Lewis, *Islam and the West* (Oxford: Oxford University Press, 1993), p. 153, poses the problem eloquently. It is "humiliation and privation, frustration and failure," he writes, that have "so far discredited all the imported solutions and made increasing numbers of Muslims ready to believe those who tell them that only in a return to their own true faith and divinely ordained way of life can they find salvation in this world and the next."

34. Akhmadkadi Akhtaev, chair of the Islamic Renaissance Party, attempts to refute this argument in "Islam i patriotizm," *Den'*, 28 June 1992, p. 4.

35. See Alexei Malashenko, "L'islam comme ferment des nationalismes en Russie," *Le Monde diplomatique* (May 1992): 4.

36. The Confederation of the Peoples of the Caucasus has opposed secession from the Russian Federation. On 10 December 1994, with Russian military action against Chechnya under way, the organization convened an emergency session in Nalchik (Kabarinda-Balkaria) to coordinate aid to Chechnya, and threatened to request members to withdraw their signatures from the 1993 Russian Federation treaty. For the moment, however, such initiatives seem to have been abandoned. Karel Bartak, "Sanglants paris de M. Boris Eltsine en Tchétchénie," *Le Monde diplomatique* (January 1995): 4-5.

37. Rajan Menon and Henri J. Barkey, "The Transformation of Central Asia: Implications for Regional and International Security," *Survival* 4(Winter 1992/1993): 85.

38. Extracts from the text of the new Russian military doctrine appear in *Krasnaia zvezda*, 19 November 1993. For an analysis see John Erickson, "Une doctrine militaire équivoque en Russie," *Le Monde diplomatique* (January 1994): 7.

39. Robert V. Barylski, "The Russian Federation and Eurasia's Islamic Crescent," *Europe-Asia Studies* 3(1994): 389-416.

40. "Russia Uneasy with Turkic Summit," *Turkish Daily News*, 19 October 1994, pp. A1 and A8 and Metin Demirsar and David Sims, "Turkic Summit: Leaders Call for a Modern-Day Silk Road," *Turkish Daily News*, 29 October 1994, pp. A1 and A8.

41. "Rivalités russo-turques," *Le Monde*, 4 November 1994, p. 1.

42. Ivo Andrić, *The Development of Spiritual Life in Bosnia under the Influence of Turkish Rule* (Durham, NC: Duke University Press, 1990), p. 38. This is the text of Andrić's doctoral dissertation, written in 1924 for the University of Graz.

43. The Turkish and Muslim population of contemporary Greece is concentrated in Thrace and on the island of Rhodes. It is estimated to number 112,665, of whom 80,000 are ethnic Turks and the remainder Muslim Slavs and Roms. Purported discrimination against the ethnic Turkish population is one of the many issues that helps keep Greek-Turkish relations in a state of permanent tension. Hans-Joachim Härtel, "Die muslimische Minorität in Griechenland," in Michael Weithmann, ed., *Der ruhelose Balkan: Die Konfliktregionen Südosteuropas* (Munich: dtv Wissenschaft, 1993), pp. 214-217.

44. "Just as the trend in the first decade of the century had been to side with the Serbs as natural allies against Vienna," writes Noel Malcolm, "so the trend now was to side with the Croats as natural allies against Belgrade." Noel Malcolm, *Bosnia: A Short History* (London: Macmillan, 1994), p. 165.

45. J. F. Brown, "Turkey: Back to the Balkans?" in Fuller and Lesser, eds., *Turkey's New Geopolitics*, p. 150.

46. Population figures are drawn from the Bulgarian census of 1992. I am grateful to Professor Ivailo Partchev of the Kliment Okhridski University for supplying me with this data.

47. A Turkish perspective on the history of the ethnic Turks of Bulgaria is provided by Bilal N. Şimşir, *The Turks of Bulgaria (1878-1985)* (London: K. Rustum & Brother, 1988). See also Wolfgang Höpgen, "Türken und Pomaken in Bulgarien," *Südosteuropa Mitteilungen* 2(1992): 138-148.

48. A review of perspectives on the problem from the Bulgarian viewpoint appears as "Natsionalniiat vupros na stranitsite na kharakterni tsentralni vestnitsi u nas prez 1991 godina," [The National Question on the Pages of Typical National Newspapers During 1991], *Sotsiologicheski problemi* 3(1992): 33-51.

49. Sabine Riedel, "Die türkische Minderheit im parlamentarischen System Bulgariens," *Südosteuropa* 2(1993): 100-124.

50. Cited from *Pressluzhba "Kurier"*, 5 June 1990, pp. 6-7.

51. Interviews with Ahmet Doğan and the MRF parliamentary delegation, 16 June 1990, 26 June 1992, and 18 June 1994, Sofia, Bulgaria.

52. For an account of this disillusionment see Radoslav Gulubov, "Akhmed Dogan, or the Iron Hawk," *Bulgarian Examiner* 4(1994): 41-43.

53. Robert Austin, "What Albania Adds to the Balkan Stew," *Orbis* (Spring 1993): 274-276.

54. See "Aid to Continue," *Balkan News and East European Report*, 16 January 1994, p. 4.

55. Fabian Schmidt, "Kosovo: The Time Bomb That has not Gone Off," *RFE/RL Research Report* no, 39, 1 October 1993, pp. 21-29.

56. Michel Roux, *Les Albanais en Yougoslavie: Minorité nationale, territoire et développement* (Paris: Editions de la Maison des Sciences de l'Homme, 1992) gives a rich analysis of the roots of the Kosovo problem focused on the failure of Yugoslav development policies.

57. For historical background see the collection by Mark Pinson, ed., *The Muslims of Bosnia-Herzegovina: Their Historic Development from the Middle Ages to the Dissolution of Yugoslavia* (Cambridge, Mass.: Harvard University Press, 1994) and Malcolm, *Bosnia: A Short History*.

58. Hugh Poulton, *The Balkans: Minorities and States in Conflict* (London: Minority Rights Publications, 1993), p. 43.

59. The text of the declaration is available in Alija Izetbegović, "Dichiarazione Islamica," *Limes* 1/2(1993): 259-274.

60. "Ima Bosne i Bosnjaka," *Bosna Press*, 2 December 1993, p. 2.

61. See Izetbegović's own, essentially moderate description of this influence in 'Alija 'Ali Izetbegovic, *Islam Between East and West* (Ankara, 1994).

62. The issue at stake for the United States seemed to be that of defining a minimally acceptable outcome. For Robert W. Tucker and David C. Hendrikson, "America and Bosnia," *The National Interest* (Fall 1993): 26-27, that meant "to get for the surviving remnant of Bosnia as much territory as we can while providing it with credible military guarantees."

63. Fredy Gsteiger, "Grosse Töne, kleine Taten," *Die Zeit*, 18 September 1992, p. 14.

64. See the interview with Şükrü Tufan, "Trostruki standardi," *Bosna Press*, 18 November 1993, p. 5.

65. Yannis G. Valinakis, "La Grèce dans la nouvelle Europe," *Politique étrangère* 1(1994): 223-22.

66. Cited in Milan Andrejevich, "Serbia's Bosnian Dilemma," *RFE/RL Research Report* no. 23, 4 June 1993, p. 17. See also E. Stitkovac, "Turska i bivše socijalističeske zemlje," *Borba*, 25 January 1992, p. 8.

67. "Turtsiia shte prati voiski, ako voina obkhvane Makedoniia," [Turkey Will Send Soldiers if War Envelops Macedonia], *Kontinent*, 10 November 1993, pp. 1 and 6.

68. Mark Thompson, *A Paper House: The Ending of Yugoslavia* (London: Hutchinson Radius, 1992), p. 286.

69. See the triumphalist but well-documented account of German support for Croatian independence by Nenad Ivanković, *Bonn: Druga Hrvatska Fronta* (Zagreb: Mladost, 1993).

70. H. T. Norris, *Islam in the Balkans: Religion and Society Between Europe and the Arab World* (Columbia, SC: University of South Carolina Press, 1993), p. 275.

5

Developments in Turkish Democracy

Clement H. Dodd

In the nineteenth century the modernizing elite of the Ottoman empire explored liberal democracy as an important part of their desire to understand and, often, to emulate the West. This elite was essentially intellectual, though often employed in the bureaucracy, in teaching, and in the developing journalistic media. Liberal democracy had the attraction of providing a means by which to make sultanic rule less arbitrary and open to participation by a wider elite than that in the sultan's immediate entourage. However, there were no other groups—save those forming the structure of Islam—with any pretensions to a role in government. There was no established Ottoman aristocracy with ancient liberties to defend or expand; nor was there a strong Muslim bourgeoisie. A good deal of commerce was in the hands of Christian subjects of the empire. Islamic influence in government was declining and was being challenged in society by the largely unsympathetic westernizing elite.

The first real attempt at liberal democracy, the 1876 constitution, was defeated by the sultan. The second, in 1908, succeeded in controlling the sultan (after the defeat of the counter-revolution of 1909) but at the expense of installing authoritarian rule by the Young Turks behind a liberal-democratic facade.

During and after the War of Liberation (1919-23) Mustafa Kemal Atatürk declared sovereignty to lay in the elected Grand National Assembly and from it derived his authority to wage the war and later to mould the new Turkish nation. This was a kind radical democracy on the pattern of the French Revolution. All power rested, in theory, in an elected assembly embodying the national will. The role of the assembly has ever since been of prime importance in Turkish constitutional thinking, though Atatürk was often constrained to sidestep and manipulate the assembly for the sake of the success of the revolution.

On his better days it seems that Atatürk believed in liberal democracy—as the hallmark of a civilized state, at least. But when he tried to liberalize the regime in 1930 religious reaction to the revolution and popular hostility were marked. The experiment had, perforce, to be abandoned in the interests of the modernizing revolution and indeed in the interests of democracy itself. Subsequently, after Atatürk's death in 1937, the Kemalist single party elite governed in a tutelary and idealist fashion on behalf of the people until such time as they could be deemed ready to operate a liberal and democratic system. This could degenerate among the less dedicated members of the bureaucratic elite into ruling the people for their own good, rather than for the their eventual participation in government, and could then appear to be little different in style from the Ottoman government which preceded it.

In 1946 a great change occurred when a multi-party system was inaugurated, bringing competition among the elite. Then, when direct replaced indirect election of deputies, the electorate began to matter much more. A new right-of-center Democratic Party proved more successful than the Republican People's Party created by Atatürk. The party held power from 1950 to 1960. Its government did not wish to abandon Atatürk's reforms, including his important secularizing policies, but restrictions on religion were eased and more attention was paid to the material needs of the peasantry. Moreover, the Democratic Party came to be regarded as the party of the newly developing bourgeoisie. Assured of its legitimacy by its support in the country and the assembly, the government became heavy-handed in its treatment of the People's Party, which had strong links with the bureaucracy, the universities, and the military.

The opposition now called for liberty and for checks on power to prevent the growth of dominant party hegemony and democratic tyranny. The military intervened in 1960 and, at the behest of the intelligentsia, allowed a constitution to be drawn up which provided for checks and balances on government by other institutions, like the newly created Senate and Constitutional Court. Outside these central institutions of state much was also expected from the universities and the media, both made more free, and from associations, including unions which would soon be given the right to strike. The military, however, reserved a place for itself among the institutions that would help control government by creating a National Security Council through which its voice could be heard.[1]

The 1961 Constitution was too liberal for what became a more and more divided society. New right-of-center governments soon clashed with the guardians of Kemalism in the Constitutional Court and in the bureaucracy. More important, new forces on the far left and far right began to be mobilized, effectively making use of the new freedoms. The military intervened again in 1971 to persuade politicians (they did not take power themselves) to restrict some of these freedoms. The major instigators of violence, the extreme left, suffered heavily. This did not stop the re-emergence of violence in the 1980s when the system returned to "normal" but now it came from both right and left. As important as the violence, including bitter clashes between right and left and the assassinations of public figures, was the increasing politicization of labor unions and other associations. Even the bureaucracy, including the police, became politicized and divided and Islamic forces became noticeably more strident. In 1961 it had been expected that administrative, legal, social, and economic structures would develop an independence that would modify political strife, not that they would be so ineffective as to become politicized themselves. In 1980 the military intervened again but this time with a very heavy hand.

Military Rule and the 1982 Constitution

The military genuinely believed that it was intervening in order to save democracy, seeing that the freedoms available in liberal democracy were being abused for illiberal and undemocratic purposes. In Europe this was given very little credence but it seems that the lessons of the 1930s had been largely forgotten. The military wanted to cleanse democracy, to restore it to its true foundations. They took the classic view that it was the will of the nation expressed through the assembly which really mattered, provided always that the secularist, populist, and nationalist norms of the Kemalist doctrine were respected. The execution of governmental policy should not be subject to corruption and other vices and social institutions should not be allowed only to look to their own interests. Politicians also had to follow not their particular or local interests but the general interest. The influence of extremist groups should not be allowed to become important simply because the major parties were evenly balanced and they should certainly not be allowed to intimidate opponents. To oversee the administration of affairs and to represent the state a strong president was deemed to be important—at one stage there was some talk of a Gaullist type presidency.

In the upshot a constitution was drawn up by a National Consultative Assembly, which was mainly chosen by the National Security Council (i.e. the military). The committee of the Assembly which drafted the constitution did consult a range of public opinion but the Assembly's draft had to be approved by the National Security Council.[2] The constitution imposed restrictions on all rights, including freedom of expression, if their exercise adversely affected economic life, security, public order and morality, and the integrity of the state. Nor should they encourage crime, revolt, or rebellion. The interpretation of rights, under the influence of these large provisos, was vested in the courts. Significantly, the president had important powers of appointment to the Constitutional Court and the military courts and appointed the chief and deputy public prosecutors. It was clearly intended that the presidency should be above politics but curiously the constitution required the president to be elected by the National Assembly—the "Assembly" tradition could not be cast aside. This was later to result in a very political presidency when Turgut Özal was elected to the office in 1989 by the Motherland Party dominated assembly.

Under the new constitution and political parties' legislation the parties were, predictably, obliged to represent the national political interest. They were not to be corrupted by, or to corrupt, professional associations or labor unions—with whom there could be no financial or other links. They could not form women's or youth organizations, nor were they allowed to recruit as members civil servants including school and university teachers. In the constitution, labor unions were singled out for attention. They were not allowed to engage in political activities, pursue political causes, or support political parties. Strikes and lock outs were also stringently controlled and were not to be politically motivated. Disputes were to be settled by a Supreme Arbitration Board under governmental supervision. Only one labor federation was recognized for bargaining purposes. One result of these measures was severe restraint of wages.

In its essentials the 1982 constitution still holds sway. However, after 1983 when competitive politics was re-introduced, there was some amelioration of the harsh regime imposed by the military. For instance, the pre-1980 political parties, which were banned by the military, have been allowed to return to the political scene. In 1987, the military did not object when a referendum was held on whether the political leaders of the 1980s, who had been banned from political activity for ten years, might return. The decision was carried by 1 per cent. Political parties set up with the encouragement of the military soon withered and the first president, the leader of the coup, General Kenan Evren, generally allowed political initiative to be taken by the elected government under Turgut Özal. A measure important for democracy taken by his government was the abolition of articles in the penal code which forbade politics based on religion or social class.[3]

Nor did the military intrude itself much into politics. By 1987 Özal was strong enough to reject the military's nominee for the post of Chief of the General Staff, a new and remarkable rejection of military influence. After a period of Motherland Party government under Özal and other leaders, Süleyman Demirel, prime minister when the military intervened in 1980, regained power in 1991 as head of the new True Path Party in coalition with the new Social Democratic Populist Party (SDPP) led by Erdal İnönü. A significant feature of this coalition government's program was the restoration of democracy, including constitutional changes. Amendments to the constitution had, in fact, been proposed by Özal when prime minister but no progress was made.

Attempts to Restore Turkish Democracy, 1991-94

In their 1991 election campaigns both coalition parties called for a radical change in the constitution mainly as a means of removing Özal from the presidency. The restoration of democracy was not the major issue but after the election Demirel and İnönü announced a redemocratization program with great flourish. It was pointed out that Turkey ranked only twenty-fourth in the world table of human rights. It was declared that in the future Turkish prisons would be made of glass. A "Democratic Package" was announced on 15 November 1991. The presidency, it was said, was not to be regarded as being a separate institution and had to be altered in character to conform with the norms of parliamentary democracy. Constitutional limitations on the participation of officials of labor unions and other associations in politics would be removed. Also, students and teachers would be allowed to join political parties, which would also be permitted to have youth and women's organizations. Civil servants would be allowed to set up unions, universities would regain autonomy, and the unpopular Higher Education Council would be abolished.

The press was also to be made more free. The constitutional reform necessary for these measures would be accompanied by legal changes to allow a wider exercise of rights to form associations and to hold rallies and meetings. There were to be no legal or *de facto* restrictions on free expression for ethnic groups, including the use of their language and the promotion of their culture within the concept of national unity. Clearly the beneficiaries in mind were the Kurds.[4] Finally, the police were to be trained to respect human rights, police stations were to be open to scrutiny, and no pre-employment "security reports" were to be imposed on candidates for government posts. These measures were close to the heart of the SDPP; it was the party's members who took the lead in seeking their implementation.

The first problem that arose was, and still is, that change to the constitution required at least a 60 per cent vote in the assembly. The coalition government could only achieve constitutional change if supported by other parties. The Motherland Party would not agree to any change that would weaken the position of Özal, so there was no chance of changing the role of the president. The religious Welfare Party had its own unique stance on a number of the democratization issues as well as on the presidency. It was therefore decided that progress could only be made on a limited front and the government distributed a package of proposals for constitutional change to the political parties for consideration.

In March 1993 five changes in the constitution were agreed in principle by the government and the Motherland Party, whose vote would be crucial for the government if progress was to be made. These were: (1) a reduction in the voting age to eighteen; (2) the reduction of the age for deputies from thirty to twenty-five; (3) freedom for political parties to recruit civil servants (including teachers) to membership, and to form youth and women's organizations; (4) freedom for political parties to establish links with unions and other organizations; and (5) the lifting of the monopoly enjoyed by the Turkish Radio and Television authority. Further meetings were scheduled for April but the sudden death of the president and the subsequent changes in leadership in Turkish politics, combined with a worsening of the Kurdish problem, resulted in these matters being left unresolved.

Of more practical significance was the determined attempt made by the SDPP minister of justice, Seyfi Oktay, to obtain legislation: (1) to prevent suspects being kept in detention for more than twenty-four hours (under existing legislation they could be kept indefinitely); (2) to ensure that in all but the most serious cases the prosecution should present its case within six months; and (3) to allow lawyers to be present at every interrogation—a practice designed to prevent torture. Although in the assembly the Motherland Party supported the legislation it was vetoed by Özal as president. He argued that the State Security Courts were too few and overworked for these measures to be practicable and that the restriction of detention could hamper investigations. Opposition to these measures developed among right-wing deputies in the Assembly, including those in the True Path Party, and Oktay had in the end to accept that those appearing before State Security Courts would for the most part be excluded from the benefits of the legislation. It was widely believed that it was in these courts that reforms were most necessary.[5]

Oktay found that his efforts to institute reform were very unwelcome to some of the top personnel in his ministry, many of whom had been appointed by Motherland Party governments. The president of the Court of Appeals openly attacked the reform bill. Not surprisingly, Oktay tried to obtain legislation to get around the veto on appointments in the Ministry of Justice which Özal had used on numerous occasions. This and subsequent "by-pass" bills were rejected by Özal, the first by-pass bill being referred by him to the Constitutional Court. They formed a background to the disruptive rivalry between Demirel and Özal during the latter's tenure as president. With the death of Özal and the election of Demirel as president the need for these by-pass bills disappeared.

These attempts to liberalize the regime by Oktay's judicial reforms ran into considerable opposition in military and bureaucratic circles, which believed that they would be regarded as concessions to the Kurds. With the military highly influential as a result of the struggle against the Kurdistan Workers' Party (PKK) there is little positive response for more human and political rights in governmental circles or in public opinion. The damning 1992 Amnesty International Report (November 1992) was largely ignored, or treated as Kurdish propaganda, as too are the often vigorous complaints made by the Turkish Human Rights Foundation. Although those in authority are often sympathetic to human rights' issues, in the present climate it is difficult to change the attitudes of those lower down. This was one of the items on the Democratization Program but little seems to have been achieved.

Another instance related to the Kurdish problem has also shown up the inadequacies of the 1982 Constitution. In 1994 seven Democratic Party deputies were successfully prosecuted, their parliamentary immunity having been lifted, for expressing separatist views on the Kurdish question. The media has also become less free in its ability to report the struggle against the PKK. There is also occasionally talk of a "creeping coup" being carried out by the National Security Council. Against this general lack of movement it must be noted, however, that the present government of Tansu Çiller has put the civil servants' rights to collective bargaining on the agenda and other unions have in fact managed to come into existence one way or another through legal devices. The control of the appointment of university rectors by the Higher Education Council has also been weakened.

Another factor in the political situation which is generally perceived to be detrimental to the development of more liberal and democratic measures is the growth of the religious Welfare Party. (The SDPP's recent decline also weakens the major protagonist for the return of liberal and democratic norms.) Whereas the political parties are still prevented from forming adjunct structures, the religious Welfare Party has them ready-made. Numerous religious organizations have developed in society, like the religious orders, charitable foundations, Koran reading courses, and the religious İmam-Hatip schools. They have no formal links with the Welfare Party but contribute indirectly but effectively to promoting its aims. The other political parties cannot, by their very nature, have ready-made social organizations of this sort.

Whilst all Muslims are by no means fundamentalist, nor, at least professedly, is the Welfare Party, the general trend in Islamic thinking is not towards the promotion of liberalism and democracy, which tend to be regarded as western secular concepts of little relevance to Muslims. The more, therefore, that Islamic organizations are successful in decrying the importance of liberalism and democracy, the more difficult it is going to be for the populace generally to come to internalize their values. This does not mean that liberal democracy is likely to disappear. The secular element in society is too strong for that. Provided there is no great national crisis it would not be possible for extreme Islamic elements to seize leadership.

Moreover the military is still strongly Kemalist, though moves to allow entry of the graduates of İmam-Hatip schools into the officer class would, if successful, presumably begin to make a difference. Islamic influence could strengthen if corruption were to grow apace and if in Islamic terms a libertarian, immoral lifestyle were to be followed by elites in a society where differences between rich and poor are marked, but where expectations are encouraged in various ways. There is at present little chance that the Welfare Party could come to power, except perhaps as a coalition partner, but a creeping religiosity has its dangers by helping to create a popular culture generally unsympathetic to liberal democracy.

Theoretical Considerations

Limitations placed on human and political rights are of course important in assessing the nature and extent of any liberal and democratic system but other underlying and more subtle factors also have to be taken into account. It is certainly important to note that the Atatürk revolution did not complete the modernization of Turkey, concentrating as it did on cultural transformation, and that the politicians of the 1950s and 1960s were allowed to mobilize the periphery, leading it into economic and social development, provided they did not attack the values and position of the Kemalist elite. This is seen to have resulted in links to the political system for the newly mobilized through the mechanisms of clientelism and patronage networks.

Such systems can break down if all demands cannot be met, or are met unfairly, and can provide recruits for extremist organizations, but even if successful they are not appropriate for liberal democracies.[6] This is mainly because they generate inefficiency in the use of usually scarce resources. There are various palliatives. Sheer size is one. Another is economic and social development on a scale that creates centers of economic power outside government. Another is an open system with marked division of powers (as in the American system) but for a country with Turkey's level of development and types of political institutions probably the best corrective is a strong and impartial public service.

This is not a simple matter, however. It is not easy, in the first place, to fit a strong bureaucracy into the theory of liberal democracy. In any large state the bureaucracy is inevitably left with many decisions in the execution of policy and these are not easy to control. Hence in some systems the top bureaucrats are political appointees, sometimes with dire consequences for subordinate appointments and for the efficient conduct of business. On the other hand a too powerful bureaucracy undermines democracy, especially if the public servants regard themselves as the guardians of the public interest, as, say, in France.

In Turkey there is said to be a strong state tradition.[7] Certainly in late Ottoman and Kemalist times many state officials set out to pursue the public interest, eventually amalgamating their quest with Kemalist revolutionary policies. These policies and attitudes often conflicted with those of the new right-of-center (and left-of-center) governments of the period 1961 to 1980. The bureaucracy, therefore, came to be transformed into an agency of government by means of wholesale dismissals and appointments when a new government took office. It could be argued that in terms of liberal democracy Turkey has had not a strong but rather a weak state, in that its bureaucrats were wedded to a belief in governmental policy, whether Ottoman or Kemalist, rather than to the underlying beliefs necessary for the maintenance of liberal democracy.[8] Rather than wait for processes of economic development to change the political environment it would be more helpful if attention were now paid to creating a more appropriate bureaucracy than the present divided and politically prone instrument. This would be a step in creating a "civic culture"—a respect for impersonal rules and procedures to accompany the development, it is to be hoped, of a "civil culture"—an assemblage of independent associations and institutions living alongside the state and cooperating with it. It may be said for the 1982 constitution that in forcing a separation between political parties and economic and social institutions it usefully broke up an unprofitable relationship which in time, it is hoped, will be allowed and encouraged to develop, but in different ways.

In the long run, however, it is the education of public opinion in the realities and difficulties of liberal democracy which is vital, not only protests about human rights, important though they are. How will this come about? The media, as almost everywhere, does not help a great deal in this regard. Inspired by western examples, the newspapers are strong on pointing fingers at corruption and other moral misdemeanors, thus unfortunately increasing the disrespect in which institutions are held. The important educational debate continues to be on secularism versus Islam. Yet there are some signs of hope. The quite rapid process of economic development, by creating centers of wealth and prestige outside of government, is slowly reducing the importance of politics and, it is to be expected, of political patronage. Politicians are becoming less antagonistic in their opposition to one another, more sophisticated, and less intense.

There are two immediate problems. One is to try to remove the social conditions under which an extreme Islamic reaction, and other such ideologies, can thrive. The other is to develop a stronger bureaucracy and one more appropriate for a liberal and democratic state as a means *inter alia* of encouraging greater respect for human and political rights at all levels.

Notes

1. The National Security Council now has the right to bring matters to the Council of Ministers on its own initiative.

2. For further details see C. H. Dodd, *The Crisis of Turkish Democracy*, 2nd ed. (Huntingdon: The Eothen Press, 1990) pp. 77-93.

3. By this measure restrictions were lifted on the left-wing labor union, the Confederation of Revolutionary Labor Unions (DISK).

4. Özal was more inclined than many of his colleagues to make concessions to the Kurds. He proposed allowing Kurdish to be used in broadcasting but without success. A Kurdish newspaper was permitted to publish but it collapsed for want of funds. Kurdish is not used officially in administration or education.

5. A clear summary of the changes is provided in A. Mango, ed., *Turkey Confidential* no. 34 (London: December, 1992), p. 5.

6. See İlkay Sunar's article in this volume for an elaboration of the argument.

7. See Metin Heper, *The State Tradition in Turkey* (Huntingdon: The Eothen Press, 1985).

8. The question is discussed in C. H. Dodd, "The Development of Turkish Democracy," *British Journal of Middle Eastern Studies* 19, no. 1(1992): 16-30.

6

State, Society, and Democracy in Turkey

İlkay Sunar

Neither socio-economic development nor cultural enrichment, if taken in isolation, can guarantee the irreversibility of democratic regimes. Even when democratic values are deeply rooted democratic regimes cannot indefinitely withstand persistent failures in socio-economic performance. On the other hand, where such values are strongly implanted, the capacity to withstand socio-economic stress is higher. In the final analysis, it is both culture and affluence together that allow for the sustained and stable growth of democracy. This is why democracy is a rarity and a "miracle" that first took root in northwestern Europe, where culture was indeed enjoined to affluence.[1] What has been called a "miracle" in western Europe is called a "model" in the case of Turkey. In the context of the Middle East the success of secular democracy in Turkey is exceptional; from a western European perspective the record is checkered. How exceptional, then, is Turkish democracy if judged by its own standards?

Nation-Building from Above

The way in which democratization is launched in a country is a "critical experience" with "character forming" consequences.[2] In Turkey, democratization was a distinct phase in a particular strategy of nation-building. The strategy was that of nation-building from above under the auspices of an elite and the phase was one of inclusion following a period of exclusion.[3] The exclusionary phase involved the creation and consolidation of a new (modern) political community that attempted to alter values, structures, and political behavior while preventing the traditional sources of values "from exercising uncontrolled and undesired influence over the development and definition of the new community." The inclusionary phase, on the other hand, involved an attempt "to expand the internal boundaries of the regime's political, productive and decision-making systems, to integrate itself with the unofficial...sectors of society rather than to insulate itself from them."[4]

In the following analysis the story of the Turkish Republic and its democratic experience is related within the framework of nation-building. "Kemalism," named after the founding father of the republic, Mustafa Kemal Atatürk, was the specifically Turkish response to under-development and traditionalism and corresponds to the experience of nation-building in Turkey. What lies at the core of this experience are its charismatic and ideological qualities. The ideological components of what we call Kemalism such as secularism, nationalism, rationalism, and republicanism are in fact profoundly modern. And yet Kemalism was a charismatic-heroic ethos initially forged during the War of Independence and eventually directed against underdevelopment as the "enemy" and toward the mission of national reconstruction.

What defined the character of the Kemalist regime and its relationship with society was precisely the combination of its modernist ideological tenets with a charismatic ethos and spirit. This character emerged from the incongruent relationship between Kemalism and traditional society (which the Kemalist republican vanguard was intent upon transforming), the choice of a strategy of national reconstruction through control rather than mobilization, and a culture based approach to social transformation rather than a socio-economic approach.

Each of these dimensions of the Kemalist regime had significant structural consequences. The conflict between the ideological tenets of Kemalism and the traditional socio-cultural environment led to the creation of an elite charged with the mission of transforming traditional culture and society. This nucleus was in turn consolidated by a sustained policy of "separating the elite and regime sectors from...the rest of society."[5] Moreover, the assumption that comprehensive and direct responsibility for national development required a "corresponding concentration of decision-making powers" within the vanguard elite led to the monopolization of the public domain by the regime. Kemalism imposed a dichotomization of regime and society and a fusion of the official and public domains. An autonomous public realm or civil society was conspicuous by its absence.

Unlike the case of revolutionary regimes, the radical nationalist Kemalist elite did not attempt simultaneously to transform all areas of social life. Instead, it focused on the transformation of critical nodal points of the old, traditional society and on preventing existing social forces from mobilizing their resentment against the regime. The consequence of this strategy was uneven change. While transformations were achieved in priority areas, in other areas the domination of traditional forces remained intact. Rural areas in particular experienced more control than transformation with a widening of the rural-urban gap the consequence.

Kemalists conceived socio-economic change as being derivative of cultural transformation. Great emphasis was placed on education, the legal system, changing the Arabic script, the Muslim calendar, and the code of dress. Simultaneously, however, the purposeful transformation and development of socio-economic institutions was neglected. An "unreconstructed" society was left to wait until cultural transformation would catch up with it; in the meantime it would continue to function in the traditional ways.

The result of this culture based conception of modernization was not only uneven development but also a ritualistic, formalistic approach to cultural change itself. In education, for instance, ritual and rote learning tended to replace critical, empirical thinking. This in turn led to the separation of cultural rituals from private life which remained largely untouched by them.

These consequences of Kemalism had additional effects with critical implications both for the political culture of the regime and for regime-society relations. They constituted the overarching profile of the early republican regime and defined the legacy of Kemalism which democratization took as its point of departure.

The Kemalist Legacy and Democratization

The legacy of the early republic was a curious mixture of modernity, tradition, and charisma. It was secular, analytical, empirical, impersonally procedural, universalist, egalitarian, and nationalist with a civic emphasis. The "carriers" of its modernist ideology were the judges, secondary school teachers, military officers, provincial governors, university professors, and the "enlightened" (*aydın*) intelligentsia. Yet alongside this "modern" Turkey there was an "unofficial country" of tradition—partly untouched, partly controlled but untransformed, and partly (and ironically) reinforced by the structural-organizational character of the early republican regime.

The mission of the Kemalist elite was the secularization of state and society. But, as the state was insulated and segregated from society, it took on the characteristics of a corporate status group equipped with exclusive powers and privileges. In this regard there was more of a continuity with the Ottoman past then a break with it. The political center was more status-embedded than role-governed and it took its cues more from its substantive goals than from impersonal procedures. Also, since its goals were based on the mission of national development, it assumed a mantle of heroism with important charismatic traits. Born during the struggle for national liberation and now charged with the mission of overcoming tradition and underdevelopment, the Kemalist state bore the characteristics of a puritanical, *"gazi"* state, so to speak. The outcome was a mixed product: the early republican state combined a clear modernist ideology with a charismatic ethos and neo-traditional structures.

The impact of the regime upon society included both a transformation of traditional culture and, simultaneously, its re-enforcement. Against the intrusion of the modernist ideology of the republic, society both adjusted tradition to modernist discourse with the use of an Islamic "idiom" and came to terms without great difficulty with the charismatic-traditional features of regime organization.[6] The response to the monopolization of the public domain by the state and the dichotomization of public (state) and private (social) spheres remained what it was in the past: the perception of state-society relations as a zero-sum game, a calculated approach to state authority, and a reliance upon dissimulation that emphasized external formalism and ritual compliance in order to preserve internal identity and independence.[7]

Once Turkey began to democratize in the aftermath of World War II a new contract was drawn up with the following terms:

1.   To guard against a contamination of the regime, communism, fascism, theocratic and fundamentalist religion, royalism, ethnic nationalism, internationalism, and cosmopolitanism were declared out of bounds.
2.   To elicit support without resorting to mobilization that might disrupt the regime, inclusionary politics would tap economic rather than ideological resources. Instead of socio-economic change being the product of cultural transformation, cultural change would become a function of socio-economic transformation.
3.   There would be a division of labor between those who would guard the ideology of the republic and those who would attend to the business of political economy. The new actors of the regime, the political parties, would provide "legitimation from below" and be accountable to the "people" while the elites would continue to provide "legitimation from above" and be accountable to the mission of the republic.

4.   Representative institutions would be upgraded without forfeiting
      the secular-national republic. A representative state, on the one
      hand, and a vigilant guardian state, on the other, would co-exist
      and cooperate.

These were the terms of the charter which formed the basis for the
transition from a regime of authoritarian consolidation to a regime of
democratic inclusion. This was "democratization from above" negotiated
within the elite to define the parameters of democratic politics.[8] It is not
surprising, then, that the story of Turkish democracy since 1950 turns out
to be the story of conflict and accommodation between the contrasting
imperatives of consolidation and inclusion.

The Consequences of Democratization from Above

In Turkey's transition to democratic politics the concern that there
should be political actors both loyal to the regime and capable of eliciting
support from a broad stratum of the population led to the emergence of
political entrepreneurs who acted upon empirical premises rather than
dogmatic ones, who used skills of persuasion and manipulation rather
than command and coercion, and who had a much greater appreciation
of discussion, experimentation, concerted action, and problem resolution.
The solution to the problem of eliciting social support that would be
consistent with the ideological core tenets of the republic (and which
would bloc the emergence of a plurality of ideological and cultural
definitions and identifications) led to the creation of a "clientelist" stratum
that served as an intermediary between the political class and the "unreconstructed" people. This stratum was the core of the regime's social
support and was drawn from occupational groups that were not directly
affiliated with the state. The transition to democracy was, in sum, pre-
mised on a set of compromises. The vanguard elite would allow an element of discretion to the party leadership in return for allegiance to the
core ideological premises of Kemalism. The party leadership would
simultaneously adopt the middle class as its client in exchange for
ideological compliance.

In the presence of a charismatic modernizing state and an unreconstructed traditional society there was no other effective way to gain social
support outside the framework of patron-client relations. Patronage was
a way of incorporating the unreconstructed "people" and upholding the
modernist tenets of the republican state without becoming isolated. Thus,
an outcome of democratization (from above) was the incorporation of

patronage by the center-right parties that dominated democratic governments between 1950-1980. It was, however, a costly phenomenon in terms
of its consequences and cultural effects. In fact;

> coalitions built on patronage thrive on the disposition of resources on
> a particularistic basis: goods and services are exchanged for loyalty
> and support. What underlies clientelist distribution of resources is a
> logic of partisan loyalty, not a logic of productivity. What lies, there-
> fore, behind a coalition of patronage is a "soft" state and a "soft"
> market. Clientele groups are subject neither to the planned discipline
> of the state nor to disciplinary competition of the market. A patronage
> coalition survives best under conditions of economic growth and be-
> gins to become undone in economically troubled times.[9]

The basis of the new politics rested on the provision of state-mediated
"material want-satisfaction" which in turn shifted legitimation from a
cultural to a performance basis. Legitimation was no longer provided
from above by an elite-defined truth and mission but rather by the
capacity of the regime to produce efficiently and to deliver fairly. This
performance was subject to ratification from below by the people.[10]

The counterpart to the bicephalous nature of the inclusionary state was
a bifurcated regime constituency. One wing of this constituency was
made up of the old, state-affiliated, salaried bureaucrats dedicated to state
autonomy and the ideological principles of the republic. The other was
the new class of market based clients that were attending to business and
pursuing patronage and economic growth. The etatist constituency was
supportive of the old Republican People's Party and the patronage
constituency was incorporated into the new Democratic Party.

The upshot of uneven socio-economic performance was the ascendance
of the client-entrepreneurial strata, the descent of the salaried, etatist
class, and the frustration of a motley of aspiring groups who could not
achieve the level of "material want-satisfaction" they believed that they
deserved. The result was often anger and rage by the excluded and the
marginalized and mobilization, initially led by the disaffected, radi-
calized splinter groups of the etatist constituency and eventually picked
up by the "dispossessed" of the "society-under-reconstruction."

The very design that had been drafted to avoid ideological conflict and
mobilization had, ironically, produced what had been most feared. Turkish politics was deeply fragmented in the 1960s and 1970s by the insur-
gence of mobilization politics and ideological "polytheism." Charismatic
politics was now back in a new form: the role of the heroic state had
been democratized and ideology was dragged into the streets in the form

of Marxist-Leninism, religious fundamentalism, populism of all sizes and colors, and ethnic nationalism.

During the 1950-1980 period Turkey first moved from incorporative to mobilization politics and then swung to the "neo-consolidationist" politics of the military and back because it lacked integrative civic politics. Nevertheless, the post-traditional politics of the 1950-1980 era in Turkey had more the characteristics of an evolving modern performance culture than the devolving features of re-traditionalization.

The Effects of Post-Traditional Democratic Politics

The attempt to win society from within as opposed to controlling it from an insulated position from above had far-reaching consequences for the regime and regime-society relations. The nature of authority relations changed from control to persuasion.

With the transition to inclusionary-democratic politics and the expansion of the political and decision-making boundaries of the authoritarian regime a new type of political actor emerged: those who staked their influence not on a charismatic mission or status-embedded power but on winning social support. Hence, this new political class was constrained by the concerns, aspirations, values, and norms of society. Its action orientation and policy initiatives were, therefore, empirical, pragmatic, calculated, and conciliatory. It relied on persuasion, manipulation, and consultation rather than being dogmatic and ideologically-informed. The new political class, in sum, staked its existence on performance, accountability, and legitimation from below (even though it relied on the resources of the state to elicit clientelist support from society).

With the expansion of production, occupational entrepreneurs that represented the new middle class emerged. They differed from the state-affiliated cadres and relied on individual initiative, achievement, and competition. They were the clients of the new patron state and were dependent on its largesse. Nevertheless, their relation to the state was defined not in terms of their status but in terms of their capacity for initiative, enterprise, and functionality.

The combined effects of entrepreneurialism were a decline in mutually exclusive relations and ritualistic, formal, and dissimulative behavior based on suspicion and estrangement and an increase in interaction built on utility, initiative, agreements, and performance (even though such interaction also had mutually manipulative and collusive aspects to it).

A new political space differentiated from the public realm and the private domain, governed by an ethos of impersonal rules and norms, and expressed in active and equal citizenship began to make inroads into popular consciousness. The effect was to diminish the distance between regime and society and to pave the way for integration and a sense of shared public identity (even though that public domain was partly exploited for private gain and partly the target of the combat troops of charismatic-mobilizational politics).

Perhaps needless to say, these were not the dominant and decisive characteristics of post-traditional political culture in Turkey. They were beginnings—the possible harbingers of a breakthrough to new forms of politics, society, and economy. They were the liberalizing and civilizing effects of a state that acted more like a patron than a liberal arbiter and manager, a society that bore less the characteristics of a civil society and more those of clientelism, and a neo-mercantile, state dependent economy that was governed more by patronage than by a competitive market or planned economy. What predominated was patron-client relations and political capitalism and what opposed this was mobilization politics governed by a charismatic-combat ethos.

The impact of post-traditionalism was double-edged: it undermined both tradition and modernity. Its modernist aspects were at odds with its traditional components. The conflicting imperatives inherent in post-traditionalism bred periodic crises, the response to which was military intervention at roughly ten-year intervals between 1950 and 1980. In the 1980s, a massive attempt was made to break out of the crisis spiral of post-traditionalism by effecting a breakthrough to liberal modernity. When, therefore, Turkey stepped into the post-Leninist world, it confronted a new set of external challenges while it was struggling with a set of its own. The internal challenge was posed by its own efforts to undertake a "liberal revolution" and the external one by the breakdown of the global postwar settlement.

The Second Transition
From Post-Traditional to Liberal Democracy?

Viewed from the perspective of nation-building, republican Turkey has been undergoing a second transition since the early 1980s. The first was the transition from the charismatic early republic to the postwar, post-traditional republic; the second has been from post-traditionalism to liberal modernism.

The issues of the late-1970s post-traditional crisis were political fragmentation, ideological polarization, and rapidly escalating terrorism and economic disintegration. The response to these problems was once again a "neo-consolidationist" military repossession of the public domain

(1980-1983). The solution was political and economic reconstruction under the auspices of the military and redemocratization and "Özalism" (1983-1993) (named after the late Turgut Özal, the "czar" of economic restructuring first under military rule and later as prime minister and president). The consequences have been significant—perhaps less than a revolution but certainly more than mere tinkering.

The immediate issue of the 1980s was economic. Yet the economic reforms of the second transition can be said to have neither succeeded nor failed. Studies of liberalization efforts in Turkey show where there have been advances, vacillations, and retreats.[11] Improvements include a reduction of micro-level state interventionism, changing priorities in public spending, financial liberalization, development of competitive exchange rates, trade liberalization, deregulation, and export promotion. There have been, however, little or no advances in fiscal discipline, increasing tax revenues, acquiring direct foreign investment, privatization, creating capital and employment, controlling monopolization, and reducing the bloated bureaucracy. Moreover, there have been retreats in income distribution, welfare system reform, inflation control, and domestic and foreign debt stabilization.

The record of economic performance is clearly spotty and erratic. Despite the decline in state interventionism, for instance, considerable protectionism and intervention continue to exist. Hence, "rent-seeking" and "rent-giving," i.e. patron-client relations, have by no means disappeared. Liberalization and growth have been fitful, relative incomes volatile, and inflation chronic.

In Turkey, economic reforms have been inconsistent and erratic because neither insular-executive nor participatory-consensual strategies could be consistently pursued or firmly implemented. This was because the political system and the civil society it has drawn upon have been fragile and weak. There is a vicious cycle here and a breakthrough to a liberal democratic cultural system is needed; a liberal economy, civil society, and democratic polity are interrelated.

The liberal political regime, civil society, and the market economy are inconsistent and incomplete in Turkey because the residue of the past continues to exercise significant influence on the style of leadership and the nature of institutions. Ideological polytheism and mobilization politics, for instance, have receded and given way to a spectrum of pragmatic parties. And yet patronage and corruption continue to be popular with a party system that is fragmented and very inadequately institutionalized. The new society is vibrant, dynamic, achievement oriented, professional—and yet it continues to approach the public domain as an instrumental arena to be exploited for private, selfish gain. Progress has been made from the concept of secularism as state control of religion to separation of state and religion and yet both continue to suspect each other of intentions to dominate. Ethnic differences are no longer denied but a sense of shared civic consciousness and integrative politics have not yet matured. The absolute level of wealth in the country has increased significantly and yet it is poorly distributed, hence becoming a source of anger and resentment. The political leadership is young and energetic and yet it lacks experience and party roots, relying too often on media-sponsored imagery and gimmicks. In sum, Turkey is an amalgam of old and new elements; there is, however, no denying that it has come a long way and that it has also some distance to cover before it emerges as a distinct type of liberal society.

Democratic Consolidation

Although good economic performance does not guarantee democratic stability, prolonged failure in economic performance can undermine it. Particularly where democratic habits are not strongly entrenched, a capacity for economic growth and an ability to resolve problems strengthens belief in democratic effectiveness and legitimacy. The current cultural cleavages in Turkey cannot solely be explained as the effects of distributional conflicts. Nevertheless, strong economic growth reduces frustration resulting from inequality and immobility, facilitates trade-offs, and hence incourages cooperation and incorporation.

The relevance of economics to the Kurdish question in Turkey has been cogently put by Morton Abramowitz. He points out that there are now more Kurds living outside the southeastern part of Turkey than inside, and notes:

> Kurds enjoy the same rights as Turks, and in the cities they are being steadily integrated into the work force. For some time, though, they will remain an economically disadvantaged minority more because of educational backwardness than ethnicity. The PKK [Kurdistan Workers' Party] war has not exacerbated tension between Turks and Kurds in the cities as many feared. Even in the very improbable event that an autonomous Kurdish area in the southeast were established, urban Kurds would not hasten to return to poverty, desolation and unemployment. Economic mobility may ultimately solve Turkey's Kurdish problem.[12]

In a similar vein, Abramowitz points out the close relationship that also exists between rapid social change, economic performance, and the rise of religious fundamentalist politics in Turkey:

The most dangerous threat to secularism comes, in fact, not from religious practices but from the rapid transformation of Turkish life. That change has created unemployment, vast income inequalities, and a squalid life for many urban dwellers. Unemployed students are particularly worrisome. With the decay of ideology and the decline of political parties on the Left and Right, fundamentalist Islam is the only radical alternative in the Turkish system. As in Algeria, the religious parties profit from domestic failures. The Welfare Party's recent success probably rests less on the inherent strengths or organizational prowess than on the failure of mainstream parties to fulfill their promises and provide benefits to the voters....The danger posed by fundamentalists thus lies in the state's inability to handle Turkey's difficult social and economic problems....if economic growth falters and the government is unable to control disorder and terrorism, fundamentalism can indeed threaten Turkey's democracy.[13]

After the transition from military rule (1983), the dominant style of politics that emerged in Turkey is perhaps best described as "delegative" or "plebiscitarian" democracy.[14] The characteristics of such rule are an executive with a wide margin of discretionary authority, mobilization of support through broad and personal appeals predominantly transmitted through the media, low levels of party-institutionalization, low levels of institutionalized consultation, low accountability to the legislature and interest groups, and unstable bases of social support.

In the initial years (1983-1985) of this system, in circumstances of limited democratization and wide executive discretion, considerable advances were made in the implementation and deepening of reforms. After 1985, however, as the restrictions were challenged and fell, as the regressive distributional consequences of the government's reform program came under attack, and as one election followed another (a total of seven elections were held between 1986 and March 1994) "policy became less coherent, macroeconomic instability increased, and a number of structural adjustment measures either stalled or reversed."[15] In 1994 Turkey was confronted with a major financial crisis. This stop-and-go pattern is typical of many developing countries undertaking market reforms. As Adam Przeworski puts it:

Given their political dynamic...[the most likely path of reforms] is one of radical programs that are eventually slowed and reversed, initiated again in a more gradual form with less popular confidence, and again slowed or reversed, until a new government promises a clean break, and the cycle starts again.[16]

The whole stop-and-go pattern rests upon a "political dynamic"—one that is shaped by the incomplete institutionalization of democracy. Under-institutionalized politics becomes the source of economic instability. Plebiscitarian/delegative democracy is both a response to the under-institutionalization of politics as well as the cause of its perpetuation. Strong executives introduce market-oriented reforms by decree and/or push them through the legislature. But since reforms entail costs, they provoke resistance. Governments are then compelled to seek political support through distributive politics and to compromise, stall, and reverse reforms. This is precisely what has happened in Turkey since 1983.

One solution is to rest reforms not on the insular power of a strong executive but rather on "widespread consultation channelled through representative institutions and ratified by elections."[17] However, in Turkey, achieving social pacts among contending parties and economic interests is a difficult task given the fragmentation of organized interest groups and political parties. There has been continual discussion and debate about the possibility of establishing some form of institutionalized social compromise and partnership in Turkey (such as the establishment of a Social and Economic Council) but with no results, for the simple reason that the institutional-organizational infrastructure needed for a "neo-corporatist" solution does not exist in the country.[18]

Turkey's political system is overwhelmingly dominated by political parties that are fragmented. There are three parties on the center-left, two major parties on the center-right, a religious and two nationalist parties on the extreme right, and a motley of small parties that span the spectrum. The divisions within the center-right and center-left are more the extensions of the clashing personalities of the leaders than the result of differences of doctrine and policy. The five parties on the center-right and left commanded more than 70 percent of the votes in the local elections held in March 1994. But because of the badly fragmented vote, the religious Welfare Party, with 19 percent of the votes, emerged as the major victor by increasing dramatically the number of mayoral positions it held and winning the municipal elections in the two major metropolitan centers, Istanbul and Ankara.

The party system constituted the central political problem of the 1970s preceding the intervention of the military in 1980 and it continues to be the central issue following redemocratization. In the 1970s, when the center-right and center-left parties could not or would not compromise and cooperate, the outcome was escalating economic and political crises, the breakdown of democratic politics, and military rule.

The...regime failure (in 1980) was the result of the inability of the centrist forces and leadership, of democrats on both sides of the political spectrum, to see the logic of escalating crisis, and cooperate and collaborate in the face of it, in order to prevent its consequences. When such cooperation did not take place, the polarization of the party system, the instability of coalition governments...the politicization of ethnic, religious and sectarian cleavages in society, and the violence...finally overwhelmed the system and put an end to it.[19]

The current situation in the mid-1990s is clearly not a replica of the 1970s. Nevertheless, in the face of extreme party fragmentation, escalating economic crisis, a deepening of primordial social cleavages, and weak governments, if cooperation (or unification) among centrist parties is not forthcoming then authoritarian temptations are inevitable. The outcome is not predetermined: to the extent to which the centrist political parties and party leaders themselves avoid the politics of confrontation and cooperate on a number of issues vital for the consolidation of economic reforms and democracy, Turkey will avoid the errors of its past.

Notes

1. See John Hall, *Powers and Liberties* (Harmondsworth: Penguin Books, 1985).

2. Martin Shefter, "Party and Patronage: Germany, England, and Italy," *Politics and Society* 7, no. 4(1977).

3. Keith Jowitt, *New World Disorder: The Leninist Extinction* (Berkeley: University of California Press, 1992). Of particular interest in Jowitt's analysis of the "system-building" approach to modernization. In structural terms, there are interesting similarities and differences between the "system-building" and "nation-building" strategies of modernization. It would no doubt be fruitful to examine the current problems of post-Leninist countries with democratization and liberalization in the light of the Turkish experience after World War II.

4. Ibid., pp 55-57, 88.

5. Ibid., p. 59.

6. See Şerif Mardin, *Religion and Change in Modern Turkey* (New York: State University of New York Press, 1990).

7. I have elaborated on these themes on several occasions. See, for instance, İlkay Sunar and Sabri Sayarı, "Democracy in Turkey: Problems and Prospects," in Guillermo O'Donnell, Philippe Schmitter and Laurence Whitehead, eds., *Transitions From Authoritarian Rule: Southern Europe* (Baltimore: The Johns Hopkins University Press, 1986) and İlkay Sunar, "Populism and Patronage: The Democrat Party and its Legacy in Turkey," *Il Politico* LV, no.4(October-December 1990): 745-757. See also Jowitt, *New World Disorder*.

8. Sunar and Sayarı, "Democracy in Turkey, Problems and Prospects."

9. Sunar, "Populism and Patronage," p. 750.

10. The effects of a clientelist politics and patronage economy on performance was uneven in terms of both growth and fair distribution. The promises of the new regime and its manner of delivery were at odds with each other. The outcome was a stop-and-go pattern of economic performance and sharp distributive conflicts in the 1960s and 1970s. For further discussion on these matters see İlkay Sunar, *The Politics of State Interventionism in 'Populist' Egypt and Turkey* (Istanbul: Boğazici University Research Papers, 1993).

11. Ziya Öniş, "Redemocratization and Economic Liberalization in Turkey: The Limits of State Autonomy," *Studies in Comparative International Development* 27, no. 2(Summer 1992).

12. Morton I. Abramowitz, "Dateline Ankara: Turkey After Ozal," *Foreign Policy* (Summer 1993): 175.

13. Ibid., pp. 177-78.

14. For the notion of "plebiscitarian" or "leader democracy" see Max Weber, *Economy and Society* (Berkeley: University of California Press, 1978), pp. 268-269. For "delegative democracy" see the remarks by Guillermo O'Donnell cited in Ergun Özbudun, *Anayasalar ve Demokrasiye Geçiş* (Ankara: Bilgi Yayınevi, 1993).

15. Stephan Haggard and Robert Kaufman, *The Political Economy of Democratic Transitions* (Unpublished manuscript, University of San Diego Graduate School of International Relations and Pacific Studies, n.d.).

16. Adam Przeworski, *Democracy and Markets* (Cambridge: Cambridge University Press, 1991) p. 179.

17. Ibid., p. 187.

18. For an analysis that explores the possibility of "social partnership" in Turkey and makes some constructive suggestions see İlkay Sunar and Ziya Öniş, *Sanayileşmede Yönetim ve Toplumsal Uzlaşma* [Managing Industrialization and Social Compromise] (Istanbul: TUSIAD Yayinlari, 1992).

19. Sunar and Sayari, "Democracy in Turkey: Problems and Prospects," p. 182.

7

The State and Economic Development in Contemporary Turkey: Etatism to Neoliberalism and Beyond

Ziya Öniş

The collapse of the communist regimes in eastern Europe created a series of new opportunities for the expansion of trade and investment in the region, particularly in countries with close cultural, linguistic, and religious ties to Turkey. The idea of the "Turkish model of development" has increasingly come into the forefront of public discussion as a possible path for the newly independent republics of Central Asia. At issue is a pattern of development based on a mixed economy combined with a democratic and secular polity.

Turkey's claim to be a model of political development rests on the durability of its democratic regime over a period of more than forty years—a record contrasting with much of the Islamic world and most countries of middle-sized gross domestic product (GDP). The central principle underlying Turkey's economic development efforts during the post-1923 republican era is the concept of a mixed economy in which the state would play a leadership role during the early stages of development but would recede into the background as private enterprise develops, matures, and becomes the dominant economic actor over time. Turkey has indeed managed to achieve a substantial degree and depth of industrialization with the relative contribution of private capital expanding drastically. Turkey has achieved growth rates of 5-6 percent per annum on average, among the highest in the developing world, particularly if we exclude the East Asian hypergrowth cases.

The growth performance is even more striking considering that in the postwar period it has been established in a predominantly democratic setting. More recently, Turkey has made a successful transition from an over-regulated and highly inward oriented economy to one that is far more open and integrated into the world markets, a process that started a decade or so before the former Soviet republics found themselves on a similar path in the early 1980s. Judged on the basis of recent growth performance and the growth trajectory over longer periods, Turkey has the most dynamic economy in the region. During the 1980s important steps were taken in the development of an infrastructural base, the most impressive of which occurred in the communications sector.

The depth of industrialization and development is also made evident by the presence of a flourishing private sector, no longer content with investing at home but increasingly involved in investment activities in neighboring countries either individually or through joint ventures, notably in major construction projects. Furthermore, Turkey is rapidly moving away from the position of a passive recipient of technology and becoming an exporter of technology itself. Another feature of Turkey's recent economic trajectory is its closer link with the European Union. While the attainment of full membership is not in sight, the onset of the customs union agreement that was to have become effective in 1995 is a major step toward a closer relationship. Even though it may fall short of full membership, this development is likely to strengthen the Turkish economy and create new avenues for investment and joint ventures among Turkish and European firms, which in turn will generate opportunities for growth in Turkey and the surrounding regions.

This justifies a close examination of the Turkish development experience with a view toward duplicating it in countries undergoing economic and political transitions. The Turkish development experience represents one of the more successful cases of development to emerge during the postwar period. The timing and sequencing of reforms is striking, with export promotion receiving priority in the early stages and the liberalization of the import regime and the capital account coming much later, once a major export push had been successfully established.

To present the Turkish case as a model of successful development might nonetheless be an exaggeration. Turkey's development experience also contains a number of important shortcomings, notably in the sphere of income distribution. A more sensible judgement would be to argue that the Turkish case does have the potential to emerge as a "model" of economic development. The potential, however, remains to be realized. Important structural weaknesses that constrain the transformation of an adequate or moderately successful performance into an outstanding success story still persist.

A major restructuring in the economic role of the state and the nature and operation of the public sector is an important precondition for improvement, judged both in terms of efficiency and equity. What is required, however, is not simply a "retreat of the state" but a restructuring of the mode of state intervention and a shift in the composition of the public sector and the rules governing its activity.

State Intervention in the Turkish Economy
in Historical Perspective

The origins of modern industrialization in Turkey can be traced back to the "etatist" era of the 1930s. Although its beginnings were evident in the immediate aftermath of the formation of the republic in 1923, the real breakthrough occurred in the 1930s. Rapid industrialization in Turkey is a comparatively recent phenomenon. Moreover, republican Turkey started its development trajectory from a position of major weakness given the virtual absence of an indigenous entrepreneurial elite. Due to the peculiar structure of Ottoman society, the Turkish elite occupied top positions in the bureaucracy and the military, while business and commercial activities were relegated to the Armenian, Greek, and Jewish minorities. The dissolution of the empire and the mass migrations that accompanied the War of Independence during the early 1920s resulted in a major reduction in the minority population. The lack of a strong entrepreneurial base was an important barrier to growth.

The great depression of the 1930s, as in the case of many Latin American countries, eliminated trade links with the external world and provided a major spurt toward import substitution in basic consumer goods in a predominantly exporting economy. The state emerged as the principal entrepreneur during this period and a number of key State Economic Enterprises (SEEs) were founded. Private enterprise also began to develop alongside state industry and a process of private capital accumulation started to manifest itself through contracts with the state. This specific phase in Turkish economic history is usually referred to as "etatism."

From a liberal or pragmatic perspective, etatism was interpreted as a development strategy in which the state is forced to undertake an active entrepreneurial role out of necessity rather than for any ideological reasons. The corollary of this reasoning is a progressive reduction in the weight of state involvement in the economy as private capital matures and assumes the leadership role in economic affairs. A qualification is called for in the sense that there were also intellectuals who interpreted etatism in a different light, namely as an alternative, non-capitalist path of economic development, inspired to a certain degree by the relatively successful Soviet experience at a time when the major industrialized countries of the West were experiencing the deepest crisis of their history. What this group of intellectuals had in mind was a vision of etatism as an "intermediate regime," a path of independent development somewhere between the capitalist and Soviet models. In retrospect, it is clear that the liberal or pragmatic conceptualization of etatism characterized or dominated the approach of the bureaucratic elite who played key roles in initiating the modern industrialization process in Turkey during the interwar era.[1]

The etatist drive of the 1930s came to a sudden halt, however, with the onset of the Second World War. Although Turkey did not actually participate in the war, the mobilization of labor and resources had detrimental effects on economic activity, and hence the 1940s proved to be a lost decade or one of relative stagnation in economic terms. Nonetheless, the process of private capital accumulation continued during the early 1940s in an environment characterized by severe shortages of many basic commodities.

The late 1940s marked the demise of etatism. The single party regime dominated by the military-bureaucratic elite came increasingly under attack both from domestic and external sources. At the domestic level, private enterprise, which had started to reach a certain degree of maturity, wanted to translate this economic power into political power and, hence, to break down the power monopoly of the bureaucratic elite. The drastic shifts in the geopolitical context in the immediate postwar period, involving the establishment of the United States as the hegemonic power and the emergence of the Cold War, were also key influences that tended to undermine the very foundations of the etatist regime and accelerate the shift to a more liberal economic order.

The year 1950 marked the transition to parliamentary democracy in Turkey. The Democratic Party (DP), which gained a large majority in the general elections, represented a broad alliance of private industrialists, commercial groups, landed interests, and the peasantry. The transition to democracy also signified a shift in the direction of a more liberal economic order. Trade liberalization, emphasis on agriculture and infrastructural development, and the encouragement of foreign capital emerged as the central pillars of the new economic strategy. This shift, accompanied by significant inflows of U.S. capital, implied a reduced role for the state in economic affairs. In fact, privatization appeared as an item on the policy agenda for the first time during the early 1950s.

In retrospect, the 1950s constituted a paradoxical case of liberalism. Contrary to original expectations, privatization did not materialize during the decade. In fact the opposite happened; new SEEs were founded and the overall weight of the state in economic affairs expanded rather than contracted.[2] What started to change, however, was the nature of state involvement in the economy. A new division of labor began to emerge between the public and private sectors. After 1950, private industry was increasingly concentrated in the final part of production of consumer goods, while the SEEs were producing intermediate and capital goods for the private sector. Hence, the economic role of the state was steadily transformed from a leadership position to a complementary or supportive role marked by a progressive shift of focus to the subsidized provision of intermediary goods and key infrastructural activities.

The liberal decade of the 1950s came to an end, however, due to careless and uncontrolled expansionism, which culminated in 1958. Turkey experienced its first major macroeconomic crisis during the postwar period, one that also marked Turkey's first ever encounter with the International Monetary Fund (IMF). An unfortunate repercussion of the stabilization episode of the late 1950s was the collapse of the democratic regime. Another dramatic implication of the crisis was a reversal of the liberal economic program and a reincarnation of etatism, combining import substitution and development planning. Import substitution under heavy protectionism was established as the dominant economic strategy during the 1960s and the 1970s in the context of successive five-year plans. The basic objective was to replace the unplanned and uncontrolled expansion of the "Menderes era" during the 1950s with a new approach involving controlled and planned industrialization.

The division of labor between the public and private sectors continued under Import Substituting Industrialization (ISI) from 1960-1979, under which Turkey managed to achieve high rates of economic growth. Yet, the strategy proved to be inherently unsustainable due to its heavy domestic market bias and fundamental neglect of exports. The planners' approach to economic policy was based on the false assumption of low elasticities or export pessimism. Both the trade and the exchange rate regime operated against exports and other foreign exchange earning activities, with the result that exports stagnated during this period. Moreover, contrary to the planners' expectations, import substitution in intermediate and capital goods could not be accomplished on the desired scale and imports of raw materials and capital goods expanded rapidly during the later years of this period. The structural trade gap which steadily deteriorated over time due to the stagnation of exports and expansion of necessary imports, coupled with the major external shocks of the mid and late 1970s, rendered a payments crisis inevitable. In the midst of acute instability and crisis during the late 1970s, ISI was abandoned followed by a forced transition to a more liberal economic regime. Again, as in the case of the late 1950s, the crisis was accompanied by a breakdown of the democratic system.

The 1980s marked attempts to renew economic growth on the basis of an export oriented strategy. Following the stagnation of the late 1970s growth recovered due to a combination of an exports push and foreign capital inflows. Respectable rates of economic growth were achieved during the decade, although in recent years macroeconomic instability has started to manifest itself once again.[3]

In retrospect, the striking fact about the Turkish development experience is that it has not been a smooth process. Industrialization has occurred and private capital has matured under state guidance. Despite these achievements, however, the process has been highly uneven, characterized by intermittent economic crises, which have also been accompanied by the breakdown of democratic order, albeit for relatively short intervals. Another interesting aspect of the Turkish experience is a pattern of policy cycles as opposed to a smooth unilinear path of development. In retrospect, it is possible to identify "etatist" and "liberal" policy phases in Turkey's contemporary economic history (Table 7.1). In that respect, it would be misleading to single out 1980 as the beginning of the liberalization efforts in Turkey, since similar projects were also evident in the 1920s and 1950s. What seems to differentiate the "liberal" and "etatist" phases is not only the nature of the trade regime and the attitude towards foreign direct investment but also the mode of state intervention in the economy.

The typical pattern is that during the liberal phases the state tends to retreat from its position as a producer of manufactured goods and to concentrate its energy in the provision of infrastructural activities directly complementary to the private sector. What is interesting, however, is that the overall weight of the public sector in economic activity does not seem to be importantly affected by the radical policy shifts that occur during the development process. In fact, a marked change in the composition of public sector activity without a corresponding shift in the overall weight of the public sector in the economy constitutes a pattern that appears to be common to the "liberal" decades of both the 1950s and the 1980s. Nonetheless, in spite of these policy cycles and the intermittent crises which gave rise to radical shifts in economic policy, rapid industrialization has occurred coupled with the development of a significant private entrepreneurial base.

To accept that significant development has occurred, however, does not rule out the possibility that development would have been even more rapid if the policy makers had made the appropriate decisions so as to avoid, for example, the crisis of the late 1950s or to engineer the transition to a more outward oriented strategy during the early 1970s.

Table 7.1

Principal Policy Phases or Policy Cycles in Turkey's Economic Development

Phase 1: The liberal era of the 1920s. Support for foreign investment. Indirect measures to encourage industrialization rather than direct state involvement in the economy. A liberal trade regime.

Phase 2: Etatism—1930-1945. The state emerges as the principal entrepreneur and the dominant agent in the industrialization process. The first five year plans are introduced during this period.

Phase 3: Liberalism of the 1950s—1950-1959. A liberalization of trade and the foreign investment regime. An emphasis on agricultural development. The major focus of the state shifts to infrastructural development.

Phase 4: The import substitution-planning era—1960-1979. Inward oriented industrialization based on heavy protectionism. Export pessimism and a restrictive attitude towards foreign direct investment. The primary focus of state activity is on industrialization via production in the intermediate and capital goods industries.

Phase 5: The neoliberalism of the post-1980 period. An emphasis on export expansion. Progressive liberalization of the trade regime and the capital account during the course of the decade. A liberal approach to foreign direct investment. The focus of state activity is increasingly shifted away from manufacturing to infrastructural activities.

Hence, Turkey's economic history illustrates the success of its development experience but also a principal weakness—the inability to undertake fundamental reforms without the constraint of crisis.

State Intervention: Changes and Continuities

The import substitution era in Turkey was characterized by a highly dirigist mode of state intervention. A large public enterprise sector existed which confined its economic activities to the intermediate goods industries. The public enterprise sector provided subsidized inputs to private industry, which was in turn primarily concentrated in the manufacture of consumer goods and durables. In addition to the direct involvement of the state as an entrepreneur in the industrialization process, a major distinguishing feature of the period involved heavy indirect or micro-level intervention in the operation of the market. The state attempted to influence the pattern of industrialization through an extensive set of instruments including tariff and quota restrictions on imports, controls over the capital account, overvalued exchange rates, low interest loans, and subsidized inputs provided by the SEEs. The planners had direct leverage over the pattern of investment through their control over the trade regime (i.e import licenses) and the system of investment incentives (i.e investment certificates).

These indirect interventions by the state rendered production for the domestic market extremely profitable. Yet the system of incentives erected under ISI not only created a major bias against exports but also, rather ironically, blocked the path for successful import substitution in more complex branches of industry. Instead of reducing the degree of dependence on imports, which was the underlying rationale of the ISI strategy, the country became more dependent on imports while exports stagnated. In spite of the comparatively rapid growth which occurred over much of the 1960-1977 period, on average 6.3 percent per annum, due to the perverse nature of the incentive structure the strategy proved to be unsustainable. Furthermore, the perverse system of incentives created widespread opportunities for rent-seeking and unproductive forms of investment when economic agents tried to take advantage of the variety of controls and regulations imposed on the price mechanism. In retrospect, Turkey could have improved its performance significantly and avoided the inefficiencies of ISI if it could have rationalized its incentive regime and moved to a more liberal, outward oriented strategy during the early 1970s, a process which actually started with the devaluation in 1970 but was unfortunately reversed during the subsequent part of the decade.

The reform process, however, became inevitable following the acute balance of payments and debt crisis of the late 1970s. The reforms of the 1980s managed to achieve a fundamental break with the ISI era thanks to a considerable reduction in the degree of micro-level intervention. Import quotas were eliminated and tariff rates declined substantially. Key relative prices such as the exchange rate and interest rates on bank deposits became flexible and were increasingly determined through market forces. The principal change on the SEE front involved the deregulation of their product prices and the elimination of the automatic link to the central government budget as the enterprises were increasingly exposed to market discipline. Parallel to the liberalization of the trade regime, restrictions over the capital account were progressively removed and a liberal foreign investment regime was introduced.

Hence, what we observe in the context of the 1980s is a much more market oriented system, far more favorable to the expansion of exports compared with the pre-1980 regime. The degree of micro-level interventionism by the state in economic affairs established a fundamental break with the past in the post-1980 period. Yet it would be rather simplistic to characterize the post-1980 reforms as a transition from the one extreme of a heavily regulated and controlled mixed economy to the opposite extreme, the neoliberal ideal of a "free market economy."

In fact, in spite of the considerable liberalization achieved during the course of the decade, a significant element of control continued to exist. For example, export subsidies, the major example of which were export tax rebates that remained intact until the end of 1988, became the principal instrument on which the export drive of the early and mid-1980s was based. Similarly, while key relative prices such as the exchange rate and interest rates were deregulated, the state continued to exercise considerable leverage over the determination of these key relative prices during the course of the decade.

It is interesting that "rent-seeking" also manifested itself under an outward regime, although perhaps on a smaller scale compared with the pre-1980 period. By the late 1980s increasing complaints emerged concerning over-invoicing of exports, frequently described in popular terms as "fictitious exports."[4] In spite of substantial liberalization, the policy regime which emerged during the 1980s was not a free market regime. Considerable micro-level interventionism continued to characterize the Turkish economy, albeit in a different form involving the use of new instruments.

The presence of rent-seeking under both policy regimes illustrates the paradox of the Turkish state, namely its relative incapacity, compared, for example, with the prototype East Asian state or South Korea, to exercise discipline over private business in return for the subsidies provided. Although the Turkish state provided considerable incentives to the private sector under both import substitution and export oriented regimes it lacked the capacity to monitor performance and avoid the abuse of the incentives by private economic agents.[5]

In spite of these qualifications, however, it is quite striking that the inward oriented regime of the pre-1980 era, based on extensive controls, was transformed to a more liberal and outward oriented system during the 1980s. Another marked change in the nature of state investment in the post-1980 period was the drastic shift of public investment from manufacturing to infrastructural activities such as transport, communications, and energy—fields which are complementary to private sector activities. In spite of this drastic change in the nature of state interventionism at the micro-level, the overall weight of the public sector in economic activity did not change significantly during the course of the 1980s. In fact, growing macro-instability and chronic inflation associated with heavy fiscal disequilibrium began to dominate the policy agenda from the late 1980s onwards. Chronic fiscal disequilibrium posed a fundamental challenge because of its negative effects on the level and composition of private investment, both domestic and foreign (Table 7.2).

In that respect the sustainability of the reform process plus the justification that the Turkish experience could serve as a "model" for the surrounding region depends crucially on the ability to create a stable macroeconomic environment. The interesting problem to pose, therefore, is why macro-instability has been an endemic problem in the Turkish economy in recent decades and why it is proving to be an elusive goal.

Dilemmas of Public Sector Reform

Turkey's inability to achieve fiscal equilibrium in recent years may be attributed to three primary causes: (a) inadequate tax revenues; (b) the heavy burden of domestic and external debt; and (c) chronic deficits in the state enterprise sector. Increasingly, in the context of the early 1990s, a consensus is emerging on the desirability of radical reform of the public sector involving both the taxation system and the public enterprise sector.

Tax reform constitutes a crucial component of the reform package. First, the level of tax revenues is inadequate; the ratio of tax revenues to GNP is the lowest in the Organization for Economic Cooperation and Development (OECD) area.[6] This pattern may be explained by the fact that the average tax rate is too high and that various loopholes and exemptions are built into the system. Both of these factors encourage widespread tax evasion and the growth of an extensive informal and underground economy. Second, the tax burden is distributed in a highly inegalitarian manner. A disproportionate portion of the income tax, for example, falls on low income groups such as wage and salary earners. Tax reform is crucial, therefore, not only for raising additional revenues for the government but also for reducing the burden of taxation on low

Table 7.2

Fiscal Disequilibrium and Macroeconomic Instability:
Comparison of Pre-1980 and Post-1980 Periods

Public Sector Borrowing Requirement as a Proportion of
Gross National Product (%), 1975, 1992

YEAR	PSBR/GNP[a]	PSBR/GNP[b]
1975	6.1	4.8
1976	8.7	6.8
1977	10.4	8.2
1978	4.1	3.2
1979	9.4	7.3
1980	10.5	8.7
1981	4.9	4.0
1982	4.3	3.5
1983	6.0	4.9
1984	6.5	5.3
1985	4.6	3.5
1986	4.7	3.6
1987	7.8	6.0
1988	6.2	4.7
1989	7.1	5.2
1990	10.5	7.5
1991	14.4	10.4
1992	12.6	9.0

(a) Old GNP series. (b) New GNP series.

Source: State Planning Organization, Main Economic Indicators, June 1993

income groups in society. The key components of a radical tax reform package would include a reduction in the average tax rate, an improvement in tax administration which would help to overcome wide-spread tax evasion, and an extension of the tax net to the rapidly growing underground or informal economy.

An interesting parallel might be drawn at this point between the Turkish case and the old-style "Latin American state," the type of state which is associated with Latin American countries which have also passed through a similar phase of prolonged import substitution followed by a major crisis and a forced transition to a liberal economic order. The common element involving the Turkish state and the prototype "Latin American state" of the pre-reform era is the inability, in both cases, effectively to tax high income groups in society.[7]

Public enterprise reform constitutes the second major component of public sector reform. The endemic problems associated with the SEEs concerning excess employment, low productivity growth, the heavy burden on the state budget, and contribution to the growth of the external debt are issues which have occupied the public agenda for many years. In fact, the recent economic history of Turkey is full of attempts to reform the public enterprise sector. During the ISI-planning era, the emphasis had been on the introduction of greater autonomy for public enterprises, thereby pressuring them to operate on the basis of commercial criteria. Attempts to introduce greater autonomy in decision making, however, have not been very successful in practice. The principal reason for this has been the reluctance of politicians to delegate real authority or autonomy to enterprise managers as long as ownership rights remained with the state. It has become increasingly evident, therefore, that in an environment where pervasive pressures for rent-seeking exists, attempts to introduce greater autonomy for public enterprises are likely to be frustrated. Hence, "privatization"—a transfer of ownership—and "closure" (or partial closure), depending on the specific cases, emerge as the principal alternatives for introducing greater enterprise autonomy. The underlying logic here is that the overload on the state needs to be reduced and the state needs to withdraw from its position as an entrepreneur or direct producer and focus its activities exclusively on fields which are complementary to the private sector.

The solutions, in principle, appear to be fairly well-established. Why then is implementation of these reforms postponed into the indefinite future? One obvious answer to this question concerns the presence of political constraints.[8] There exist important, powerful, and well-organized groups in society whose immediate interests would be hurt by an extensive tax reform or a widespread privatization program. This explanation probably has somewhat greater relevance in accounting for the delay in tax reform than in the privatization program.

Increasingly, opposition to privatization is fading. In the past, private business was a key component of the pro-public enterprise coalition because of the benefits derived in the form of subsidized inputs. More recently business has broken away from that coalition and is favoring extensive privatization because in a much more open and liberal foreign trade regime it is possible to import inputs at a cheaper price from external sources. From the business point of view, then, the costs associated with chronic deficits and the uncertainty created by high and variable rates of inflation tend to outweigh the possible benefits to be derived from the continued provision of intermediates by SEEs. Even labor unions are increasingly favoring privatization, provided that safeguards concerning employment and social security are built into the program.

The highly fragmented nature of the party system in Turkey acted as a major political constraint on the extensive and rapid privatization of the early 1990s. The pattern which has emerged in Turkey in recent years is the gradual convergence of the principal political parties of the right and the left on the desirability of market oriented solutions, although differences remain on some issues or over the choice of specific instruments. In spite of the convergence on basic solutions, in a fragmented party system and especially in an environment of coalition government, no party in government is willing to shoulder the costs of transition associated with an extensive privatization program, such as the increase in unemployment which would inevitably result in the short-term from the sale of an enterprise or its closure.

Apart from the political factors which constrain radical reform of the public sector, there are some fundamental economic considerations which also work against speedy reform. One important factor is the availability of domestic savings to absorb a large public enterprise sector. This is accentuated by the fact that the capital market, in spite of its rapid surge in recent years, is still in the early stages of development.

The success of privatization itself depends crucially on the environment in which it is implemented. It is increasingly recognized that macroeconomic stability and an effective regulatory framework against monopolistic practices are crucial ingredients of a successful privatization program. Thus, even if we agree that privatization and a reduction in the entrepreneurial role of the state are desirable objectives, the manner and the environment in which they are implemented are crucial for effectiveness and sustainability.

Privatization implemented in an environment of chronic fiscal instability may lead to sales which fail to reflect the true value of the assets sold. Furthermore, the use of privatization proceeds to close budget deficits is a dangerous practice because it is a short-term solution. In the long-run, the public sector may find itself confronted with larger fiscal deficits as profitable enterprises are gradually sold off and the more problematic enterprises are left within the orbit of the public sector. It is imperative, therefore, that privatization proceeds are directed towards activities such as productive investment or reduction in external debt which will make a permanent rather than short-term contribution to economic welfare.[9] Successful privatization requires prior reforms to reduce macroeconomic instability in the first place. In other words, either a major tax reform or selective government expenditure cuts must precede an extensive privatization effort.

A second major requirement for successful privatization involves the introduction of a more competitive environment and a regulatory framework designed to eliminate monopolistic practices. Otherwise the sale of public monopolies, in the absence of adequate safeguards, is likely to decrease social welfare by worsening income inequality and failing to improve economic efficiency. Finally, a crucial precondition for the success and durability of the reform process concerns the design of adequate safeguards for social safety needs. It is imperative that a social insurance system is created to protect the losers in the privatization program. In the absence of such safeguarding mechanisms an extensive privatization program is likely to generate widespread resentment that may jeopardize the future of the program.

The important message that emerges from this discussion is that the desirability of privatization as such does not guarantee that a program will necessarily be successful in terms of realizing its ultimate objective of increasing social welfare. Rapid or shock-treatment approaches to privatization, without the necessary preconditions, may result in highly perverse outcomes. A gradualist path to public sector reform, therefore, may be preferable to a shock-treatment approach. It is quite clear that fiscal instability in the Turkish economy, as in many other contexts, is a structural problem and an issue which can only be addressed effectively over a period of time. To expect immediate solutions to public sector reform are not realistic given the dilemmas that have been outlined. The fact that the problems cannot be solved over a short period, however, does not justify a delay in the reform process which may well aggravate the problems of fiscal disequilibrium.

The Transition to Post-Populism: A New Economic Role for the State

Chronic fiscal instability has been an endemic problem in the postwar period. Turkey experienced two major macroeconomic crises during the late 1950s and late 1970s and fiscal disequilibrium has reappeared as a major problem during the present phase of neoliberal reform. This is not to suggest that a third major crisis is inevitable. In the late 1950s and late 1970s Turkey experienced balance of payments crises as much as fiscal crises. Current fiscal instability may not lead to similar crises, considering the much greater foreign exchange earning capacity of the economy compared with the earlier periods. Nonetheless, the fact that a crisis is not inevitable does not reduce the importance of working toward macroeconomic stability. A stable macroeconomic environment will have a positive impact on productive investment, a key source of rapid and sustainable economic growth, as well as on the income distributional profile.

From a political economy perspective, the origins of endemic fiscal disequilibrium might be traced to the "overload" imposed on the state during the industrialization process. Originally, in the absence of a private entrepreneurial base, the state emerged as the principal entrepreneur and became the engine of growth during the primary phase of import substitution in the etatist era of the 1930s. Following the transition to democracy and a multi-party system in 1950, the state was forced progressively to undertake additional functions. In addition to a direct entrepreneurial role, the state emerged as a key provider of subsidies to nascent private industry. The public enterprise sector, in the post-1950 period, increasingly concentrated its activities in the intermediate goods industries and made an important contribution to private accumulation through the provision of subsidized inputs. During the import substitution era the functions of the state were enlarged as it sought to influence the pattern of industrialization through an extensive set of controls. While the liberalization of the post-1980 period led to a significant decline in the degree of intervention, considerable micro-level interventionism has continued to prevail.

In addition to intervention designed to influence the production and accumulation process, the state needed to deal explicitly with income distributional objectives. The transition to parliamentary democracy in the 1950s, in the context of a highly unequal distributional profile, implied that the state was confronted with significant populist pressures for redistribution. Newly industrialized East Asian countries like South Korea and Taiwan possessed a major advantage over Turkey in that their major take-off phase, in terms of rapid economic growth, started from a position of low income inequality. The initial set of land reforms in both countries played a key role in creating a relatively equal distributional profile. The combination of the egalitarian distributional pattern plus the existence of an authoritarian state which could repress pressures from labor and other subordinate groups meant that the South Korean or the

Taiwanese state could concentrate its attention almost exclusively on the longer-term objectives of growth and productivity. Turkey, in contrast, did not possess this comfortable option of abstracting itself from distributional considerations. In this respect, significant parallels may be discerned with Latin American cases such as Brazil, which also experienced comparatively early transitions to parliamentary democracy in the context of high income inequality. Turkey's Gini coefficient during the post-1950 period has consistently exceeded the 0.5 mark and as a result pressures for income redistribution have been an endemic feature of its political economy.[10]

The response to these pervasive distributional pressures involved the development of an "underdeveloped welfare state." In an environment where electoral constraints became particularly pressing, governments used the large public sector as an instrument for the distribution of patronage and the erection of an electoral base of support.[11] An illustration of the way the underdeveloped welfare state operated involved the creation of excess employment in the SEE sector in response to political pressures. Such practices were clearly in conflict with both efficiency and productivity objectives. High support prices for the numerically very significant farming community constituted yet another example of a populist redistributional practice. In fact, populist redistribution mechanisms became particularly important in an environment where direct redistributional measures such as tax reform proved to be politically unfeasible. The result was pressures in the direction of expanding government expenditures without a concomitant increase in government revenues. Given the populist pressures for expanding government expenditures, successive governments have resorted to short-term solutions such as high monetary rates and/or high cost domestic and external borrowing that in turn have contributed to growing fiscal instability.

The problems that the SEE sector has confronted also become more readily comprehensible when they are interpreted in the light of these political economy considerations. The origins of the perennial problems of the SEE sector might be traced to the fact that it was given contradictory objectives in the first place. In their entrepreneurial role, SEEs were expected in principle to be commercially profitable and to operate according to market oriented criteria. But, at the same time, they were expected to contribute to private accumulation indirectly through the provision of subsidized inputs. The realization of this objective necessitated underpricing their products, clearly in direct contradiction with the initial objective. Furthermore, the SEEs had to satisfy explicit social or redistributional objectives through pricing, employment, and location policies. Not surprisingly, these contradictory objectives proved to be incompatible and the result was a marked deterioration in their performance, the most visible manifestation of which was chronic operating deficits and the burden they imposed on the government budget.

The long-term solution of this dilemma clearly involves the reduction of the overload on the state by the creation of a new equilibrium or a new "post-populist state" which can intervene in the economy more effectively by concentrating on a small number of well-defined objectives. The important point to emphasize is that the greatly overextended state which characterized the ISI era, and continued to exist during the neo-liberal era in a modified form, was not a "strong state" in economic terms—compared with the East Asian developmental states for example. This is not to suggest, however, that the model of the East Asian developmental state, in its pure form, was ever feasible in the Turkish context. In an environment where democracy is a major objective in its own right and where income inequality has reached unacceptably high levels, a government cannot withdraw itself from redistributional considerations and focus all its energy on longer-term productivity and accumulation objectives. While the prototypical East Asian development model is not the natural alternative, fundamental restructuring of the state and its mode of intervention is nonetheless desirable in the Turkish context, a process which we describe as the transition from "populism" to "post-populism."

The key question is what type of state should emerge in the "post-populist" phase and what type of new functions it should be asked to perform. First of all, a reduction of the overload on the state requires it to withdraw gradually from its direct entrepreneurial role. In this respect, a well-designed privatization program sensitive to the pitfalls described earlier constitutes a necessary condition for transforming the state and helping it to play a more effective role in support of an externally competitive market economy. In the new system, the state would seek to contribute towards productivity and accumulation objectives by performing a complementary or supportive role as opposed to a direct entrepreneurial role. This does not imply, however, a transition to a minimalist state since there exists considerable scope for state intervention in this complementary role. The key functions of the state may include infrastructure investment, human capital formation, the support or the restructuring of key infant industries through selective or strategic intervention, and collaborative arrangements with the private sector over the introduction or dissemination of new technologies.

What is crucial for the success of the new form of state interventionism is that the system of support and subsidies be truly selective such that both the private and public sectors are forced to operate in a genuinely competitive environment under tight budget constraints. State intervention in this scheme means the imposition of equal conditions or standards on both the private and public sector. A push for privatization in the public sphere, while at the same time maintaining pervasive soft budget constraints for private firms through an extensive set of subsidies, clearly constitutes a double standard. Dual standards of this type would continue to impose a heavy burden on the budget and would also have negative repercussions for productivity growth. In the new system proposed, the private sector would be expected to share some of the functions of the government to a much greater degree. For example, private firms would be expected to share the burden of investment in education and the research and development effort rather than imposing the whole burden on the state.

Another key function of the post-populist state would be to set standards of performance. The institutional capacity of the state needs to be improved in order better to monitor private sector activities, exercise discipline over the private sector, and close off avenues for rent-seeking. The state has a crucial regulatory role to perform in terms of setting legal and quality standards. In fact, the persistence of an entrepreneurial role inhibits the state from focusing more explicitly on regulatory activities that may contribute in the long-run towards the achievement of both efficiency and equity objectives. To enable the state to perform this regulatory role more effectively it needs to build strong institutions within the state bureaucracy and to develop civic or non-governmental institutions. The development of these institutions, implying a more active and participatory role for interest associations, is also important for making state institutions more accountable and providing a democratic constraint on rent-seeking activities.

Finally, does the transition from a "populist" to a "post-populist" state imply that the state should not concern itself explicitly with income distributional objectives? In contrast to neo-conservative writers like James Buchanan, who also argues for a reduction in the size of the state and a change in the scope of state activity, the position adopted here is that a better income distribution should definitely be one of the priorities of the post-populist state.[12] An improvement in the income distributional profile should emerge as a clearly defined long-term objective, as opposed to one which can be realized over a very short period of time. The instruments used need to be quite different from those associated with the populist or underdeveloped welfare state. As opposed to the artificial creation of employment within the public sector, direct instruments ought to be utilized in order to accomplish income distributional goals. Examples of such "direct" instruments include tax reform, expansion of educational opportunities and health care, the institution of a well-developed system of social security and employment insurance, and a regional policy. An attempt can be made to develop a broad consensus on the post-populist approach to welfare by demonstrating that the costs and contradictory outcomes associated with populist measures of income distribution tend to aggravate rather than reduce income inequality. Hence, in the new environment, the public sector would continue to play an important role in a mixed market economy but the nature of the public sector and the composition of its activity would be radically different from the previous era.

Conclusions

For several reasons, the Turkish development experience is worth investigating from a comparative perspective. First, it is an interesting case in the dynamics of economic development in which the weight of "public" and "private" changes quite drastically over time. Second, it represents a case of rapid industrialization in the context of a broadly democratic environment. Third, it constitutes a comparatively successful transition from a heavily regulated and inward oriented economy to a more liberal economy with a high degree of exposure to the discipline of the world market. Fourth, the country has been the most dynamic in the region in which it is located in recent years. The coexistence of rapid development and democratic polity is particularly striking. Whilst one may claim that the economic performance of the East Asian newly industrialized countries has been superior to Turkey on the basis of various economic criteria including growth, income inequality, and the absence of macroeconomic crises, in one crucial respect their performance has been inferior. Their outstanding growth performance has been established in a highly authoritarian setting and the transition to democracy in these countries has been a very recent phenomenon, in fact a feature of the late 1980s.

A relatively successful case of economic development, however, does not necessarily justify the label of a "model." Leaving aside the questions of context and transferability, the central problem with the concept of the Turkish model is that Turkey's development experience, in addition to its major strengths, also embodies a number of important structural deficiencies. Turkey is still trying to emerge from semi-peripheral status and graduate into the ranks of newly industrialized countries or the core group of advanced industrialized countries. It is still in the transitional stage in that some of the key structural problems that one tends to associate with semi-industrial, semi-peripheral economies continue to manifest themselves in Turkey, including, among others, an overextended

Table 7.3

**A New Role for the State in Comparative Perspective:
Nature of State Intervention under Three Policy Regimes**

Import Substituting Industrialization	Neoliberal-Populist	Post-Populist
Extensive public enterprise sector plus heavy indirect state interventionism to assist inward oriented industrialization

Key instruments: tariffs, quotas, price controls on SEEs, subsidies

Inward oriented trade regime. Populist redistribution mechanisms.

Widespread rent-seeking in a heavily controlled environment | Somewhat reduced but still extensive SEE sector.

Significant reduction in the degree of indirect interventionism over price mechanism.

Outward oriented but not free trade or free market environment.

Export subsidies important.

Populist redistribution mechanisms still in force.

Export oriented rent-seeking | Significantly reduced direct entrepreneurial role for the state.

Liberal trade regime supported by highly selective, strategic interventionism.

Outward oriented. Highly selective system of subsidies.

Direct redistribution mechanisms.

Emphasis on the elimination of unproductive forms of rent-seeking. High degree of government accountability. |

public sector, chronic inflation, inadequate investment in manufacturing and technology creation, a high degree of income inequality, unemployment, major regional imbalances, and low levels of welfare provision. An excessive proportion of the labor force, namely more than 40 percent, is located in rural areas, although the contribution of the agricultural sector to GNP is less than half of this figure. Furthermore, the reform process which successfully began in the early 1980s is still incomplete, particularly with respect to public sector reform. Considering these weaknesses, it might be more appropriate to describe Turkey as a country in a transitional stage, one on the verge of transformation from peripheral status to joining the core or near-core group of industrialized countries or newly industrialized countries in the world economy.

Turkey's transition from peripheral to core status will not necessarily be a smooth process nor one that can be accomplished over a short period of time without significant social dislocation. In retrospect, one of the central prerequisites for the transformation from semi-peripheral to core status involves a transformation of the state—a transformation that does not imply simply a retreat but rather a new mode of state intervention and composition for public sector activities. The central objective of this new type of "post-populist state" would not necessarily be the achievement of a high rate of economic growth per se but the generation of "balanced growth," that is growth which is sensitive to key social objectives such as income distribution, environmental concerns, and interregional balance. The restructuring of the state in this transition also necessitates a strengthening of civil society and its institutions to render operation of the public sector and state intervention in the economy more accountable. The type of regulatory discipline exercised by a highly centralized bureaucratic machinery, as in the East Asian setting, might be accomplished jointly and in a more democratic manner by state and civil society institutions such as interest group associations.

Defining the contours of a new type of state, however, does not mean that the transition to such an equilibrium will inevitably be a smooth and relatively painless process. The dynamics of the reform process require serious attention in this context. A good example is the debate over the privatization of the SEEs. Privatization is a highly desirable instrument in terms of reducing the excess load on the state in the medium or long-run. Yet the manner in which privatization is implemented or the type of environment in which it is put into practice will have a crucial bearing on its effectiveness, judged in terms of both efficiency and equity objectives.

In conclusion, although Turkey is a country which embodies the potential to emerge as a "model," a number of important shortcomings in its economic structure need to be overcome before it can claim to be a leading example of economic development. In one respect, however, the label "Turkish model of development" serves a useful purpose. The need to present itself as a model to neighboring countries, and particularly to the Turkic republics, can serve as a form of collective self-discipline in the domestic sphere which could, in turn, have positive consequences for speeding up and completing the reform process over the coming years. In that respect, the psychological repercussions of the notion "Turkish model"—of a society setting new standards for itself and trying to realize those standards—should not be underestimated.

Notes

1. On the broad economic history of Turkey in the twentieth century see Henri J. Barkey, *State and the Industrialization Crisis in Turkey* (Boulder: Westview Press, 1990); Korkut Boratav, *Türkiye İktisat Tarihi, 1908-1985* [Economic History of Turkey, 1908-1985] (Istanbul: Geçek Yayınevi, 1989); William Hale, *The Political and Economic Development of Modern Turkey* (London: Croom Helm, 1981), pp. 100-117; and Çağlar Keyder, *State and Class in Turkey* (London: Verso Press, 1987). On the different interpretations associated with the term "etatism" see William Hale, "Ideology and Economic Development in Turkey, 1930-1945," *British Society for Middle Eastern Studies Bulletin* 7, no. 2(1980): 100-127.

2. For a detailed account of the 1950s, dominated by the Democratic Party, and for evidence concerning the expansion rather than the contraction of the state enterprise sector, see Hale, *The Political and Economic Development of Modern Turkey*.

3. Comprehensive analyses of the Turkish experience with neoliberal reforms include Tosun Arıcanlı and Dani Radrikl, eds., *The Political Economy of Turkey: Debt, Adjustment and Sustainability* (London: Macmillan Press, 1990) and Merih Celasun and Dani Rodrik, "Debt, Adjustment and Growth: Turkey," in Jeffrey D. Sachs and Susan M. Collins, eds., *Developing Country Debt and Economic Performance: Country Studies* vol. 3 (Chicago: Chicago University Press, 1989). On the political economy of the neoliberal era see Ziya Öniş and Steven B. Webb, "The Political Economy of Policy Reform in Turkey in the 1980s," in Stephan Haggard and Steven B. Webb, eds., *Voting for Reform: The Politics of Structural Adjustment in New Democracies* (Oxford: Oxford University Press, 1994), pp. 128-186.

4. For evidence concerning the over-invoicing of exports see Celasun and Rodrik, "Debt, Adjustment and Growth: Turkey."

5. The nature of the East Asian state has been extensively investigated. Key contributions include Alice Amsden, *Asia's Next Giant: South Korea and Late Industrialization* (Oxford: Oxford University Press, 1989); Frederick Deyo, ed., *The Political Economy of New Asian Industrialism* (Ithaca: Cornell University Press, 1987); Leroy Jones and Il Sakong, *Government, Business and Entrepreneurship in Economic Development: The Korean Case* (Cambridge, Mass.: Harvard University Press, 1980); Robert Wade, *Governing the Market: Economic Theory and the Role of Government in*

East Asian Industrialization (Princeton: Princeton University Press, 1990); and Jung-en Woo, *Race to the Swift: State and Finance in Korean Industrialization* (New York: Columbia University Press, 1991). For a comparison of the East Asian and the Latin American state see Paul Cammack, "States and Markets in Latin America," in Michael Moran and Maurice Wright, eds., *The Market and the State: Studies in Interdependence* (London: Macmillan Press, 1991), pp. 138-156 and Rhys Jenkins, "The Political Economy of Industrialization: A Comparison of Latin American and East Asian Newly Industrializing Countries," *Development and Change* 22, no. 1(1991), pp. 197-231. The key characteristic associated with the East Asian state, namely a high degree of state autonomy plus highly institutionalized business-government collaboration, has been absent in the Turkish case. In retrospect, the Turkish case is much closer to the Latin American cases. As opposed to the East Asian state and rather like the Latin American cases, the Turkish state has enjoyed a comparatively low degree of autonomy and a correspondingly limited ability to discipline the private sector and close off avenues for rent-seeking.

6. For evidence on this point see the recent OECD reports on Turkey. Detailed examinations of the nature of the tax system and its principal deficiencies include Cevat Karataş, "Public Debt, Taxation System and Government Spending Changes in Turkey, 1980-1990," Paper presented to the Conference "Change in Modern Turkey: Politics, Society and the Economy," Manchester, England, May 1993 and İzzettin Önder, et al., *Türkiye'de 1980 Sonrası Vergi Politikası* [Tax Policy in Turkey in the Post-1980 Era] (Istanbul: TÜSES Foundation, 1991).

7. For evidence concerning the relative weakness of the Latin American state's ability to tax upper income groups and the characterization of the Latin American state in general see Albert Fishlow, "The Latin American State," *Journal of Economic Perspectives* 4, no. 2 (1990): 61-74; Eliana Cardoso and Ann Helwage, *The Latin American Economy* (Cambridge, Mass.: MIT Press, 1992); Paul Cammack, "States and Markets in Latin America," in Michael Moran and Maurice Wright, eds., *The Market and the State: Studies in Interdependence* (London: Macmillan Press, 1991), pp. 138-156; and Jenkins, "The Political Economy of Industrialization." From a comparative perspective, striking similarities may be detected between the development experiences of key Latin American cases, such as Brazil, and the Turkish case, such as prolonged import substitution followed by a crisis and forced liberalization. Two key differences, however, deserve emphasis. Foreign capital has played a much more important role in countries like Brazil and Mexico than in Turkey. The democratic regime in Turkey has proved to be far more durable, in spite of periodic breakdowns, compared with the Latin American cases (excluding the unique case of Mexico), which have been characterized by long periods of military rule.

8. For an analysis of the slow pace of privatization in Turkey see Ziya Öniş, "Privatization and the Logic of Coalition Building: A Comparative Analysis of State Divestiture in Turkey and the United Kingdom," *Comparative Political Studies* 24, no. 2(1991): 231-253.

9. For detailed examinations and evidence on the Turkish privatization experiment so far see Cevat Karataş, "Privatization and Regulation in Turkey: An Assessment," *Journal of International Development* 4, no. 6(1992): 583-605 and Sven B. Kjellstrom, "Privatization in Turkey," *World Bank Policy: Research and External*

Affairs Working Papers (Washington D.C.: The World Bank, 1990). Kjellstrom argues that privatization proceeds in Turkey in the late 1980s have been used primarily to cover the budget deficit and suggests that this objective came to dominate the more fundamental objectives such as improvement in economic efficiency.

10. For evidence on income distribution in Turkey see Gülten Kazgan, *Türkiye'de Gelir Bölüşümü: Dün ve Bugün* [Income Distribution in Turkey: Today and Yesterday] (Istanbul: Friedrich Ebert Foundation, 1990). Turkey is closer to the Latin American high income inequality cases such as Brazil and Mexico than to the East Asian low inequality cases of Taiwan and South Korea. For evidence concerning income distribution in East Asia and the importance of this factor for the developing state's ability to concentrate almost exclusively on long-term growth objectives see Deyo, ed., *The Political Economy of New Asian Industrialism.*

11. For an excellent discussion of the populist-clientelist practices in Turkey which started during the Democratic Party era of the 1950s and continued to manifest themselves in subsequent periods see İlkay Sunar, "Populism and Patronage: The Democrat Party and its Legacy in Turkey," *Il Politico* LV, no. 4, (October-December 1990): 745-757.

12. On the public choice perspective of the state and arguments in favor of a minimalist state see James Buchanan, *Essays on Political Economy* (Honolulu: University of Hawaii Press, 1989).

8

Black Sea Economic Cooperation

N. Bülent Gültekin
Ayşe Mumcu

The venture for regional integration among countries surrounding the Black Sea was initiated by Turkey in 1991. On 25 June 1992, Albania, Armenia, Azerbaijan, Bulgaria, Georgia, Greece, Moldova, Romania, Russia, Turkey, and Ukraine signed the declaration of Black Sea Economic Cooperation (BSEC) committing themselves to multilateral cooperation in the region based on the principles of a market economy. The principal purpose of the BSEC was to encourage political stability and well-being through economic cooperation. Such cooperation was expected to lead to welfare gains for participating countries, taking advantage of their geographic proximity, complementary economies, and the new opportunities created through a continuing reform process and structural adjustment.

The BSEC was regarded as a contribution to the shared aspiration of its members for integration with the world economy. For this reason, it was established to be harmonious with other international and regional organizations. Articles V and VII of the declaration explicitly state that the BSEC is not an alternative to existing integration projects but a complementary process aimed at achieving a higher degree of integration with the European and world economies. The cooperation does not discriminate against third countries in the sense that any state which recognizes the provisions of the declaration can become a member or be partially involved in joint projects. While the BSEC's goal was to forward economic development and refine the institutions needed for the emergence of functioning market economies, it was also a signal to the rest of the world that the members were committed to outward oriented economic policies.

Economic cooperation was to be promoted gradually, in view of the specific conditions and problems of the member countries in transition to the market economy. Cooperation among the member countries was expected to occur above all in economic relations—including trade and industrial cooperation, science and technology, and the environment —and to encompass a wide range of areas such as transportation and communication, information technologies, exchange of economic and commercial data, standardization, energy, mining, tourism, agriculture and agro-industries, veterinary and sanitary protection, health care, and pharmaceutics.

The BSEC assumed that the initiative of the private sector would be the driving force for cooperation among members. The role of government was to create the necessary legal, economic, commercial, and fiscal framework to remove barriers to the free exchange of goods and services in the region; to improve the business environment by facilitating the free movement of operatives; and to provide an appropriate environment for the free flow of capital by taking precautions to prevent double taxation. The governments were also to take an active role in the implementation of joint projects for the development of infrastructure in the region and for the protection of the environment, particularly preservation of the Black Sea.

Regional Integration Arrangements

Since the 1957 treaty of Rome, which set out a common market model for the western European countries (the European Community—EC), regional integration has been a vivid issue in the agenda of policy makers. The success of the EC was followed by the European Free Trade Agreement (EFTA) formed by six European countries in 1960, the Australia-New Zealand Closer Economic Relations Trade Agreement (ANZCERTA) which was signed in 1983, and the Canada-U.S. Free Trade Agreement (CUSTA) of 1989 leading to the North American Free Trade Agreement (NAFTA) including Mexico as a third member.[1] There have been many other regional integration attempts among developing countries such as the Latin American Free Trade Association (LAFTA), the Andean Pact, the Central American Common Market (CACM), and the Association of South East Asian Nations (ASEAN), but these regional integration arrangements have shown slow progress compared to those among developed countries.[2]

The Economics of Regional Integration

Regional integration arrangements assume several forms; the degree of integration increases as it moves from preferential trading areas to economic unions.[3] There are three steps of integration: to assure the free flow of goods and services; to allow mobility of production; and to harmonize fiscal and monetary policies in the region. In practice, emphasis has been given to the first step.

The theoretical work on regional integration has focused on the costs and benefits to both member and non-member countries. Recently, with the polarization of world trade around three regions (western Europe, North America, and East Asia) more attention was given to the effect of regionalism on multilateralism. The question is whether regional integration arrangements will accelerate the ultimate goal of the General Agreement on Tariffs and Trade (GATT) negotiations (i.e. free trade all over the world) or hamper it by dividing the world into trading blocs.

In terms of the effects of integration on member countries, the volume of intra-regional trade is expected to increase as barriers to trade are removed.[4] Jacob Viner suggested that the increase in the volume of trade after its liberalization in the region consisted of two distinct effects, namely, trade creation and trade diversion.[5] Trade creation occurs when high-cost domestic production is replaced by low-cost imported goods from a member country. Trade diversion occurs when low-cost imports from the outside world are replaced by high-cost imports from the member country after removal of tariffs. It is assumed that liberalization of trade in the region is economically efficient if trade creation is greater than trade diversion, and inefficient otherwise.

A typical example of trade diversion was the effect of EC enlargement on agricultural trade. After beginning participation in the EC, southern European countries stopped importing grains from costly northern European sources in exchange for exporting costly Mediterranean products to them, which had been supplied by cheaper sources previously. Generally, the trade creation/trade diversion ratio tends to be high if tariffs of outside countries and/or tariffs of prospective members are high before the integration and the tariffs on external trade are low after integration. Trade diversion will also be small if member countries are natural trading partners. For example, the inclusion of Mexico in NAFTA will not cause much trade diversion since 71 percent of Mexico's imports were from the U.S. and 82 percent of its exports were to the U.S. in 1991.[6] In particular, a free trade area can avoid possible trade diversion by not forcing its members to have a common external trade policy as opposed to a customs union.[7]

There are some other potential gains that can be obtained through free trade. James Meade and Richard Lipsey pointed out that the price of imported goods will decline with the removal of tariffs even though the cost of production is high, hence resulting in fewer distorted consumption patterns in the importing country.[8] This argument can be extended to the case of imported intermediate goods, which will improve efficiency by reducing the cost of production.

Besides static gains, the member countries will also benefit from the dynamic gains associated with free trade. Competition in the region will increase as tariffs are reduced and markets expand. As monopolistic and oligopolistic market structures become exposed to outside pressures inefficient firms will disappear. Competition will encourage research and development, stimulating new investments. With access to a larger market, small countries especially will enjoy the economies of scale created by a greater degree of specialization, greater utilization of plant capacity, learning by doing, and the development of a pool of skilled labor and management. These cost reductions can reduce trade diversion in the long run.

In theory, the gains from regional integration can be increased by following different trading patterns. If the countries are complementary then inter-industry trade may expand on the basis of differences in resource endowments, hence providing comparative advantage. If they are competitive, in other words if they are similar in terms of factor endowments, production structures, and consumption patterns, then trade creation can be achieved on the basis of intra-industry trade, product differentiation, and economies of scale.

No matter what form regional integration takes, it creates discriminatory trade liberalization, thereby affecting non-members. The extent depends on how the bloc sets its external trade policies. Paul Krugman argues that since the terms of trade of the region improve at the expense of the rest of the world, outsiders will be hurt without any overt increase in protectionism.[9] On the other hand, Augusto De la Torre and Margaret Kelly suggest that non-member countries may benefit from integration if the external trade policy of the bloc is not hostile. This benefit will come in the form of increased demand for outside imports by member countries, lower-cost exports supplied from the region, and access to a larger market.[10]

The Experience with Regional Integration

Since the 1960s, the world economy has experienced the integration of industrialized countries (North-North) such as the EU and CUSTA, and of developing countries (South-South) such as LAFTA and CACM. Recently there has been an attempt by developing countries to join one of the rich clubs, NAFTA being a good example of this "North-South integration." Past experience shows that North-North integration has been more successful than South-South integration. This contrast is explained not only by the differences in the purpose of integration but also by the divergent techniques used in implementation, the diverse levels of development of the member countries, and the conflicting national policies pursued by the member states.

Regional integration among industrial countries aimed to improve the welfare of participating countries by removing barriers to trade. The slow progress made in the GATT negotiations led the industrial countries to seek liberalization of trade through regional arrangements. These arrangements generally cover trade in goods and services and provide free movement of capital through liberalization of financial services and intra-regional investment. Free movement of labor is still subject to restrictions except in the EU. Trade barriers were removed across-the-board within a specified period of time except in sensitive sectors, where they are either subject to common policies or were extended over a longer period.[11] Other policies, such as subsidies, standards, customs procedures, government procurement, investment, and competition law, have also been an important part of these arrangements. Agreements were implemented on and in some cases ahead of schedule.

The success of regional integration among industrial countries is explained by the similarities of their economies. Trade liberalization in these arrangements mostly led to an intra-industry trade specialization, that is trade in differentiated products. With the partial exception of ANZCERTA, the industrial countries that are engaged in regional trade agreements have previously been each other's major trading partners. This has a potential impact in reducing trade diversion.

The regional integration arrangements in developing countries, on the other hand, became very popular in the 1960s and extended import substitution development strategies to a larger region reaching beyond national boundaries.[12] In this way, a "training ground" would be provided to firms to gain competitiveness in the world market and exploit economies of scale. With the emergence of the debt crisis in the 1980s, the import substitution development strategies were abandoned, subsequently causing lessened interest in regional integration. In recent years, however, interest has been revived, this time supporting outward oriented and market based development strategies.

The performance of regional trading agreements among developing countries was very weak. This is attributable both to structural elements limiting the scope for potential gains and the low degree of implementation. Initial deadlines for the removal of barriers to intra-regional trade were postponed. In addition, there was a differential treatment of tariffs depending on the country of origin. Also, the reductions on trade barriers were made on a product-by-product basis which required periodic negotiations and a high degree of consensus. This lack of spontaneousness in implementation often resulted in biased selection of products, giving enough power to member countries to exclude the relatively sensitive sectors. Among all the regional integrations within the developing world, CACM is the only one that showed significant progress in terms of the increase in intra-regional trade. Intra-regional exports in CACM increased from 7 to 26 percent in the 1960-70 period.[13] Its relatively successful performance was attributed to the usage of across-the-board tariff reductions, establishment of a common external tariff, and the initially weak position of import competing sectors in the member countries.[14]

There were also inherited structural elements that limited the scope for potential gains from regional integration among developing countries. First, the member countries had highly protected industries with little intra-regional trade occurring prior to the agreement. Secondly, developing countries were similar in factor endowments which overruled trade creation based on comparative advantage. Additionally, they could not exploit the advantages of intra-industry trade based on economies of scale and product differentiation as the industrial countries did (their markets were smaller and per capita incomes were lower). Finally, underdeveloped capital markets, barriers to entry, and differential tax and regulatory environments among member countries have seriously constrained the capacity to reallocate resources.

The recent attempt of developing countries to enter the industrial countries' groups (North-South integration) is motivated differently. It provides secure future access to a large and stable market. As it is often argued in the case of Mexico's entrance in NAFTA, a commitment to such a regional integration ensures the irreversibility of hard-fought policy reforms and increases the credibility of national economic policies. In addition, this kind of North-South integration can allow a developing country to import the institutions of a well-functioning market economy from its industrial partner.

A thorough study of regional integration by De la Torre and Kelly concludes that two key conditions have to be met to maximize the gains from the integration process; maintenance of outward oriented development strategies and provision for across-the-board intra-regional liberalization with an automatic timetable.[15] Outward oriented development strategies would ensure relatively low and uniform levels of protection vis-a-vis third countries and reduce the present trade diversion effect. Across-the-board intra-regional liberalization will avoid the biased selection of products. The BSEC countries declared their commitment to the first condition.

The Economies of the Members of the BSEC

As of 1994, the BSEC had eleven members. Six are the republics of the former Soviet Union—Armenia, Azerbaijan, Georgia, Moldova, Russia and Ukraine; three are post-communist countries of eastern Europe—Albania, Bulgaria and Romania; and the final two are Greece and Turkey, which adopted outward looking development strategies more than a decade ago.

Table 8.1 gives the selected economic indicators for the member countries in 1992. The total population of the region is around 325 million, and per capita Gross Domestic Product (GDP) for 1992 is $2,650. Greece has the highest per capita GDP with $7637 and Albania has the lowest[16]. Among the members only Greece and Turkey recorded positive growth rates, of 1.3 and 5.5 percent respectively. From 1991 to 1992 all the post-communist countries experienced a decline in their GDP, mostly due to the collapse of CMEA (Council of Mutual Economic Assistance) trade and the breakup of the USSR. With the liberalization of prices, the rate of inflation increased dramatically in these countries during 1992, and continued because much needed macro and structural adjustment programs were not complete. All the countries in the region have open economies with a high total trade to GDP ratio. This is especially true for the republics of the former Soviet Union, which carry the legacy of the centrally planned Soviet system.

Former Soviet Union Republics

The breakup of the USSR in 1992 had a disruptive effect on the economies of the republics. Under the centrally planned economic system of the USSR, each state had a role in the economy specializing on certain industries (not necessarily those in which it had comparative advantage) and supplied these products to the rest of the republics.

Table 8.2 gives the structure of net material product (NMP) in 1991 for the republics of the former Soviet Union. Azerbaijan, Georgia, and Moldova are the major suppliers of agricultural products. Azerbaijan is also endowed with large oil supplies and has a broad-based industry operating in ferrous and non-ferrous metallurgy, petroleum equipment, electrical engineering, chemicals, petrochemicals, as well as agro-indus-

Table 8.1

Members of the BSEC, Selected Economic Indicators, 1992

	Pop. ('000)	Per Capita GDP U.S. $	Real GDP Growth	Inflation Cons. Prices	Total Trade/ GDP
Albania	3,400	n.a.	-15.00%	n.a.	15.69%
Armenia	3,645	2,000.00	-37.40%	1500%	84.45%
Azerbaijan	7,202	2,370.00	-26.00%	1350%	103.57%
Bulgaria	8,470	1,051.98	-7.70%	110%	108.86%
Georgia	5,478	2,000.00	-35.00%	1000%	56.99%
Greece	10,200	7,636.87	1.30%	16%	56.15%
Moldova	4,360	2,762.00	-21.00%	1277%	54.13%
Romania	22,760	777.58	-15.40%	210%	55.37%
Russia	148,770	4,325.00	-20.00%	1350%	44.00%
Turkey	58,584	2,637.30	5.50%	67%	24.33%
Ukraine	51,900	3,560.00	-16.00%	n.a.	36.00%

Georgia's data are for 1991 except for inflation rate. Armenian trade data are for 1990. Albania and Azerbaijan's trade data are for 1991. The Romanian and Bulgarian inflation rates are over retail price. Ukraine's data are for 1991 and total trade ratio to GDP only includes intra-regional trade. Russia's trade data are for 1989.

For the republics of the former Soviet Union, per capita GDP is calculated by purchasing power parity standards.

Source: World Bank Country Reports 1989-1993; EIU Country Profile

tries. Georgia's main industrial activities include engineering, aircraft and car manufacture, light and food industries, chemicals, and computers. A large part of the industry in Moldova is accounted for by agro-industry and the rest entails production of household appliances and high technology electrical goods. Armenia is a supplier of a wide range of consumer and non-specialized producer goods. Russia's industry is the most diverse one, and Russia is endowed with rich natural resources—it is the second largest energy producer in the world. Ukraine has a very large and diverse industrial sector specialized in heavy industry, chemical industries, textiles, and fuel and energy related industries. It also has significant coal deposits.

Table 8.2

FSU Republics: Structure of NMP, 1991

	Armenia	Azerbaijan	Georgia	Moldova	Russia	Ukraine
NMP (M rubles)	12,253	20,370	16,961	18,753	425,200	210,600
Real Growth rate in NMP	-11.80	-1.90	-25.00	-18.00	-5.00	-11.00
NMP by origins (%)						
Agriculture	32.21	41.10	41.80	41.70	18.34	28.70
Industry	43.18	37.10	34.40	44.50	43.13	43.10
Construction	14.37	8.40	10.10		12.32	13.80
Transportation & Communication	2.55	3.30	5.90	3.80	7.57	4.50
Other Material Services	7.69	10.10	7.80	10.00	18.64	9.90

NMP (Net Material Product) is in current prices.
For Moldova, the share of Industry in NMP also includes Construction.

Source: World Bank Country Reports, 1992

The centrally planned system in the former Soviet Union created very large scale and dependent industries in each of the republics, which in turn made inter-republican trade an essential part of economic growth and development. Most of the republics are dependent on Russia for the supply of energy and to each other for the supply of intermediate inputs. Among all the republics, Russia is the least dependent on interstate trade, accounting for 59 percent in 1990. In contrast, the other republics' inter-republican trade constituted more than 80 percent of the total trade; Russia was contributing almost 60 percent for each, followed by Ukraine with a share of around 20 percent on average. Table 3 gives the distribution of inter-republican trade by destination.

The major macroeconomic imbalances which arose after the breakup were aggravated by disruptions in inter-republican trading patterns within the former Soviet Union. In addition, the collapse of trade as a result of the dissolution of the CMEA affected them severely, particularly Russia whose imports from non-former Soviet Union sources (primarily the CMEA) fell by 46 percent in 1991. For example in Armenia, the inter-republican exports as a percentage of NMP fell to 12.43 percent in 1992 from 29.49 percent in 1991. On the imports side this decline was from 36.14 percent to 18.03 percent. The disruption in inter-republican trade led to shortages of many essential inputs and left all of the republics with a slump in production. Export markets have collapsed as well. In all republics of the former Soviet Union 1992 was characterized by a drastic fall in economic activity and large increases in prices. The decline in real NMP in 1992 was 50 percent in Armenia, 26 percent in Azerbaijan, 24 percent in Moldova, and 16 percent in Ukraine. In Georgia output fell by 28.3 percent in 1991; in Russia output has continued to fall in 1992 and was estimated to be 15 percent below the level of mid-1991 which itself represented a substantial drop from 1990.

The Trade Regime in the Former Soviet Union Republics

Although inter-republican trade was very high in volume in the former Soviet Union, there were strict state regulations and restrictions to trade. Inter-republican trade was carried out by state orders. The bilateral agreements among republics determined prices (which were substantially lower than world prices), the types of goods, the quantities of exports and imports, trading enterprises, origin, destination, and timing. This system lacked necessary incentive mechanisms, so it often caused delays in the deliveries of goods which compounded the decline in output. It also prevented economies from gaining comparative advantage in their respective industries vis-a-vis third countries.

Trade with countries not formerly part of the USSR was subject to severe restrictions. Export taxes, licenses, and the surrender system for hard currency were common practices in all the former Soviet Union republics. For example, export taxes in Azerbaijan were between 5 and 50 percent, which had an unweighted average of 28 percent. In Ukraine, export taxes were averaging about 45 percent through 1992. Also, exports to countries not formerly part of the USSR were subject to the surrender system, where firms had to pay a percentage of the hard currency earned from their exports. The exchange rates used were in fact considerably lower than market exchange rates, imposing an implicit export tax. Even though Russia began to use the market rate after July 1992, traders tended to use barter trade as a means of transaction in order to avoid holding rubles in a high inflation environment. Imports from the rest of the world were still subject to high tariffs. Azerbaijan eliminated tariffs on existing imports originating from non-former Soviet Union countries in August 1992.

The strong economic interdependence of the former Soviet republics called for an immediate reform in the trade pattern. For the near future these countries will be dependent on each other for the supply of energy and other intermediate inputs. Further disruption in trading patterns would compound existing supply constraints and could undermine the reform process. There is a need for transitional regulations to restore and sustain inter-republican trade. At the same time, however, these economies need restructuring and reallocation of resources. Most sectors of the economy are not in a position to compete in foreign markets. The trade that was taking place through state orders assumed heavily controlled prices that were substantially lower than world prices. Also, very low transportation costs distorted trade considerably. In the transition period, the introduction of world prices in the valuation of tradable goods and services would leave these republics with terms of trade gains and losses. Oil pricing in Russia is particularly important, since most of the republics depend on Russia for oil supply. However, introducing world prices would also provide the right signals to the industries in terms of their competitiveness, and lead to restructuring and the reallocation of resources.[17]

More Economies in Transition: Albania, Bulgaria, and Romania

Besides the six republics of the former Soviet Union, three members of the BSEC—Albania, Bulgaria, and Romania—are in transition to a market economy as well. Therefore, they are facing more or less the same problems as the republics of the former Soviet Union, with the exception

Table 8.4

Albania, Bulgaria, and Romania:
Structure of NMP in 1991

	Albania	Bulgaria	Romania
NMP by origins (%)			
Agriculture	44.60	14.20	22.70
Industry	32.70	56.80	45.20
Construction	6.40	9.10	5.20
Transportation & Communication		9.40	5.40
Other Material Services	16.30	10.50	21.50

Bulgaria's data are for 1990.
For Romania, the structure of GDP is provided and the data are for 1992.
Albania's data are for 1989 and transportation and communication is included
in other material services.

Source: World Bank Country Reports 1989-1992; EIU Country Profile

that they have much more independent economies. As in the case of the inter-republic trade in the former Soviet Union, the post-communist countries had very strong trade links with each other. This institutionalized trade relationship was organized through the CMEA. While providing a ready market for growing economies, it insulated these countries from international competition. As in the former Soviet Union, trade was directed by state orders, which led to an inefficient allocation of resources. The CMEA did not increase the welfare of its members in the Vinerian sense because the major part of trade was diverted. It helped the industrialization of its members' economies, but by 1980s they could no longer keep up with the pace of industrial progress in the West. With the collapse of communist rule the CMEA lost its importance but left the socialist countries with uncompetitive and inefficient industrial structures.[18]

From the 1980s there was a persistent decline in the GDPs of most of the communist countries. Albania's GDP declined by 30 percent and 15 percent respectively in 1991 and 1992. Bulgaria experienced a decline of 2.9 percent and 7.7 percent in the same years and in Romania these figures were 13 percent and 15.4 percent. All of these countries without exception suffered from balance of payments problems, and especially

Table 8.5

FSU Republics: Total Trade and Distribution of Inter-Republican Trade by Destination and Origin in 1992

	ALBANIA		BULGARIA		ROMANIA	
	Export	Import	Export	Import	Export	Import
TOTAL TRADE (million $)	208	612	2,592	2,973	4,036	5,582
Geographic distribution of trade						
Central & Eastern Europe	n.a	n.a	17.39%	16.64%	13.30%	1.50%
EC	34.13%	63.39%	40.84%	53.23%	36.02%	37.49%
Industrial Countries	41.34%	72.22%	49.76%	59.22%	46.65%	50.16%
Middle East	1.92%	2.12%	14.67%	3.51%	15.01%	15.51%
Former USSR	n.a	n.a	n.a	n.a	14.44%	14.52%

Source: IMF, Direction of Trade Statistics Yearbook, 1993

with convertible currency countries. Solving these problems is not easy since in no case are exports likely to become competitive in convertible currency markets in the near term. The CMEA countries are negotiating to straighten out their trading relations once again, but this time based on international prices which will obviously create terms of trade deterioration for most of them.

Albania is the poorest country in the region. Agriculture accounts for the largest part of NMP but it has a diversified industrial base in light and fuel industries. Seventy-five percent of Albanian exports are industrial goods and it imports mostly capital and some consumer goods. Both Bulgaria and Romania developed an industrial economy under the communist regime at the expense of agriculture. They both specialized in heavy industry, such as fuels, metallurgy, and machine building. With the collapse of CMEA trade, shortage of oil and other hard currency imports arose and forced these countries to change their trading pattern. Greece and Turkey became the fastest growing foreign trade partners for all three of these countries.

Two Market Economies: Greece and Turkey

Greece and Turkey are the two members of the BSEC which adopted market economies more than a decade ago. Although this difference between the members of BSEC on the institutional level postpones integration in many areas, it provides an opportunity to the economies in transition to benefit from the experience of these two countries.

Greece has been a member of the EU since 1981. The 1991 data on the structure of the GDP shows that agriculture accounted for 16.3 percent of GDP at factor cost, industry including construction accounted for 27.4 percent, and the service sector contributed 56.3 percent. Greece depends heavily on agriculture and textiles for exports. In 1991, 26.1 percent of the dollar value of the exports was accounted for by fresh and processed foods, while 23.6 percent was provided by textiles and clothing. Since Greece joined the EU exports have been moved away from fresh produce to processed foods and beverages. On the import side, automotive industry, fuel, meat and diary product, electrical equipment, and appliances are important items. Greece mainly trades with EU partners (primarily with Germany, Italy, and France)—commerce with the EU accounts for two-thirds of its total trade.

Turkey became predominantly an industrial country in the last decade. The share of industry in GDP has increased to 26 percent in 1992 from 19 percent in 1970. These figures for agriculture were 16 and 31 percent, respectively. Turkey has a well-diversified manufacturing base. The

Table 8.6

Structure of GDP and the Distribution of Trade in 1992

	GREECE	TURKEY
GDP by origin Agriculture	16.3	15.72
Industry	20.8	26
Construction	6.6	6.72
Transportation & Communication	7.4	12.32
Other services	48.9	39.24
Total Trade		
Export (million $)	9540	14468.6
Import (million $)	23152	22879
Export by Destination (% of total)		
Germany	23.11%	26.49%
Italy	18.01%	13.96%
France	7.22%	5.66%
UK	6.92%	5.31%
US	4.04%	6.72%
EC	64.11%	53.35%
Middle East	6.52%	15.69%
Central and Eastern Europe	10.13%	6.18%
Former USSR	1.29%	4.43%
Imports by origin (% of total)		
Germany	20.20%	18.26%
Italy	14.21%	4.02%
France	7.84%	6.00%
UK	5.52%	5.39%
US	3.66%	9.86%
EC	62.74%	46.71%
Middle East	8.40%	14.24%
Central and Eastern Europe	2.76%	4.88%
Former USSR	1.85%	4.60%

The data on the structure of the GDP of Greece are for 1991.
Source: IMF, Direction of Trade Statistics Yearbook, 1993

textile industry is the largest sector, contributing around 20 percent of the output and employing one-third of all workers in manufacturing. Turkey adopted an export-led growth strategy in 1983. This transition was coupled with an economic reform package which included a devaluation of the Turkish Lira and transition to a flexible exchange rate regime, elimination of quantitative restrictions on imports, promotion of exports through subsidies, improved efficiency in the State Economic Enterprises, and liberalization of credit markets and the banking sector. Exports as a percentage of GNP rose from 6 percent in 1970 to 12 percent in 1991. Besides the increase in trade volume, the composition of traded commodities has also been changed since the implementation of the reform program. Before 1980, two-thirds of exports were agricultural. In 1991 industrial products provided 78 percent of total exports. The Organization for Economic Cooperation and Development (OECD) countries have been the largest foreign trade partners, accounting for over 60 percent of Turkey's foreign trade. In 1992, 53 percent of total exports went to the EU, of which 26 percent was to Germany. The recession in western Europe and increased competition from Asian producers in textiles and clothing forced Turkey to diversify the geographic distribution of its foreign trade. Eastern and central Europe are becoming new competitors to Turkey in western European markets but they also offer it new export opportunities.

Potential Gains from Economic Cooperation in the Black Sea Region

The BSEC consists of countries that complement each other. Examining current trade relations in the region, it is possible to make one of two immediate observations; there is either too much or too little trade among the members of the BSEC. Except for Greece and Turkey, the rest of the members had close trade relations with each other in the past and continue to do so. However, this close relationship is not really a good substitute for natural trading partners. Under communist rule the regimes had protected industries and all trade was organized through state orders. Some of the industries are not internationally competitive and as a result much of current trade is diverted trade. New trade patterns established through cooperation in the region can eventually overcome this trade diversion.

As opposed to the rather heavy trade flows that the post-communist countries had among themselves, they had very little trade with Greece and Turkey. Table 8.7 gives the data on Turkey's trade with the other members of BSEC. The largest trade volume is with Russia, which only

Table 8.7

Turkey's Trade with the
Members of BSEC (million $)

	1992		1993	
	Export	Import	Export	Import
Albania	19	0.9	12.3	0.4
Armenia	3.2		3.8	0.1
Azerbaijan	99.8	35	34.5	17.3
Bulgaria	70.5	222.2	24.2	100.1
Georgia	10.6	5.6	7.2	14.1
Greece	142.5	87.3	56.3	62.4
Moldova		1.7	0.2	11.9
Romania	170.8	254.6	72.4	139.6
Russia	438.3	1035.7	224	721.6
Ukraine	34.5	89.4	19	149.6

The data for 1993 presents only the first half of that year.
Source: Central Bank of Turkey statistical archive.

accounted for 3 percent of Turkey's total exports in 1992 and 4.5 percent of its imports. The total trade of Turkey in the Black Sea region accounts for approximately 7 percent of its foreign trade calculated as a whole during 1992. This is a rather low trade level. It can perhaps be explained at least in part by the restrictive trade regimes pursued by many post-communist states, caught up as they are with the manifold difficulties of transition and restructuring.

Even though the post-communist countries abolished many of the protectionist policies which they had maintained for decades, the current financial situation in the republics of the former Soviet Union represents a major constraint on trade. This is so above all else because of the lack of access to convertible currency. As a consequence it will almost certainly require a good deal of time before trade in the region begins to develop dynamically and becomes more vital. The legal infrastructure that is badly needed in order to facilitate the transfer of money and capital within the region has yet to be developed. For this reason among others, the countries of the region have given high priority to the establishment of the Black Sea Trade and Development Bank (BSTDB). In a first phase of development the BSTDB will seek to finance both intra-regional and extra-regional trade, with the goal of encouraging and facilitating the transfer of foreign capital and investment resources into the region.

It has already been agreed that Special Drawing Rights will be used as the accounting unit of the BSTDB's capital. Half of this fund could be paid in their own currency by the countries who are undergoing economic transition. The share of capital was determined as 16.5 percent for Greece, Russia, and Turkey; 13.5 percent for Bulgaria, Romania, and Ukraine; and 2 percent for Albania, Armenia, Azerbaijan, Georgia, and Moldova. As individual countries complete their transition, or at least achieve a certain level of stability, they will be allowed to increase their capital share. The goal is to allow each member to have an equal share in the BSTDB. Since the paid-in capital of the BSTDB will initially be quite low, it has also been decided that it will be used to finance trade rather than investments. It is hoped that when utilized in this way it will be most effective in helping to increase the levels of potential trade in the region—that is, to help work around the blockages presently created by the lack of access to convertible currency. As it enhances its reputation in the international finance community, it can also begin to allocate available credit to short and long-term projects within the region. The BSTDB will likewise function as a guarantor. This is a very important task, due to the fact that from the outside the Black Sea region is generally seen as a high-risk area of great potential instability. The warranty provided by the bank has the potential partially to overcome the reluctance born of such perceptions and to increase the amount of foreign funds channeled to the region.

For the BSEC, the establishment of a real free trade area would seem to be a distant prospect. Greece, of course, is an EU member, and Turkey is expected eventually to enter into the EU Customs Union. These associations limit the potential of both Greece and Turkey for developing dynamic trade regimes with third country partners. Neither Athens nor Ankara is permitted to abolish its tariffs on imports from other members of the BSEC. The option of forming a full-fledged customs union among the members of the BSEC is not feasible for the same reasons. Initially, intra-regional trade could be improved by the establishment of some kind of preferential trade area. When one evaluates the future, long-term prospects of the BSEC, however, one must consider other available alternatives. In the near future none of the BSEC countries, with the exceptions of Greece and Turkey, have a realistic prospect of joining the EU as full members. Their options are therefore somewhat limited. They may either choose unilaterally to liberalize trade (as Chile did with some considerable success) or they may attempt to increase the gains from free trade through cooperation. It has been argued with some force that unilateral trade liberalization may well come to dominate free trade areas, especially in the case of small countries.[19] In the transition period, however, a preferential trade area may provide a sufficient level of protectionism.

In addition to its effects on intra-regional trade, closer integration promotes internal and external foreign direct investment. This is so above all due to the enlarged size of the market. Foreign direct investment can also contribute to the growth of intra-industry trade between member countries. Once barriers to trade are removed, integration should lead to a considerably more efficient allocation of foreign direct investment. If member states harmonize their tax policies, as well as other regulations governing the operation of multinational enterprises, the result would be strengthened bargaining power for all members and a generally more buoyant economic environment. Integration may also create a diffusion of rents that is associated with foreign direct investment among member countries.

The most important benefit may come from economic cooperation in areas where significant externalities and public goods exist. Cooperation may take different forms, such as the simple exchange of information, joint projects on environmental issues, transportation, and communication, harmonization of tax systems and public administrative rules, and the establishment of joint institutions.[20] This seems to be the direction in which these countries are moving.

Notes

1. EFTA was formed by Austria, Finland, Iceland, Norway, Sweden, and Switzerland. Turkey joined it in 1992. EFTA is negotiating free trade agreements with the Czech Republic, Slovakia, Hungary, Poland, and Israel.

2. For a detailed review of present regional integration arrangements see Augusto De la Torre and Margaret Kelly, *Regional Trade Arrangements* (Washington, D.C.: International Monetary Fund, 1992).

3. In a preferential trading area, tariffs on intra-regional trade are lower than those on extra-regional trade. In a free trade area, member countries abolish all tariffs and quantitative restrictions in intra-regional trade, retaining their individual trade policies against non-member countries. Customs union also requires common trade policies against non-members. One may speak of a common market if in addition to customs union the free movement of labor and

capital is allowed between the member countries. An economic union exists when fiscal and monetary policies are harmonized within the region as well.

4. The effects of regional integration on member countries is examined under the assumption that the alternative is the status-quo.

5. Jacob Viner, *The Customs Union Issue* (New York: Carnegie Endowment for International Peace, 1950), pp. 41-55.

6. G. C. Hufbauer and J. J. Schott, *North American Free Trade: Issues and Recommendations* (Washington, DC: Institute for International Economics, 1992), p. 48.

7. The country can always unilaterally reduce the tariffs to the non-member country and continue to import from the lowest cost country.

8. R. Lipsey, "The Theory of Customs Union: Trade Diversion and Welfare," *Economica* 24 (1957): 40-46 and J. E. Meade, *The Theory of Customs Unions* (Amsterdam: North-Holland, 1955), pp. 44-52.

9. P. Krugman, "The Move Toward Free Trade Zones," *Policy Implications of Trade and Currency Zones* (A Symposium Sponsored by The Federal Reserve Bank of Kansas City) (Kansas City, 1991), p. 10.

10. De la Torre and Kelly, *Regional Trade Arrangements*, p. 6.

11. In the EC, agriculture, coal, steel, and shipbuilding are subject to common policies.

12. The regional integration arrangements among developing countries also emerged as a reaction to regional integration among industrial countries in order to gain bargaining power in multilateral negotiations.

13. Jaime De Melo and Arvind Panagariya, eds., *New Dimensions in Regional Integration* (Cambridge: Cambridge University Press, 1993), p. 13.

14. S. Edwards and M. Savastano, "Latin America's Intra-Regional Trade: Evolution and Future Prospects," in D. Greenaway et. al., eds., *Economic Aspects of Regional Trading Arrangements* (New York: New York University Press, 1989), pp. 195-197.

15. De la Torre and Kelly, *Regional Trade Arrangements*, p. 39.

16. It was not possible to obtain exact data for Albania's per capita GDP, but *World Tables-1993* reports that it is in the lower-middle income range.

17. As we mentioned before, the establishment of industry in the former Soviet republics did not necessarily reflect comparative advantage. An example is provided by the World Bank country report on Ukraine, which examines the competitiveness of existing industries. The composition of output at world prices reveals engineering, food processing, agriculture, iron and steel, and chemicals to be the most important industries in the economy. Overall, 16 percent of the total output at domestic prices is comprised by negative value-added sectors at world prices. Furthermore, the report found that almost one-twelfth of all Ukrainian inter-republican exports are from negative value-added sectors, with sugar refining the most striking example.

18. J. Brada, "Regional Integration in Eastern Europe: Prospects for Integration Within the Region and with the European Community," in De Melo and Panagariya, eds., *New Dimensions in Regional Integration*, p. 321.

19. Ibid., p. 166.

20. To date the BSEC countries have been exchanging information in various fields. A unit was created within the State Institute of Statistics of Turkey to compile and analyze basic data. This initial information on the BSEC members is required for the harmonization of foreign trade and the preparation of conditions for the adoption of free trade agreements.

Concerning cooperation in transportation, there is a proposal for the creation of a "ring" corridor along the coast of the Black Sea, as well as a radial network emerging from the ring corridor. There is also a project for the enlargement, modernization, and construction of new sea ports.

In telecommunications, there are continuing projects that were begun before the establishment of the BSEC. Two of them are fiber-optic submarine cable systems, one connecting Bulgaria, Moldova, Romania, and Turkey and the other connecting Russia, Turkey, Ukraine, and Italy. Both projects are scheduled to be completed by 1996.

9

Turkey and the European Union: A Multi-Dimensional Relationship With Hazy Perspectives

Heinz Kramer

The European Union (EU—formerly the European Community) is that part of the world into which Turkey is today most strongly integrated, although it is not a member. In economic terms, the EU covers about half of Turkey's trade relations. In 1992, 51.7 percent of Turkish exports and 43.9 percent of its imports involved EU member states. These figures can be taken as being roughly representative of the magnitude of trade relations between the two sides over the last twenty years, with a short and exceptional period in the early 1980s when trade relations with Middle Eastern countries covered a significant share in Turkish foreign trade.[1]

What has changed tremendously during this period is the composition of Turkish exports. In the early 1970s Turkey was an exporter of agricultural produce and raw materials, whereas since the mid-1980s the country's exports to the EU were concentrated in manufactured goods. Textile and clothing still represent the bulk in this respect but over the last ten years Turkey has been able considerably to diversify the composition of industrial exports.[2]

The EU's share is about 55 percent of direct foreign capital investment in Turkey. The EU countries account for about 43 percent of the total number of firms with foreign capital, and the EU is the area in which most Turkish firms abroad exist and where most Turks outside Turkey live. Hence, it is only natural that most Turks travelling abroad also go to European destinations.

Beside this strong economic integration there exists a considerable number of narrow political bonds as well. First and most prominent ranks the Association Agreement with the former European Community (EC), followed by NATO membership and association status in the Western European Union (WEU). Furthermore, Turkey is a member of other politically relevant European institutions including the Council of Europe and the Conference on Security and Cooperation in Europe (CSCE). This network of bonds between western Europe and Turkey offers a very wide range of possibilities for intensive cooperation and dialogue with the EU and its member states.

This points to the more fundamental bases of a relationship that has always been importantly political and strategic in character. In the cold war years, EC members wanted to bind closer to the West a country that was deemed to be an indispensable ally in countering the strategic threat from the east. The Turkish political and economic elite, on their side, saw EC membership as the final objective that would make Turkey's "westernization" irreversible. Hence, Turkey's relations with the EU have always been influenced at least as importantly by strategic and political factors as by economic developments. With the approaching possibility of an eventual Turkish membership in the EU, cultural and religious considerations have increasingly been added to the picture.

The Contractual Framework

Relations with the EU are basically governed by the stipulations of the Association Agreement of 1964 (Ankara Agreement) which has been supplemented and specified by an Additional Protocol in 1972.[3] This is the oldest association relationship in which the EU is engaged. The objective of the Association Agreement is the establishment of an extended customs union between Turkey and the EU. Furthermore, in Article 28 the agreement foresees the possibility of an eventual Turkish membership in the EU if and when Turkey is able to perform the necessary obligations. Hence, association can be regarded as a preparatory measure for membership. There is, however, no automatic accession to the EU foreseen once the customs union has been fully established. For this to occur, another decision by the institutions of the EU will be necessary.

Contrary to common ideas about a customs union, the Ankara Agreement does not only cover trade of manufactured goods. It also includes trade of agricultural products, free movement of workers, freedom of settlement for professions, freedom of trade in services and capital transactions, stipulations about the harmonization of tax systems, rules of competition, and other economic legal regulations. Furthermore,

EU transport policy will be made applicable to Turkey, trade policy vis-a-vis third countries will be coordinated, and the general economic policy of both sides will be guided by the same principles. Hence, this type of customs union comes fairly close to the establishment of a common market between the EU and Turkey, an additional indication that the relationship was not intended to stop here. The stringency of the stipulations covered by the agreement varies, however, with regard to the various subject areas. In trade of manufactures, it is foreseen that Turkey will gradually abolish customs duties and equivalent barriers to trade by 1995 at the latest. Up to that date, Turkey is also obliged gradually to apply the EU's common external customs tariff in trade with third countries. For the bulk of manufactured products, however, both measures were already to have taken effect, again in a gradual manner, by 1985. The EU, for its part, would abolish all barriers to trade in manufactures—with some temporary exceptions concerning textiles and petroleum products—upon the coming into effect of the Additional Protocol.[4]

In all other areas covered by the Agreement and the Additional Protocol stipulations are less stringent. However, the Association Council as the governing body of the agreement had been asked to take actions in order to secure the timely implementation of the stipulated measures, which were regarded as necessary complements to the establishment of the customs union for manufactures. Exceptions to this are the free movement of workers, which should have been established by 1 December 1986, and the agricultural sector where Turkey should by 1995 have organized its agricultural policy in such a way as to ensure that free trade in agricultural products would become possible.

Implementation of the Ankara Agreement: A Story of Failure and Misperception

The implementation of the Ankara Agreement and the Additional Protocol never really took off until the early 1990s.[5] The EU abolished all customs duties and non-tariff barriers (NTBs) for Turkish manufactures by 1973. An important exception, however, was trade in textiles and clothing which later came under the EC textile policy in the framework of the international Multi-Fiber Arrangement. Presently it is regulated by so-called voluntary self-restraint agreements concluded between Turkish textile exporters and the Brussels authorities. As the political task of aligning Turkey's agricultural sector with the Union's Common Agricultural Policy (CAP) has never been taken up by the association's institutions, trade in agriculture is still restricted by the CAP's very effective

NTBs, although in 1987 the EC abolished all customs duties for agricultural imports from Turkey. Hence, as of 1994, the EU restricts imports from Turkey in those sectors where the country's actual export potential is the greatest.

Another issue of Turkish concern is the non-fulfillment of obligations concerning free movement of labor. At the beginning of 1973 the German government issued a ban on the recruitment of migrant workers from non-EC countries and the other member states soon followed suit. This was later supplemented by the introduction of visa requirements for Turks visiting Germany and other EC countries. Since then, immigration into the EC has been possible for Turks only when an already legally settled worker is being joined by family members. The German government, with the silent accord of all its partners in the EC, did its utmost to prevent the terms of the Association Agreement from taking full effect.

Since about four-fifths of all Turkish migrant workers in the EU lived and continue to live in Germany, the issue actually became less one of EU policy than of bilateral German-Turkish relations within the multilateral framework of the association relationship. Germany's partners in the EU were only too willing to leave the issue to the Germans and did not really develop a position of their own.[6] As a result, only a gradual improvement of the situation of Turkish workers and their families who were already legally living in the Community could be achieved.[7] In November 1986 the EC proposed a definite regulation of the issue of freedom of movement of labor according to which immigration of new workers would virtually be suspended for the duration of the association relationship. The Turkish government of course rejected this proposal and since then the issue has been pending.

In the beginning, it was basically economic and social concerns that motivated the German government to adopt its restrictive attitude towards free movement of labor. In a time of severe economic difficulties, a constant inflow of low skilled labor was regarded as an unwelcome burden on the German economy and the German welfare system.[8] In more recent years, however, the issue of free movement of labor for Turks has increasingly become intermingled with European domestic political issues such as policy towards asylum-seekers and the resurgence of racist xenophobia in Germany and elsewhere. Added to this is the religious or cultural factor. A strong public reaction to the idea of incorporating Islam as a legitimate element of "European civilization" has developed recently. This will make a solution of the problem much more difficult than it was fifteen years ago.

If one adds to all this the inability of the EU to pass the fourth Financial Protocol agreed upon in principle already in 1981, which foresees aid to Turkey in the amount of 600 million Ecu (European

Currency Unit), one can easily come to the conclusion that the EU and its member-states did not undertake strong efforts to make the Ankara Agreement and the Additional Protocol a success. Financial aid was intended as a means to prepare the Turkish economy for the customs union and to ease the negative repercussions of that development on Turkish industry. Until 1980, the EC provided financial aid of a total amount of 705 million dollars in the form of three consecutive Financial Protocols of five years duration each, which were concluded in the framework of the Association Agreement.[9] The 1980 Financial Protocol became a victim of the consequences of the third coup by the Turkish military leadership of 12 September 1980. Later, after political normalization in Turkey since 1983, its implementation was constantly blocked in the EC's institutions by Greece due to the perennial Greek-Turkish conflict.

It is not only the EU and its members that are to be blamed for the non-performance of the Ankara Agreement and the Additional Protocol. Turkey did even less in order to implement the provisions foreseen for the establishment of a customs union. Only two reductions of tariff rates for imports from the EC, in the magnitude of 10 per cent each, were executed in 1973 and 1976 respectively. The adjustment to the EC's common external tariff was not begun at all and the process of reducing quantitative restrictions on imports from the EC also came to an end in 1976 after hardly having taken off. Furthermore, Turkey pressed for greater EC concessions in agricultural trade without showing any signs of readiness with regard to an adaptation of its agricultural policy to the conditions of the CAP. In 1978, finally, when the EC did not respond favorably to Turkey's demands, the Turkish government even proposed a five-year moratorium on the association in order to reassess the whole undertaking.

The main reason for Turkish behavior was that the goal of establishing a customs union with the EC came under severe criticism in Turkey during the 1970s. The Turks suddenly realized that the gradual opening of their economy to European competition ran contrary to the established policy of planned national economic development by way of import substitution. The discussion became increasingly exacerbated by its intermingling with the quickly deteriorating general domestic political and economic situation in Turkey.[10]

The debate showed that a large part of Turkey's political and economic elite had a somewhat misleading idea of the goals and mechanisms of a customs union. In their view, this undertaking basically was a mutual exchange of economic sacrifices and benefits which should support Turkey in its economic development, as the weaker partner, by granting it a lasting preferential position in the EC's pattern of foreign trade relations. This position, however, did not take into account that a customs union is not an instrument of guided national economic development. The underlying logic of a customs union is indirectly to promote economic development in the whole area by improving the efficiency of the allocation of productive factors through trade liberalization, thereby improving the general welfare and the production structure in the union. This does not say very much about how resulting development gains are distributed among the participants of the customs union. Hence, the establishment of a customs union does not guarantee that Turkey will get more, in relative terms, than the EU. This, however, was exactly what the Turkish side was (and still is) looking for.[11]

When the EC started to grant similar trade concessions to other countries, especially in the framework of its "global Mediterranean policy" established after 1975, Turkey saw itself deprived of the expected benefits from the EC's trade liberalization measures of 1973.[12] Turkey increasingly perceived its own obligations for trade liberalization as one-sided sacrifices without any beneficial reciprocal measures from the EC. This assertion, however, has never been proven empirically and should be regarded more as an essentially political argument to justify Turkish reluctance in fulfilling its obligations under the agreement.[13] The fact that third parties might have been involved in the same field of trade with similar conditions can hardly be taken as an indication that real harm was inflicted upon Turkey's foreign trade with the EC.[14]

After the economic policy turn-around in Turkey of 24 January 1980, Ankara's attitude towards the development of the association relationship was more influenced by political events and considerations than by economic interests. Turkey opened its economy towards international competition in the 1980s without, however, giving any special attention to its obligations under the Ankara Agreement. This approach was main- ly justified by pointing to the non-compliance of the EC with regard to financial aid, free movement of workers, and trade restrictions for textile and clothing. On a broader level, it was the Turkish anger at recurrent EC criticism of Turkey's democracy and human rights record which guided Ankara's policy towards Brussels. Added to this was a deep Turkish disappointment about the EC members' inability to stop Greece from using its membership in the Community to undermine EC-Turkey rela- tions.

Turkey's Application for Membership in the EC: A Premature Attempt at Changing the Rules of the Game

By the mid-1980s the establishment of the customs union seemed to have become a failure, free movement of labor seemed impossible, and financial aid was recurrently blocked by Greek vetoes in EC institutions. The association relationship had seemingly reached an impasse. Given this situation, voices in Turkey proposing a policy switch in the direction of application for membership grew.

It was mainly the country's Istanbul-based business community that advocated such a move.[15] It expected from such a development a lasting improvement of its position in an EC market that had become more attractive for Turkish business as a result of the general policy of economic liberalization. Contrary to the situation of the 1970s, this time all parties, including the Social Democratic Populist Party, also supported this policy approach, although less for economic reasons than to protect and stabilize the recently-regained civilian democracy. Initially the government of Turgut Özal, and especially the prime minister himself, favored foreign policy alternatives and tried to establish closer links with the Islamic countries of the Middle East and with the U.S. When this orientation did not bring about the expected results, the Turkish government joined in the general opinion of the Turkish economic and political elite concerning membership in the EC.

The new Turkish attitude met with great reluctance on the side of the EC. Here, all members were of the opinion that for various reasons a Turkish application for membership was untimely. The Twelve had only begun the process of digesting the so-called southern enlargement, i.e. the accession of Greece, Spain, and Portugal. In addition, the EC had just started the process of overcoming a long period of internal stagnation or "Eurosclerosis" by initiating a common internal market by the end of 1992 and by streamlining its internal decision-making procedures with the adoption of the Single European Act in 1986. Under such circumstances hardly anyone in the EC's political circles was ready to contemplate another enlargement, and even less so if this would mean the membership of a large and less economically developed country like Turkey. Such a step only promised new financial burdens and further complications.

Özal, however, had made up his mind and was determined to become the one Turkish politician after Atatürk who actually anchored his country in Europe. Hence, on 14 April 1987, the Turkish minister of state for relations with the European Community, Ali Bozer, officially presented Turkey's application for membership to the acting president of the Council of the European Community, Belgian prime minister Leo Tindemans.[16] Turkish expectations to become a member, however, did not materialize. In spite of strong Turkish lobbying at various levels to convince EC members of the necessity and profitability of Turkish accession, on 5 February 1990 the Twelve declared that the country was not yet ripe for accession. The position of the EC Council of Ministers

was basically a confirmation of the official "Opinion" of the EC
Commission on the Turkish application, which had been published on 18
December 1989. In its Opinion, the Commission put forward a series of
social and economic realities that prevented a positive prognosis for the
success of a Turkish EC-membership. More in passing and in very general terms, the Commission also pointed to some political problems
which additionally complicated a positive reply to the Turkish request.
Instead, the EC proposed an intensification of relations based on the
existing Association Agreement.[17] For this purpose, and following a
request of the EC Council, in June 1990 the Commission presented a
comprehensive package of measures in the fields of trade relations,
economic and industrial cooperation, financial aid, and political dialogue
in order to improve EC-Turkey relations.[18]

Almost Back to Square One:
New Attempts at Finalizing the Customs Union

It took until November 1992—and it required a complete turnover of
the European political landscape and a change of government in
Turkey—for this proposal to be implemented. After the opening of the
"iron curtain" western Europe's foreign policy preoccupation turned east.
Furthermore, the end of the strategic East-West confrontation seemed
significantly to reduce the political importance of Turkey for western
European security policy interests. It was only after the second Gulf War
and after the demise of the Soviet Union that Turkey's geographic
location took on new geopolitical value for western interests. This was
acknowledged by a declaration of the European Council, the bi-annual
summit meeting of the EC's heads of state and government, at its Lisbon
meeting in June 1992, which stated that "the Turkish role in the present
European political situation is of the greatest importance."[19]

As a consequence of this change of attitude, the EC undertook serious
efforts at normalizing relations with Turkey. This was reciprocated by the
new Turkish coalition government under prime minister Süleyman
Demirel which had succeeded the Motherland Party government in the
Turkish elections of November 1991. As a result of Turkey's newly
enhanced strategic image and upgraded geopolitical position, Demirel
and his social democratic coalition partners took a more pragmatic
approach in relations with the EC. For them, the new situation offered a
chance of strengthening Turkey's bonds with the West in general and the
EC in particular. At a meeting of the Association Council on 9 November
1992 both sides agreed to restart the implementation of the provisions
laid down in the Association Agreement.

The Turkish government confirmed its readiness to finalize the establishment of a customs union with the EC by 1995. The EC, on its side, agreed to the creation of an intensive political dialogue with Turkey on the highest level and showed its willingness to enhance economic and industrial cooperation. Since then, both sides have been busy implementing these basic decisions to improve a bilateral relationship which had gone through a period of severe political estrangement during the preceding decade.

Political dialogue started in February 1993 with a visit of Turkey's deputy prime minister Erdal İnönü to Brussels, where he met with the presidents of the EC Commission and Council. In March, a common steering committee between the EC and Turkey was set up in order to prepare for the completion of the customs union. Its work resulted in a list of topics to be discussed and resolved in order to meet the 1995 deadline. This list was formally agreed upon as a working program for both sides at another meeting of the Association Council in November 1993. It includes the following points:

- free circulation of goods, abolition of all existing customs duties and equivalents, removal of quantitative restrictions and provisions applying to processed agricultural products as well as to products under the legal jurisdiction of the European Coal and Steel Community;
- implementation of the EC's common external tariff on goods from third countries and cooperation between customs authorities;
- common trade policy, i.e. adaptation of Turkey's trade regime to the preferential and other trade agreements concluded by the EC with third countries as well as to special EC trade-regimes in certain industrial sectors (textile, coal and steel, etc.);
- cooperation on the harmonization of agricultural policy and provisions for reciprocal preferential market access;
- mutual minimization of restrictions on trade in services, especially concerning telecommunications, financial services, transport, and tourism;
- harmonization of commercial legislation regarding competition policy, state aid, anti-dumping legislation, intellectual and industrial property rights, and public procurement;
- institutional provisions concerning decision-making and dispute-settlement procedures;
- financial issues and investment promotion;
- social issues;

- economic, industrial, monetary, environmental, scientific, and cultural cooperation and collaboration in curtailing drug-trafficking.[20]

This working program is a Herculean task. It amounts to nothing less than doing everything necessary for the implementation of a functioning customs union between Turkey and the EU that has not been done since the conclusion of the Additional Protocol in 1972. It seemed highly unlikely that all that has been neglected over the past twenty years could now be made up for within one year's time. If this could really be done, it would be an indication of either the huge developmental progress which Turkey has made since then or that the EU and Turkey overestimated the difficulties for establishing their customs union and chose an unrealistically long time-table in the Additional Protocol.

A closer look at the topics of the working program, however, shows that this fresh start can fairly quickly run into serious problems. This will not so much be the case with regard to trade liberalization. Turkey has made substantial progress in general trade liberalization during the 1980s and even concerning its obligations under the Additional Protocol. It resumed the process of gradual tariff reductions towards the EC in 1988 and in 1994 there remained only a last step of 10 or 20 per cent. Problems could, however, arise with regard to some still highly protected sectors with a strong economic and political position like automobiles and pharmaceuticals.

The establishment of a customs union under the present circumstances, however, cannot be reduced to the complete abolition of customs duties between the two sides plus the implementation of the EU's Common Customs Tariff (CCT) by Turkey. First, all internal barriers to trade have to be abolished. This means that Turkey must completely eradicate its system of raising import levies for financing of the Mass Housing Fund. This fund is the last remaining of what was once a whole system of extra-budgetary fund raising for various purposes introduced by the former Motherland Party government of late president Özal when he was prime minister. Fund levies and customs duties, however, are still important contributions to the Turkish budget, which is nevertheless constantly running a rising deficit. Hence, the Turkish treasury may face some problems in finding compensations for the loss of income caused by the establishment of a customs union. Turkey has already indicated that it expects some type of financial compensation from the EU and it has presented a figure of about three billion dollars for the sake of discussion.[21]

However, the EC too has to make some corrections in its trade policy applied to Turkey, mainly trade in textiles and clothing. The practice of imposing voluntary trade restraints on Turkish exporters clearly contravenes the stipulations of the Additional Protocol and will have to be abolished prior to 1995. Hence, EU authorities may face some major problems with respect to their textile policy unless the negotiations about the implementation of the working program lead to a reconfirmation of the safeguard clause of Article 60 of the Additional Protocol in such a manner as to provide a further legal basis for trade restrictions.

Second, the establishment of a customs union does not only mean the application of the EU's CCT by Turkey. It would also imply the application by Turkey of all the preferential trade agreements which the EU has concluded with third countries and the adaptation of all Turkish trade agreements with other countries to the respective EU situation. Otherwise, there would be the possibility for firms from third countries to circumvent EU and/or Turkish import regulations to the detriment of either EU or Turkish producers, unless technically complicated procedures concerning rules of origin were implemented.

The opening of the Turkish market towards the EU, however, has proceeded much faster than the adaptation to the CCT. Steps of 40-50 percent still have to be taken. Full compliance to adapt the Turkish customs tariff to the generally much lower CCT and to apply the EU's preferential trade regimes with third countries within one year's time may cause even more serious problems to Turkish industry than those created by abolishing trade restrictions for EU-exports. EU trade preferences are granted to a number of third countries which are direct competitors in sectors of industry that are still strongly protected in Turkey—for example textiles and clothing, processed agricultural goods, and household appliances.

In short, the establishment of a customs union between Turkey and the EU, given the latter's status as one of the strongest trading blocs in the world, is about to create severe adaptation problems for Turkish industry. Turkey may, however, not be well prepared to shoulder this burden given the fairly short period of time until the realization of the scheme and the still high level of protection for some very important industrial sectors. Vivid complaints by industrialists representing the sectors that are expected to be most seriously affected concerning the scope and speed of the realization of the customs union scheme can already be heard in Turkey.[22] What could be expected as a "solution" to this problem is, first, a prolongation of the adaptation of Turkey's customs tariffs with regard to preferentially treated third countries, and second some negotiated exceptions for the full implementation of the customs union scheme by 1995. What most probably will happen is an increase in the sophistication of Turkish NTBs for certain sectors or across the board in order to diminish the negative consequences of a formally open market.

Another problematic issue will be trade in agricultural produce which, according to the Association Agreement, should be included in the customs union. For this to happen, however, Turkey would have to adapt its national agricultural policy to the CAP in such a way as to allow for the abolition by the EU of its non-tariff trade barriers in agricultural trade. In essence, this would mean that Turkey would have to apply EU market regulations and price policy in most of its agricultural sectors without, however, taking part in the CAP. It is hardly foreseeable that the country will be ready and able drastically to change its national agricultural policy before 1996. For this to happen more time will definitely be required and complicated negotiations between Turkey and the EU will be necessary.[23] By 1996 we are likely to see only a somewhat limping customs union restricted mainly to trade in manufactured goods between the EU and Turkey and with many transitional measures and exceptions concerning other areas.

The creation and full functioning of a customs union, however, does not only require trade related measures. Of equal importance are activities concerning the regulatory framework of production such as anti-trust policy, state aid, and taxation—measures designed to enable undistorted competition between industries within the large market. In these areas, much work remains to be done in EU-Turkey relations prior to the start of a full-fledged customs union even for industrial products. There is, for instance, at present no Turkish equivalent to the EU's competition policy, although legislation in that direction has been prepared for years. The same holds true for the issue of industrial and intellectual property rights, which has gained increasing importance in recent years with the establishment of a large business of industrial counterfeit products in Turkey.

Given the fairly short time span in question, the fact that the proper functioning of the association has been interrupted for fifteen years is now being very negatively felt. It is doubtful whether the Turkish and the EU administrations will be able to make up for that delay. In 1994, the Union already had to undertake great efforts to bring its entry nego- tiations with four EFTA members to successful conclusions. Taking up the whole range of measures needed for the timely completion of the customs union with Turkey could create administrative bottlenecks. In the same regard, it is doubtful if the administrative measures taken by prime minister Tansu Çiller, who created three new bodies for the coordi- nation and supervision of relations with the EU, will really enhance efficiency on the Turkish side.

It should be noted that the new approach to completing the customs union between Turkey and the EU only marginally includes the issues of free movement of labor and financial aid. A change of the EU's position regarding the former is not in the works, given the deterioration of the EU's labor market and the climate of xenophobia in some member states. Turkey, however, seems to be ready to accept this for the time being. This attitude may change fairly quickly if as a result of fully opening Turkish markets to foreign competition redundancies become a large-scale phenomenon in Turkish industry.

A similar argument would apply with respect to financial aid. As a result of the economic development of the last decade, Turkey is no longer in a position to depend on foreign aid for the financing of its economic development. It can now use the international financial markets for this purpose. Hence, the implementation of the fourth Financial Protocol has predominantly become an issue of the political climate of the relationship and a test case for the willingness and ability of EU members to overcome Greece's stubborn attitude regarding a lasting and fundamental improvement of EU-Turkey relations. What will, however, almost certainly become an issue in negotiations over the completion of the customs union is the question of compensation for the financial disadvantages, in budgetary terms as well as in terms of current account balance, which Turkey is about to experience as a consequence of completely opening its market to imports from the EU as well as other countries.

It has already been argued by Turkish officials that Turkey would be the only country to have established a customs union with the EU before becoming a member, and hence it would be deprived of the financial privileges that all new member states—including Portugal, Spain, and even Great Britain—enjoyed during the transitional period of the accession process. For this reason Turkey should also benefit from EU financial assistance for a certain period during which Turkish industry fully adapts to the consequences of the customs union. If the EU is ready to accept this argument, member states would have to look for ways of overcoming Greece's principled resistance to larger financial transfers from the EU to Turkey.

Elements of Politicization in the EU-Turkish Relationship

The likely problems which may arise in the process of completing the customs union clearly show that this issue cannot be regarded as a basically technical one.[24] It is embedded in the broader political framework of Turkey-EU relations, as has always been the case with the development of the Association Agreement. From the Turkish point of view the customs union is still strongly related to the question of Turkish membership in the EU, as had been confirmed by minister of foreign affairs Hikmet Çetin during the meeting of the Association Council in November 1993. From the point of view of the EU, the completion of the customs union cannot disguise serious concerns with regard to the Cyprus issue, Turkish democracy, and eventual Turkish accession, as was stated by Çetin's EU-counterpart on the same occasion.[25]

With regard to these issues, the positions of Turkey and the EU have constantly differed. None of them can be regarded as completely solved. At the level of official relations, however, they have been thrust into the background to a certain extent due to new international developments after the demise of the Soviet Union. As no real political efforts at coming to terms on these issues have been undertaken by either side, however, a deterioration of Turkey-EU relations due to developments external to the association framework proper can always occur. A closer look at these issues of contention seems to be appropriate in order fully to understand the complexity of the relationship.

The "Greek factor" and the Cyprus issue

The perennial Greek-Turkish conflict became an issue in Turkish-EC relations after Greece had achieved EC membership.[26] The majority of the Turkish political public is convinced that Greece abuses its membership in the EU in order to spoil Turkish-EU relations. It is equally convinced that the EU institutions as well as Greece's partners do not put up sufficient resistance against this.

In general terms, the Turkish view is not completely unfounded given, for instance, Greece's stubborn resistance against the application of the EC-Turkey Association Agreement and the Additional Protocol on its bilateral relations with Turkey. It took the EC more than seven years after the accession of Greece on 1 January 1981 and it required a temporary Greek-Turkish rapprochement (the so-called "Davos process") to achieve Greece's consent in signing the respective protocol for the application of the Association Agreement.[27] This is but one example of Greece's continuous attempts at blocking any new movement in EC-Turkey relations by pointing both to the unsolved Cyprus problem and to what in Greek eyes is an unsatisfactory human rights situation in Turkey.

What is, however, either a fundamental Turkish misconception or an exaggeration of the real situation is the evaluation of the reaction of Greece's partners to Athens' behavior. It is misleading to interpret this reaction as active support for Greek ambitions. More often, the remaining EU member states have tried hard to change Greece's attitude, but they are bound by the EU's decision-making rules. Most of the decisions for the implementation of EU activities within the framework of EU-Turkey association need unanimity in the EU Council, i.e. Greek consent. There is also no chance of changing the rules because this, too, requires an unanimous decision of the Council. This situation is certainly deplorable from the Turkish point of view but it seems unfair to blame Greece's partners in the EU.[28]

Greece's attitude is strongly linked to the Cyprus issue.[29] Since its entry into the EC, Greece has sought to rally its EC partners behind its national position in the struggle with Turkey. This effort was not successful until the late 1980s. It was only in preparation for the meeting of the Association Council of 25 April 1988 that the Greek government succeeded in getting a formula included in the EC's opening statement that "the Cyprus problem affects EC-Turkey relations." This, in return, led to the boycotting of the meeting by the Turkish foreign minister. Subsequently the issue of the "Cyprus formula" in the EC opening statement became a point of disagreement between Turkey and the EC. The EC nevertheless hardened its position by including this formula in the presidency's conclusions of the Dublin meeting of the European Council of 25-26 June 1990. The Turkish government immediately denounced the EC's position by repeating its opinion that the Cyprus question is not connected to EC-Turkey relations. It declared that the EC had given up its constructive approach regarding the Cyprus issue and instead sided with Greece, thus losing any political credibility concerning international efforts to achieve a negotiated solution.[30]

A new facet has been added to the Cyprus issue in the context of Turkey-EC relations with the application for the accession of the Republic of Cyprus to the EU dated 3 July 1990. This move may have been induced by the stated position of the Dublin European Council meeting. The Turkish-Cypriot government supported by Ankara argued that the application was illegal from the point of view both of Cypriot constitutional law and international law.[31] The Council ignored the Turkish concerns and passed the Cypriot application to the Commission for the preparation of an "Opinion," adding another complication to the already very difficult situation regarding its political position in the eastern Mediterranean.

In its "Opinion" of 30 June 1993 the Commission declared that Cypriot membership in the EC was possible in principle and would most likely not pose any special problems in the social and economic field.[32] It was, however, also of the opinion "that Cyprus's integration with the Community implies a peaceful, balanced and lasting settlement of the Cyprus question" in order to "create the appropriate conditions for Cyprus to participate normally in the decision-making process of the European Community and in the correct application of Community law throughout the island."[33] The EC was ready immediately to start talks with the Cypriot representatives for the preparation of smooth negotiations once this occurred. If, however, future intercommunal talks under the auspices of the UN did not lead to a political settlement of the Cyprus question, the EC would reassess the situation "in view of the positions adopted by each party in the talks" and reconsider the issue of Cyprus's accession to the EU in January 1995.[34]

The Council of Ministers, at its session on 4 October 1993, accepted the Commission's "Opinion" without qualifications and in late November of the same year a first round of preparatory talks between Commission officials and the government of the Republic of Cyprus took place in Nicosia. Furthermore, the EU decided to attach an observer to future intercommunal talks without, however, having been able to define the observer's task beyond generally getting first-hand information about the behavior of the Cypriot parties during the negotiation process. In order not to upset Turkey too much by this decision, the EU Council explicitly stated that "observer" did not mean "participant" or "interlocutor."

These developments in EU-Cyprus relations have nonetheless created a new situation in the EU-Turkey-Greece triangle which may soon have serious repercussions on the development of overall EU-Turkey relations. What seems evident are the growing cross-pressures on the EU from Athens and Ankara with Greece, as always since 1981, enjoying the advantages of EU membership. It seems doubtful, however, that the situation contains sufficient incentives for both Athens and Ankara to undertake serious bilateral efforts to find a comprehensive solution for their conflicts. In the long run, as an unwelcome result of all of this, the EU's status as an international political actor could be considerably damaged.

For Turkish spectators, however, the situation will continue to evoke the impression of a partisan EU position with regard to Greek-Turkish relations, and of a certain application of double-standards by the EU with regard to Turkey and Greece respectively. Although this impression is to some extent objectively justified, the underlying factors cannot be changed because Greece is a member of the EU and Turkey is not.

Turkey's Process of Democratization and the Kurdish Problem

Over the last decade the state of democracy and human rights in Turkey has been another recurrent issue in EU-Turkey relations. This contrasts sharply with the situation that prevailed during most of the first fifteen years of the association relationship. Although the respective negotiations leading to the Ankara Agreement of 1964 and to the

Additional Protocol of 1972 took place in the immediate aftermath of military interventions which were accompanied by restrictions on human and political rights this did not significantly influence the negotiating climate. Nor did the serious deterioration of the domestic political situation in Turkey during the second half of the 1970s, which was also accompanied by a general loss of personal security for many citizens, create major concerns in western European political circles, not to speak of repercussions on EC-Turkey relations.[35]

This changed almost overnight with the third military intervention in September 1980. Since then the western European public (particularly in Germany), the EC's institutions (especially the European Parliament), and organizations like the Council of Europe have continually monitored human rights in Turkey. They found many flaws in Turkey's human rights record even after the return to civilian political rule with the elections of November 1983. These elections were not regarded as having been fair and free. As a result, the European Parliament refused to re-establish official contacts with the newly-elected Turkish parliament. Furthermore, many stipulations in the new Turkish constitution of 1982 were regarded as being undemocratic, especially those concerning parties and trade unions. Added to this was a recurrent complaint by EU institutions and the general western European public about severe violations of human rights by Turkish authorities, especially the systematic torture of persons detained for political reasons.[36] These constant complaints seriously hampered a rapid normalization of EC-Turkey relations during the 1980s. Many in the Turkish public regarded these reservations on the side of the EC as unfounded and a result of misinformation, or as a sign of political ill-will. It should be noted, however, that such criticism was never a one-sided western European affair. There has always been strong domestic criticism of the prevailing standards of democracy and human rights in Turkey, which was not only the expression of "separatists" or "radicals" but could be found in circles of the Turkish "moderate left" as well. Western European complaints about the situation in Turkey were also, to a certain extent, a reflection of the domestic Turkish political debate inasmuch as this was not suppressed by the state authorities. In this sense, the sometimes harsh rejection of western European criticism by Turkish officials was also directed at certain domestic groups.

Since the end of 1991, western European criticism about insufficient human rights and democratic standards in Turkey has calmed somewhat. It was acknowledged that during the last years Turkish governments have brought about significant improvements in this respect. Nevertheless, the situation is widely regarded as being not fully satisfactory.[37] There is concern in EU circles about how effectively and rapidly further

progress can be made given severe resistance from parts of the bureaucracy and the "law and order apparatus" of the state. The position of
these groups is strengthened by the fact that they also find support in the
Turkish parliament. Optimism still prevails in the EU, however, as can
be seen in the latest *Turkey-Report* of the European Parliament submitted
by the Belgian parliamentarian Raymond Dury.[38]

Strongly related to the issue of "democratization" is the problem of the
Kurdish minority in Turkey and its treatment by Turkish authorities.
Recently, this issue has come to outrank "democratization" in the
hierarchy of western European public concern with regard to EU-Turkey
relations.[39] A satisfactory reconciliation of western European and
Turkish views of this problem seems to be very difficult. There certainly
are some misunderstandings or misjudgements on the side of western
Europeans, as Turkish official and public opinion suggest time and again.
The main underlying factor, however, seems to be conceptual differences
regarding the substantial content of the notions of "minority" and
"nation-state" and the relationship between them.[40]

Other Europeans have difficulties in sharing the Turkish view that
there are no minorities in the country except those explicitly mentioned
in the treaty of Lausanne of 1923. This is a narrow legal approach to the
phenomenon of identity which is mainly based on the Turkish state doctrine of the indivisibility of the Turkish nation and state. It should be
noted, however, that this approach does not deny the existence of Kurds
in Turkey—it only denies their legal status as a minority.

In the prevailing and overwhelmingly accepted Turkish doctrine the
nation and the nation-state form an inseparable whole which, if coupled
with the principles of political democracy and rule of law, renders
meaningless any differentiation between citizens based on ethnic
criteria.[41] This Turkish (majority) position with regard to the links
between "minority," "nation," and "nation-state" is, however, but one
possible view of the substantive meaning of these concepts and their
linkage. This definition mainly holds true for nation-states which are
organized upon the principles of a "unitary state" whereas nation-states
that are organized upon the principles of a "federal state" display a
different understanding.

The mainstream European approach to the issue of minorities and
their relation to the state does not always and automatically mean that
each and every group which is termed a minority is also granted the
right of special treatment. Generally speaking, in most of the western
European countries there is a certain public acceptance of the argument
that any minority has a right to expect that its claim to special treatment
be open to public political debate and, if necessary, democratic political
decision.

In this perspective it is the behavior of the Turkish state authorities toward persons and groups, be they Kurds or Turks, that deviates from the official line which should come under criticism, rather than the official position defending the principle of the unitary state. The state authorities' reactions to the various concrete manifestations of the Kurdish issue go far beyond fighting separatist terrorism and include severe violations of human rights, an evaluation which can also be found in the Turkish press. It is even indicated in an report about the infamous "Newroz" events of March 1992 which has been published by the Social Democratic Populist Party, a member of the governing coalition.[42]

The Turkish approach towards the Kurdish problem also contrasts with another emerging consensus in most EU countries about the treatment of ethnic minorities—one which has been accelerated by the end of the East-West conflict and its unleashing of long-suppressed ethnic conflicts in various central and eastern European states. Today, the majority of the western European public is of the general opinion that every ethnic group of a certain size should have a right to maintain, develop, and express its specific ethnic identity. Opinions vary in and between EU member states as to the ways and means according to which this should be accomplished. The spectrum of possibilities offered in public debate on the issue varies from a general right to political self-determination to granting limited rights to a vaguely defined "cultural autonomy." The treatment of ethnic minorities within EU member states varies accordingly.

The preceding reflections put into perspective the most prominent issue in west European-Turkish disagreements on the Kurdish problem: the activities of the Kurdistan Workers' Party (PKK) and the reactions of the Turkish state to these activities. The governments of EU member states, the leading parties of these countries, and other officials of the EU and its member states have seldom if ever shown any sympathy for the PKK and its terrorist activities. Official and other political criticism which has been directed at the anti-terrorist activities of Turkish authorities has always complained about an overstepping of the limits set by the rule of law and about violations of human rights with respect to the civilian population in southeast Anatolia. Turkey has never been denied the right to defend its political and territorial integrity against separatist terrorism.

It would, however, be misleading if the Turkish government and public would interpret the most recent ban on the PKK and other Kurdish organizations in some EU countries as an unconditional official support for Turkish policy on the Kurdish problem. Western European official and public opinion will continue to differentiate between a legitimate fight against separatist terrorism on the one hand and an overstepping of the limits of the constitutional state and violations of human rights on the other.

As long as the Turkish government continues its present approach to curbing the separatist terrorism of the PKK mainly by means of large-scale military operations which severely affect large portions of the civilian population in the region, western European criticism will not stop. The same holds true with regard to a continuation of repressive state measures in other parts of Turkey such as censorship and closure of the press, which are mainly justified as necessary concomitants to the fight against Kurdish separatism. Generally speaking, it is hardly conceivable that the western European public will ever accept a military solution to the Kurdish problem.

All this, certainly, will continue negatively to affect the climate of official EU-Turkey relations. It remains to be seen if and how far such intervening political factors will be pushed into the background in official relations due to overriding strategic and political considerations deriving from a re-evaluation of Turkey's key position in the emerging new "European architecture."

The New "European Architecture" and the Future of EU-Turkey Relations

The basic decisions of completing the customs union within the framework of the Ankara Agreement, of establishing a comprehensive political dialogue between Turkey and the EU at the highest level, and of granting Turkey association status in the WEU can all be interpreted as a decision to continue with relations between Turkey and the EU on the path which has been set in the last forty years. This, by implication, would mean either that the basic conditions informing the relationship continue to be the same or that a change in these conditions, in the opinion of both sides, does not justify altering the relationship. Given the dramatic changes in the international framework which has guided EC-Turkey relations in the past, only the second assumption seems valid. The only other possibility is that both sides have refrained from a reassessment of the new international situation and its impact on their relationship and preferred, for the sake of convenience, to continue as if nothing serious had happened.

The approach of the EU member states to relations with Turkey is still dominated by strategic considerations. Under the present international situation it is, however, no longer a real and present Soviet threat which determines western Europe's interest. This has been replaced by a more diffuse idea of European strategic interests and a related Turkish role with regard to the situation in the Middle East and to possible developments in Central Asia. In this new environment, Turkey is ascribed the role and function of a stabilizing element and a political and social model to curb fundamentalist Islamic tendencies as well as the more far-reaching strategic ambitions of radical members of the Islamic world.

It is unclear how much this perception of Turkey's new role is the result of a genuine western European strategic analysis or how much it is simply an adaptation to U.S. analysis and interests within the framework of the Atlantic Alliance.[43] Given the fact that EU member states, within the framework of their special system of foreign policy cooperation, have hardly been able to devise strategic positions with regard to the future European architecture, it would be a real surprise if this reassessment of European strategic interests in Turkey would have taken place in a more thorough way. Official public statements by EU representatives show, in any case, a certain vagueness in defining specific western European interests beyond ascribing to Turkey a loosely defined role as a "bridge" or as a socio-political model for other countries.[44]

A closer look at the broader political issues and the actors involved in this new Turkish role gives rise to some doubts about the validity and coherence of the new strategic approach of the EU members in their relations with Turkey.[45] Moreover, it seems highly plausible that in the longer run relations between the EU and Turkey will be much more influenced by developments within Europe and Turkey than by the possible strategic roles Turkey could play or be assigned in the Middle East or Central Asia. Given Turkey's continued strong interest in becoming an undisputed part of Europe, the strategic choices and substantial political decisions for building a new European architecture will become the decisive issues for the fate of EU-Turkey relations.

The complete break-down of the system of bipolar East-West strategic rivalry eliminated the basis upon which western European governments tended to evaluate the necessity of close EC-Turkey relations within the larger framework of the western alliance system. It also tremendously altered the circumstances under which Turkey, after the Second World War, decided on how to implement its basic political goal of "westernization." At the same time, both sides were confronted with a new international environment containing fundamental challenges with important implications for the future of their mutual relationship. A simple continuation of old strategic choices no longer seemed possible.

For the EU and its member-states, the new situation poses the fundamental challenge of a redefinition and reconstruction of the "European order." In the end this comes down to the task of re-defining Europe's identity. The first task implies an answer to questions about the borders of Europe, as well as to questions concerning the organizing principles of the new order or architecture, including its security dimension but not limited to that. To be more precise, it is mainly the question of the eastern border of Europe that has to be resolved, whereas the question of organizing principles has to do with the choice between a system based on the politics of "regional community building" and one built on nation-states, alliances, and power balances.

The second challenge has to do with the political and economic substance of strategies devised to implement guidelines established according to answers to the first challenge. In more concrete terms, this comes down to the issue of the way in which the EU can and should cohabit with the rest of Europe. In a somewhat superficial and misleading manner, this issue is presently being discussed within the EU as a choice between "deepening and widening."[46]

For Turkey, the change in the international situation also tends to raise the issue of identity. The emergence of the new Turkic republics in Central Asia and Transcaucasia from out of the former Soviet Union, together with a renewed Turkish public awareness of kin-groups in the Balkans as a result of the fighting in Yugoslavia, have called efforts to restrict a "Turkish identity" to the Anatolian heartland into question. One should also add the domestic revival of Islam as a factor that is causing a reevaluation of Turkish identity among a wide stratum of the population. The struggle between "moderates" and "fundamentalists" over the organization of a proper Islamic society in most countries of the Arabic-Islamic world has not been without effect on the Turkish population, as shown by growing tensions between "secularists" and "Islamists" within and among various strata of Turkish society.

At the same time, Turkey is confronted with the need fundamentally to reorient its foreign policy. The immediate strategic threat from the north has gone, but it has been replaced by a variety of low to medium-scale conflicts among Turkey's immediate neighbors in the Caucasus. A possible extension of the Balkan wars, the still unresolved issue of regional hegemony in the Gulf area, and the continuing Russian strategic interests in the Black Sea and Central Asian regions tend to increase Turkish feelings of uneasiness. The situation raises the question of the reliability of past strategic alliances in the face of new security challenges.

It is the possible intersection of these simultaneous processes of redefining identity and reorienting foreign policy, in both western Europe and in Turkey, that creates the major challenge for the future of EU-Turkey relations. The more "community-like" the future European architecture wishes to be, the more restricted its geographic scope has to be. This would leave a number of other European states as outsiders, among them Turkey. The more such an image of Europe determines the respective political perceptions of Turkey's public, the greater is the chance that Turkey's effort to redefine its own national identity will move in the direction of a greater emphasis on "Turkishness" and "Islam." Extremes in the respective western European and Turkish processes of identity-building could reinforce each other and lead to increased mutual estrangement.

On the other hand, a European architecture which is more "European" in geographic terms and less of a "community" in political terms could eventually incorporate all European countries, with the notable exception of Russia. Turkey's inclusion would not pose insurmountable difficulties as long as the country can keep its basically secular political and social system. The stability of the system would indirectly be supported by the perspective of becoming part of the European political order. The crucial, but at present highly uncertain, feature of such an architecture would be its ability to ensure enough economic and political cohesion to guarantee the implementation of common rules for a peaceful settlement of conflicts among its constituent parts.

This is basically an abstract discussion of fundamental political issues that western Europe and Turkey must confront simultaneously as a consequence of the collapse of the USSR. As such it can only give a meager idea of where the strategic choices for the development of the EU-Turkey relationship in the years to come will be situated. Simply following the lines of the past may be the best choice for the time being given the high degree of uncertainty connected with future developments. This, however, will hardly relieve responsible politicians on both sides of the need thoroughly to reassess the goals and the structure of the mutual relationship once the future conditioning framework of this relationship assumes clearer and more predictable patterns. This reassessment will be a primary task for the newly established high-level political dialogue between Turkey and the EU.

In any case, the political process of redefining the basis and the broader substance of the relationship will be significantly influenced by the general attitude in EU countries concerning Turkey's Europeanness. The question whether Turkey and its citizens are or should be integral parts of Europe presents the most intricate and delicate problem for the conduct of the relationship. This problem goes far beyond that of eventual Turkish membership in the EU, although it is one of the most challenging (though rarely discussed) issues in that context.

For the sake of clarification it seems necessary to remind ourselves that the question of membership has been decided in principle long ago. The stipulations of Article 28 of the Ankara Agreement in which the possibility of a Turkish accession to the Community is regulated do not mention the issue of Turkey's Europeanness as a prerequisite of membership. Nor does the "Opinion" of the Commission on Turkey's request for accession mention this topic as having any relevance to the problem. Nevertheless, many Turks feel that the final decision about their place in the emerging new European order will be decisively influenced by this problem—and they are right in feeling so.[47]

It can hardly be denied that a majority of western European politicians and even more members of the general public are of the opinion that in a cultural and historical perspective the Turks are not really Europeans and that Turkey is not an integral part of Europe. This perception can be regarded as the result of a process of European identity-creation which has unfolded since the Middle Ages. Over centuries the "Turk" and the Ottoman empire were assigned the role of "the other," which was by definition that of the "non-European."[48] More recent political experiences with Turkey as a reliable partner of the western security alliance and a country associated to the EC, together with a multitude of personal contacts with "westernized Turks" at the elite level, have not contributed to a substantial revision of this deeply rooted European view of the "Turk."

This position can correctly be regarded as highly irrational. It nonetheless constitutes an important "objective" factor for the evaluation of the perspectives of Turkey's relations with the rest of Europe and especially with the EU. As long as this mixture of cultural prejudice and religiously motivated fear of an "Islamic Threat" to the "Christian West" continues to influence western European perceptions of Turkey, its wishes to become an integral part of the EU will encounter difficulties unknown to other European states.

Europe's basically reluctant or hostile approach towards Turkey, consciously or subconsciously, tends negatively to influence the evaluation of other issues that are of political and economic relevance to the question of Turkey's eventual membership in the EU. Economic problems, democratic deficiencies, and political conflicts quickly become welcome scapegoats for a much more fundamental and deeply-rooted unwillingness to accept Turkey as a member of an "European" Union and of European "civilization" as well.[49] It seems at least doubtful that Turkey's new geopolitical and strategic position, together with general uncertainty about the future development of the Eurasian political landscape, will in themselves generate enough momentum to change the negatively biased European perception of Turkey and the Turks.

Notes

1. Figures are taken from State Planning Organization, *Main Economic Indicators-Turkey, August 1993* (Ankara: State Planning Organization, 1993). For a detailed assessment of EC-Turkey trade relations in the past see Canan Balkır, "Turkey and the European Community: Foreign Trade and Direct Foreign Investment in the 1980s," in Canan Balkır and Alan M. Williams, eds., *Turkey and Europe* (London: Pinter, 1993), pp. 100-139 and Heinz Kramer, *Das wirtschaftliche Element in den Beziehungen der EG zur Türkei-eine Bestandsaufnahme* (Ebenhausen: SWP, 1987).

2. For a concise analysis of structural change in Turkish foreign trade during the 1980s see Anne O. Krueger and Okan H. Aktan, *Swimming Against the Tide: Turkish Trade Reform in the 1980s* (San Francisco: ICS Press, 1992). Regarding trade with the EC see Halis Akder, "Constant-Market-Share Analysis of Changes in Turkey's Exports to the EC (1981-1985)," *Yapı Kredi Economic Review* 1, no. 2(1987): 33-42.

3. For the text of the Ankara Agreement see *Official Journal of the EC* no. 217, 29 December 1964; for the text of the Additional Protocol, ibid., no. 293, 27 December 1972. Whereas the Ankara Agreement sets the framework and guiding principles of the relations, the Additional Protocol regulates the details of the establishment of the customs union.

4. A short but fairly comprehensive overview of the stipulations in the Ankara Agreement and the Additional Protocol is given by Haluk Günuğur, "Customs Union with the European Community," *Economic Dialogue Turkey* no. 39, September 1993, pp. 112-116.

5. For a comprehensive account of the (non-)realization of the customs union scheme see Heinz Kramer, *Die Europäische Gemeinschaft und die Türkei: Entwicklung, Probleme und Perspektiven einer schwierigen Partnerschaft* (Baden-Baden: Nomos Verlagsgesellschaft, 1988). For a Turkish view of the issue see Mükerrem Hiç, "The Evolution of Turkish-EEC Relations and Prospects of an Early Application for Membership: A General Survey," in *Dış Politika/Foreign Policy* 9 nos. 1-2(1981): 49-80.

6. For details of the EC's efforts to prevent full implementation of the association's stipulation concerning free movement of labor see Kramer, *Die Europäische Gemeinschaft und die Türkei*, pp. 216-233 and Nusret Ekin, "Turkish Labour in the EEC," in Werner Gumpel, ed., *Die Türkei auf dem Weg in die EG. Möglichkeiten und Probleme einer Vollmitgliedschaft der Türkei in der Europäischen Gemeinschaft* (Munich: R. Oldenbourg Verlag, 1979), pp. 77-98.

7. A fairly comprehensive overview of the present legal state of Turkish workers in the EU, also taking into consideration the most recent judgements given by the EU's Luxembourg based European Court of Justice, is given by Christian Rumpf, "Freizügigkeit der Arbeitnehmer und Assoziation EG-Türkei," *Recht der internationalen Wirtschaft* no. 3(1993): 214-223.

8. For details of Germany's policy on migrant-workers at the time see Ray C. Rist, "Migration and Marginality: Guestworkers in Germany and France," *Daedalus* 108, no. 2(1979): 95-108.

9. For details of this aid see *European Investment Bank, 25 Years (1958-1983)* (Luxembourg: European Investment Bank, 1983), pp. 75-6.

10. This issue is discussed by Atilla Eralp, "Turkey and the European Community in the Changing Post-War International System," in Balkır and Winters, eds., *Turkey and Europe*, pp. 28-31. For details of the Turkish debate see Erol Esen, *Die Beziehungen zwischen der Türkei und der Europäischen Gemeinschaft unter besonderer Berücksichtigung der innertürkischen Kontroversen um die Assoziation 1973-1980* (Pfaffenweiler: Centaurus-Verlagsgesellschaft, 1990), pp. 92-166 and İlhan Tekeli and Selim İlkin, *Türkiye ve Avrupa Topluluğu* vol. 2 *Ulus Devletini Asma Çabasındaki Avrupa'ya Türkiye'nin Yaklaşımı* (Ankara: Ümit Yayıncılık, 1993), pp. 166-238.

11. For an overview of the economic theory of customs union see the classical text of James E. Meade, The *Theory of Customs Union* (Amsterdam: North Holland, 1955). For a more up-to-date overview see Willem Molle, *The Economics of European Integration: Theory, Practice, Policy* (Aldershot: Dartmouth, 1990), pp. 83-113. The Turkish debate about the compatibility of Turkey's development strategy with the intended establishment of a customs union with the EC is reflected in Osman Okyar, "Turkish Industrialization Strategies, the Plan Model and the EEC," in Osman Okyar and Okan H. Aktan, eds., *Economic Relations Between Turkey and the EEC* (Ankara: Hacettepe University, 1978), pp. 14-53 and Mükerrem Hiç, "The Importance of Turkey's Development Strategy for Her Integration into the EEC," in Gumpel, ed., *Die Türkei auf dem Weg in die EG*, pp. 19-46.

12. A short introduction to this issue and its link to EC-Turkey relations is given by Heinz Andresen, "The European Community's Mediterranean Policy," in Okyar and Aktan, *Economic Relations*, pp. 60-71.

13. Turkey's continually growing trade deficit with the EC, which was put forward to substantiate its arguments, most likely was a result of the country's rigid policy of import substitution. This policy systematically discriminated against exports and therefore undermined the international competitiveness of Turkish producers in general.

14. For an argument along these lines see, for instance, Erol Manisalı, "Turkey and the EEC: An Assessment of Obligations and Interests," in Institute of Economic Development, *Problems of Turkey's Economic Development* (Istanbul: Istanbul University Faculty of Economics, n.d.), pp. 129-142.

15. This big-business attitude was clearly revealed during a special "hearing" of the Great Turkish National Assembly on 18 May 1984 and it was also expressed during a visit of a delegation of representatives of Turkish industry to the EC Commission in November 1985. On this issue see "Relations Between Turkey and the EEC" (special edition), *İKV (İstanbul Kalkınma Vakfı) Magazine*, June 1984 and *Turkish Daily News*, 10 November 1985, p. 4.

16. For a more detailed account of the EC-Turkey relations which led to the application for membership see Eralp, "Turkey and the European Community in the Changing Post-War International System," *Turkey and Europe*, pp. 31-36 and Kramer, *Die Europäische Gemeinschaft und die Türkei*, pp. 84-111 and 120-150.

17. Commission of the European Communities, *Commission Opinion on Turkey's Request for Accession to the Community*, Brussels, 20 December 1989 [SEC (89) 2290 fin./2] and Commission of the European Communities, *The Turkish Economy:*

Structure and Developments, Brussels, 18 December 1989 [SEC (89) 2290 final, Annex].

18. For details of this so-called "Matutes-package," named after the member of the EC Commission in charge of relations with Turkey, see Commission of the European Community, *Commission Communication to the Council Concerning Relations with Turkey and a Proposal for a Council Decision about a Fourth Financial Protocol*, Brussels, 12 June 1990 [SEC (90) 1017 final].

19. "Conclusions of the Presidency," *Agence Europe* no. 5760, 28 June 1992, p. 5. Since then, this position has been repeated by EC authorities on various other occasions.

20. For a short account of the November 1993 meeting of the Association Council see *Agence "Europe"*, 10 November 1993, pp. 9-10.

21. It seems doubtful whether the problem can be solved by simply declaring the Mass Housing Fund a forms of fiscal tariff. According to the Additional Protocol, under certain conditions it could then be maintained for some time, as has been suggested by a Turkish scholar. See Haluk Günuğur, "Customs Union with the European Community," *Economic Dialogue Turkey* no. 39(September 1993): 112-116.

22. Representatives of these industrial sectors are among those who advocate a less speedy and more phased approach towards the completion of the customs union. See *Briefing*, no. 966 (Ankara, 29 November 1993), p. 14.

23. An idea of what will be necessary and how much change and adaptation may be involved can be inferred from State Planning Organization, *Turkish Agriculture and European Community Policies-Issues, Strategies and Institutional Adaptation* (Ankara: State Planning Organization, 1990).

24. In this section I rely on earlier research which has only recently been published. See Heinz Kramer, "EC-Turkey Relations: Unfinished Forever?" in Peter Ludlow, ed., *Europe and the Mediterranean* (London: Brassey's, 1994), pp. 190-249 and especially pp. 224-238.

25. See *Briefing*, no. 965 (Ankara, 22 November 1993), pp. 9-10 and *Agence "Europe"*, 10 November 1993, pp. 9-10.

26. One has to note, however, that Greece has always been an important factor shaping Turkey's policy towards the EC. This can, for instance, be very clearly shown with regard to the Turkish decision to apply for association in 1959. See Mehmet Ali Birand, "Turkey and the European Community," *The World Today* 34, no. 2(1972): 52-61.

27. For details see Constantine Stephanou and Charalambos Tsardanides, "The EC Factor in the Greece-Turkey-Cyprus Triangle," in Dimitri Constas, ed., *The Greek-Turkish Conflict in the 1990s: Domestic and External Influences* (London: Macmillan, 1991), pp. 207-230 and Heinz Jürgen Axt and Heinz Kramer, *Entspannung im Ägäiskonflikt? Griechisch-türkische Beziehungen nach Davos* (Baden-Baden: Nomos Verlag, 1989), pp. 54-55.

28. For a similar view from a Turkish scholar see Haluk Günuğur, "Certains problèmes juridiques qu'entraînera l'adhésion de la Turquie à la CEE," *Turkish Yearbook of Human Rights* 7/8 (1985/1986): 119-136, and especially p. 122.

29. As with regard to the issues of the bilateral Greek-Turkish conflict, I refrain from a substantial analysis of the Cyprus question proper. I content myself in this paper with discussing the implications of these issues for the development of EC-Turkey relations.

30. See the statement by the undersecretary of state of the Turkish foreign ministry Turgay Özceri in *Newspot*, no. 28, 12 July 1990, pp. 3 and 6.

31. See the text of the Turkish-Cypriot memorandum of 12 July 1990 and the text of a complementary note of 3 September 1990 in Necati Münir Erteкün, ed., *Le Statut de deux peuples à Chypre* (Lefkosa: Public Information Office of the Turkish Republic of Northern Cyprus, 1990), pp. 31-45. This position, of course, has been fully supported by the Turkish government in a letter by Turkey's foreign minister, Ali Bozer, to the Italian foreign minister as the acting president of the EC's Council of Ministers. See *Newspot*, no. 30, 26 July 1990, p. 2.

32. See Commission of the European Communities, *Commission Opinion on the Application by the Republic of Cyprus for Membership*, Brussels, 30 June 1993, Doc. COM(93) 313 fin.

33. Ibid., p. 22.

34. Ibid., p. 23. One should note that this occurred after Greece's period of EU presidency, which covered the first half of 1994, came to an end. During this time Athens undertook serious efforts at promoting Cypriot membership.

35. For a more detailed account of the developments that occurred in the late 1970s see Lucille W. Pevsner, *Turkey's Political Crisis* (New York: Praeger, 1984); Clement H. Dodd, *The Crisis of Turkish Democracy*, 2nd ed. (Huntingdon: Eothen Press, 1990); and Mehmet Ali Birand, *The Generals' Coup in Turkey: An Inside Story of 12 September 1980* (London: Brassey's, 1987).

36. Details of the western European reaction to the domestic political situation in Turkey can be found in Kramer, *Die Europäische Gemeinschaft und die Türkei*, pp. 84-111. See also the contributions in *Die Türkei-ein demokratischer Rechtsstaat* (Ankara: Konrad-Adenauer Stiftung, 1989).

37. A short account of the reconsolidation of Turkish democracy is given by Metin Heper, "Consolidating Turkish Democracy," *Journal of Democracy* 3, no. 2(April 1992): 105-117. See also Turkish Democracy Foundation, *Development and Consolidation of Democracy in Turkey* (Ankara: Sevinç Matbaası, 1989). For a different position see Mehmet S. Gemalmaz, *The Institutionalization Process of the "Turkish Type of Democracy:" A Politico-Juridicial Analysis of Human Rights* (Istanbul: Amaç Yayıncılık, 1989).

38. See European Parliament, Doc. A3-0193/92 (with Annexes), 21 May 1992, in which it is stated that relations between the EC and Turkey, which "in future will play an ever more important, even a decisive, political role in an especially endangered region, should be strengthened and revitalized." (p. 29) Due to controversies between the groups in the European Parliament over how to react to the anti-Kurdish moves of the Turkish government, the report had been removed from the parliament's agenda twice since its presentation in committee. It was finally approved at the November 1992 session after a controversial debate. For the text of the final resolution see OJ, No. C 337, 21.12.1992, pp. 218-225.

39. For a short but comprehensive overview of the history of the Kurdish issue in Turkey see Michael M. Gunter, *The Kurds in Turkey: A Political Dilemma* (Boulder: Westview Press, 1990). The best treatment of the Kurdish issue in a broader perspective is Martin van Bruinessen, *Agha, Shaikh, and State* (London: Zed Books, 1992).

40. In taking this position the author denies Turkish claims that western European opinion leaders are victims of the disinformation campaigns of Kurdish separatist organizations and their fellow travellers. A careful reading of the leading western European dailies such as *Le Monde, Financial Times, The Independent, The Times, Neue Zürcher Zeitung*, or *Frankfurter Allgemeine Zeitung* gives no justification to the claim of one-sided reporting about the Kurdish issue in Turkey. There is certainly no significant difference when reportage and commentary is compared with Turkish publications like *Turkish Daily News* or *Briefing*.

41. This Turkish state doctrine is embodied in the Turkish Constitution of 1982 in article 3 which, according to article 4, is not open to amendment. Even a proposition toward that end is prohibited.

42. Detailed descriptions of the behavior of the Turkish state authorities, especially the Turkish army, can be found in Ismet G. Imset, *The PKK: A Report on Separatist Violence in Turkey (1973-1992)* (Ankara: Turkish Daily News, 1992).

43. This new view on Turkey's strategic role after the end of the Cold War was first developed in the U.S. and heavily promoted by its government. For a comprehensive account see Graham E. Fuller and Ian O. Lesser (with Paul B. Henze and J.F. Brown), *Turkey's New Geopolitics: From the Balkans to Western China* (Boulder: Westview Press, 1993).

44. This can, at least, be inferred from the draft papers which the British presidency of the EC prepared in summer 1992 to further the process of normalization in relations with Turkey prior to the November meeting of the Association Council. See the reports in *Agence "Europe"*, 4 May 1992 and 20-21 July 1992.

45. See Philip Robins, "Between Sentiment and Self-Interest: Turkey's Policy Toward Azerbaijan and the Central Asian States," *Middle East Journal*, 47, no. 4(1993):593-610 and Heinz Kramer, "Die Türkei: Eine Regionalmacht mit Zukunft?," in Albrecht Zunker, ed., *Weltordnung oder Chaos? Beiträge zur internationalen Politik* (Baden-Baden: Nomos Verlag, 1993), pp. 109-125.

46. For a much more intelligent approach to the two-fold challenge see William Wallace, *The Transformation of Western Europe* (London: Pinter, 1990), pp. 92-107.

47. This Turkish concern is an expression of the broader problem of defining Turkey's identity as "western." It goes back to the foundation of the republic by Atatürk as a political and social entity which was intended to be completely different from the former Ottoman Empire and its society, which was basically founded in Islam. A representative contemporary example of this Turkish endeavor in the context of the application for membership in the EC is the book by then Turkish prime minister Turgut Özal, *La Turquie en Europe* (Paris: Plon, 1988). For a more scholarly but comparable approach to the problem see Metin Heper et al., eds., *Turkey and the West: Changing Political and Cultural Identities* (London: I. B. Tauris, 1993).

48. For an elaboration of this argument see Iver B. Neumann and Jennifer M. Welsh, "The Other in European Self-Definition: An Addendum to the Literature on'International Society," *Review of International Studies* 17, no. 4(1991): 327-348.

49. Although public comments on the issue of Turkey's membership are seldom explicit on this point, one should note that it is only with regard to Turkey that the "cultural issue" is mentioned as a problematic factor in the context of the enlargement debate. See for instance European Parliament, EP 141.136/fin./add. (Opinion of the Committee on External Economic Relations for the Political Committee on Enlargement of the European Community and Relations with other European Countries), Luxembourg, 14 May 1991, pp. 5-6.

10

Turkish Communities in Western Europe

Faruk Şen

The Turkish population in the European Union (EU) (not including the new members as of 1 January 1995—Austria, Finland, and Sweden) is about 2.5 million. There are also more than 2.7 million Turks in western Europe including Switzerland, Austria, and the Scandinavian countries. This figure represents 24.4 percent of all foreigners within the EU, making the Turks the largest single minority group. With a population of 1,918,395 (as of the end of 1993), Turks are also the largest minority group in the Federal Republic of Germany.[1] The countries with the next highest levels of concentration of Turks are France, with 240,000 Turkish citizens, and Holland, with 215,000 Turkish citizens.[2]

Approximately 4 percent of Turkish citizens live within the borders of the EU. The number of Turkish citizens living in the EU comes to half of the population of Denmark, six times that of Luxembourg, two-thirds that of Ireland, or one-fourth the population of Portugal or Greece.

The mass migration of Turks to western Europe began in 1961, following the ratification of the recruitment agreement between Turkey and Germany. Subsequently, Turkey also concluded such agreements with the Netherlands, Belgium, and Austria in 1964, France in 1965, and Sweden in 1967. In the period between 1961-1973 these Turks formed a homogenous group of mainly male laborers. After the European community (EC) countries stopped recruiting workers—particularly in 1973—the process of migration experienced important structural changes.

Although labor migration from Turkey to western Europe came to a halt with the curtailment of recruitment in the early 1970s, migration continued with family reunifications for the next two decades. In the 1990s, Turkish migration to western Europe has been mainly family

Table 10.1

Population of Turks in
Selected European Countries

Countries	Population
Germany	1,918,000
Netherlands	215,000
France	240,000
Belgium	85,000
Denmark	30,000
Austria	150,000
Switzerland	73,000
United Kingdom	20,000
Sweden	50,000
Total	2,781,000

Source: Statistisches Bundesamt, (Federal Statistics Office),
Wiesbaden; Sopemi-Netherlands 1992, Amsterdam; Yurtdışı
İşçi Hizmetleri Müdürlüğü (Office for Workers' Services
Abroad), 1992 Annual Report, Ankara, 1993

formation rather than family reunification, the latter having been
practically completed in the 1980s.

A trend of increasing immigration is observed by way of family
formation, meaning a new marriage between a migrant (or migrant's
child) with a partner in the country of origin, leading to migration of the
latter to the country of settlement of the former. This tendency is
especially to be observed among the Turks in Germany and the Netherlands.[3] A rough estimate of expected migration by family reunification
of Turks to the Netherlands is 950 in 1996. However, migration by family
formation for the Turks in the Netherlands was expected to be 2,000 men
and 2,000 women in 1994; high variant estimates of family formation
were 3,200 men and 3,600 women for Turks in 1994.[4]

Table 10.2

Population of Turks in Germany between 1961-1992

Year	Population	Year	Population
1961	6,500	1977	1,118,000
1962	15,300	1978	1,165,100
1963	27,100	1979	1,268,300
1964	85,200	1980	1,462,400
1965	132,800	1981	1,542,300
1966	161,000	1982	1,580,700
1967	172,400	1983	1,552,400
1968	205,400	1984	1,425,800
1969	322,400	1985	1,400,400
1970	469,200	1986	1,425,700
1971	562,800	1987	1,466,300
1972	712,300	1988	1,523,700
1973	910,500	1989	1,612,700
1974	910,500	1990	1,675,900
1975	1,077,100	1991	1,779,600
1976	1,079,300	1992	1,854,945

Source: Statistisches Bundesamt (Federal Statistics Office), Wiesbaden

Even though migration from Turkey to western Europe might continue at a relatively slow pace through family formation, it is evident that the majority of the Turkish population in Europe intends to settle and remain permanently. The negative economic conditions, unemployment, and dissatisfaction of the Turkish returnees once back home have influenced many Turks in Europe and decreased the tendency to return.[5] The policy toward foreigners at the beginning of the 1980s in Germany and "The Law of Promotion of Voluntary Repatriation for Foreigners" (the so-called 10,500 Deutschmark Law) put into force between 1983-1984 created a

Table 10.3

Turkish Workers Recruited Officially Annually by Selected European Nations and Total Emigration of Labor 1961-1992

	Germany	Belgium	France	Holland	Total*
1961-1973	648,029	15,309	45,336	23,359	790,289
1974-1980	9,412	834	10,668	1,836	125,257
1981-1984	409	20	19	42	206,426
1985	23	7	4	5	47,353
1986	17	-	3	12	35,608
1987	27	2	4	18	40,807
1988	85	1	6	19	53,021
1989	51	3	7	21	49,928
1990	62	15	14	31	47,707
1991	49	2	33	22	53,020
1992	1,685	7	21	21	60,000

* covers Germany, the Netherlands, Belgium, France, Austria, Sweden, Switzerland, Denmark, Saudi Arabia, Libya, Iraq, Australia, Kuwait, Jordan, CIS (former Soviet Union), and others.

Source: Yurtdışı İşçi Hizmetleri Müdürlüğü (Office for Workers' Services Abroad), 1990, 1991 and 1992 Annual Reports, Ankara

feeling of insecurity among Turks and fuelled a repatriation movement.[6] This law rewarded return migration with a payment of 10,500 German Marks (DM) per returnee and 1,500 DM per child. Growing hostility towards foreigners, along with the German government's promise to transfer social security payments immediately without a two-year waiting period, led more than 370,000 Turks from Germany to return to Turkey between 1983-85.[7]

Public and political authorities in Turkey have approached labor migration in the last three decades more or less as a way to reduce the pressure of unemployment at home. After the oil-crisis of 1973 the Turkish government viewed emigration as a way to improve the balance of payments. Labor migration was made a part of development plans, and although not admitted openly it was placed in the balanced development model.[8] According to balanced growth theory, labor migration can reduce economic differences because the transfer of labor allows the emigration area to catch up economically with the immigration area. Development in these areas could be launched by migrants' remittances, savings, and investment.

The particular stage of development—an import substitution industrialization strategy—that Turkey was experiencing in the 1960s and 1970s explains the role played by labor migration abroad. The macro-impact of labor migration was felt in four specific areas: the contribution of remittances to foreign exchange availability; the widening of the internal market; the role of migration in the solution of the employment problem; and the role of both labor exports and workers' remittances against the uneven pattern of development that import substitution industrialization implies.[9]

Turkish government policy recognized the relationship between labor migration and underdeveloped regions, thus granting priority for recruitment abroad to applicants from provinces designated as underdeveloped and areas of natural disaster. However, on the whole recruitment of Turkish workers was done according to the demands and needs of the labor-importing countries.[10] Some attempts by the Turkish government to channel migration included preserving shares in the annual recruitment for Village Development Cooperatives and a ban on emigration for those workers who were already fully employed in the Zonguldak coal mines and in some shipyards.[11]

The Impact of Migration on Turkey

The flow of migrants' savings (remittances) to Turkey has been and still is substantial, but there is no magic or automatic process which transforms remittances into the kind of economic development that makes emigration stop. This depends to some extent on the amount but more on the way that remittances are utilized. In reality, over the years only a negligible part of the massive flow of remittances has been channelled into direct productive investment in the industrial sector in Turkey. Other efforts of the Turkish government to channel remittances to employment generating activities have by and large failed.

Table 10.4

Workers' Remittances to Turkey between 1964 - 1992

Years	Millions ($)
1964-1975	5,927.9
1976-1980	6,713.2
1981	2,489.7
1982	2,186.6
1983	1,553.6
1984	1,881.2
1985	1,774.2
1986	1,694.8
1987	2,101.6
1988	1,839.5
1989	3,138.0
1990	3,337.0
1991	2,819.0
1992	3,008.0

Source: Yurtdışı İşçi Hizmetleri Genel Müdürlüğü, 1990 Yılı Raporu, Ankara, 1991, p. 167; The Istanbul Chamber of Commerce, Economic Report, Publication No: 1991-28, p. 148; Türkiye in Figures, Turkish Confederation of Employer Associations, Ankara, May 1993

Turkish migrants have transferred a significant amount of remittances to Turkey: annually $1.5-2 billion (U.S. dollars) during the 1980s and even more at the end of the decade. These funds have been used to finance the foreign trade deficits, especially since 1970. It should also be mentioned that workers' remittances provided Turkish policy-makers with more freedom in making economic policy.

Table 10.5

Workers' Remittances as a Share of Export Earnings and of Import Payments, 1970-90 (millions US-$)

Years	Total Transfer	Imports	Exports	Share of Imports	Share of Exports
1970	273	948	589	28%	48%
1971	471	1,171	677	40%	69%
1972	740	1,563	885	47%	84%
1973	1,183	2,086	1,317	57%	89%
1974	1,426	3,778	1,532	38%	94%
1976	983	5,129	1,960	19%	50%
1977	982	5,796	1,753	20%	56%
1978	983	4,599	2,288	21%	43%
1979	1,634	5,069	2,261	34%	75%
1980	2,071	7,667	2,910	27%	72%
1981	2,500	8,900	4,700	29%	53%
1982	2,186.5	8,843	5,746	24%	38%
1983	1,553.7	9,235	5,728	17%	27%

(continues)

Table 10.5 (continued)

Years	Total Transfer	Imports	Exports	Share of Imports	Share of Exports
1984	1,881.2	10,757	7,133	17%	26%
1985	1,774.3	11,613	7,958	15%	22%
1986	1,696.0	11,105	7,457	15%	22%
1987	2,102.0	14,158	10,190	14%	20%
1988	1,865.0	14,335	11,662	13%	15%
1989	3,229.0	15,792	11,625	20%	27%
1990	3,337.0	22,302	12,960	14%	25%

Source: Turkish Central Bank, 1986; The Istanbul Chamber of Commerce, Economic Report, Publication No: 1991-28, pp. 131, 148

Labor migration to western Europe undoubtedly relieved unemployment pressures in Turkey, but the reason for the improvement was not that it was predominantly unemployed workers who went abroad. A considerable literature suggests that most Turkish migrants were already employed in Turkey before their departure (at least during the first years of mass labor migration) and that about one-third of those who chose to migrate were skilled workers. Table 10.6 gives a hypothetical calculation of unemployment levels with and without migration in selected Mediterranean countries. As table 10.6 shows, it is clear that there is a link between migration and unemployment. It is not clear, however, just how strong and consistent the relationship actually is. Migration, one could posit, does not significantly contribute to the solution of the unemployment problem. This is at least what seems to be so in the case of Turkey.

At the beginning of the 1970s, with large-scale labor migration nearly at an end, western European countries enacted family reunification laws. Such schemes set up a framework to allow Turkish workers in western European countries to be joined by their families. The population structure of Turks living within the borders of the EC changed soon afterwards. At present, only a third of the general Turkish population is gainfully employed, while the remaining two-thirds is composed of spouses, children, and other family members.

The term that Germans used to designate foreigners provides an indication of their status and the length of time foreigners intended or were expected to stay in Germany. At the beginning they were called "guest workers," stressing the temporary nature of their employment. Subsequently they were called "foreign workers" and since the family reunification program of 1974 they have been referred to as the "foreign resident population" or even "foreign fellow citizens." The term "fellow citizens" raises the whole question of the status of foreigners in Germany, as they by no means have all the rights of the "citizen."

Looking at the demographic structure of the Turkish population in Germany, where the largest Turkish community in Europe lives, we see that no less than 55 percent of the Turks are male.[12] Altogether Turks are a young population group, particularly when compared with the age profile of the host country. The statistics reveal that 35.7 percent are younger than eighteen years old. Approximately one-half of the Turkish population is between twenty-five and forty-five years old and only 5 percent are older than sixty.[13] As of 30 September 1990 there were about 258,851 foreign migrants who were sixty years old or older in Germany, of whom 25,777 were Turkish. This represents only 1.6 percent of the total Turkish population in Germany.[14] Among those who were older than sixty, 47,000 were pensioners as of 1 January 1991.[15]

Table 10.6

Turkish Population in the FRG According to Age Structure as of 30 September 1990

Age	Turkish Population	Percent
0 - 17 years	597,619	35.7%
18 - 20 years	127,766	7.6%
21 - 29 years	332,779	19.9%
30 - 39 years	192,503	11.5%
40 - 49 years	249,202	14.9%
50 - 54 years	100,419	6.0%
55 - 59 years	49,846	3.0%
60 - 64 years	17,960	1.1%
65 and above	7,817	0.5%

Source: Statistisches Bundesamt (Federal Statistics Office), Wiesbaden, 1992

There are no models or studies to determine the economic impact of migration in host countries. However, there is some general agreement concerning the major economic effects of migrant workers in the 1960s and 1970s. For instance, the availability of foreign labor sustained high levels of non-inflationary economic growth. Migrant workers helped to hold down wage increases. Additional assembly lines were built to employ unskilled workers and native workers enjoyed upward mobility. "Migrant workers' savings also helped to restrain inflationary pressures and boost exports."[16] Turkish migrant workers, who consisted mostly of men in the 1960s, remitted 30-50 percent of their earnings to Turkey, which reduced the demand for goods in the Federal Republic of Germany and increased the demand for German goods in Turkey.[17] Even though it is believed that the workers' remittances have had inflationary effects in Turkey, they also served to meet the foreign account deficits and eased the balance of payments problem to an important extent.

Table 10.7

Unemployment With and Without Workers' Migration in Mediterranean Migrant Sending Countries, 1973

	Unemp. 1000s	Unemp. rate (%)	Emigration as % of Unemp.	Unemp. Rate w/o Emigration
Turkey	724	4.5	18.8	5.1
Spain	362	2.7	26.5	3.4
Portugal	180	5.3	18.9	6.2
Greece	35	1.1	31.4	1.4
Yugoslavia	382	4.2	26.2	4.8

Source: OECD, The Future of Migration, Paris, 1987

Furthermore, the so-called rotation principle allowed the management of the labor supply as a private and public economic policy tool. Migration became a tool of labor market policy. However, as a result of family reunifications, migrant workers began to make demands on housing, education, and health services in the 1970s. Public financing of such demands and the infrastructure costs of absorbing the migrants increasingly appeared on the agenda in the 1970s and 1980s.

The German economy witnessed a period of rapid growth in the late 1980s. This gave way to complaints of labor shortages, despite the large-scale influx of refugees and asylum-seekers. The situation changed drastically with the dissolution of the eastern bloc and the subsequent unification of Germany. The 1990s have been marked by a rise in unemployment and the Turks are among those who are most affected by unemployment in Germany (13 percent).[18]

The German population is expected to decrease significantly in the next forty years despite unification. This decrease has its implications, especially on social security payments. Studies indicate that German workers would have to spend about 40 percent of their income on pension contributions without the presence of a mainly young migrant population.[19] Foreigners, particularly Turks, offer a young labor force that makes important contributions to the welfare of German society and counteracts the negative effects of an ageing population.

According to a 1990 study, although foreigners do incur costs initially (in the form of language courses, social benefits, etc.), their social security contributions far exceed, in the long run, the amount spent on them. This study also brings to light the fact that they brought approximately fifty-seven billion DM into the economy, directly or indirectly, in the form of taxes and social security payments. In contrast, only sixteen billion DM was spent on foreigners in the form of social benefits, including expenses for asylum-seekers. The remaining forty-one billion DM accrued to the German state as revenue.[20] Experts suggest that the German welfare state could not be maintained without the major economic contributions of the migrant community.

The average Turkish household in Germany is made up of 4.1 persons, more than the average German household, with 2.35 persons. The average net income of the Turkish household is 3,650 DM. The total income of Turkish workers amounts to approximately eighteen billion DM per year. When regular costs such as rent and security payments are subtracted, the consumption volume that remains totals 10 billion DM a year.[21] Turkish workers paid approximately 470 million DM within the framework of the "*Solidaritätsabgabe*" ("Solidarity Contribution," that is money removed from monthly wages for the restructuring of the former German Democratic Republic) in 1992. The total sum of solidarity payments made by all foreign workers in Germany exceeds 1.7 billion DM.[22]

It is not only as taxpayers that Turks contribute to the German economy; they also contribute as consumers. In addition, 34.6 percent of Turks in Germany have secured a savings contract with German construction societies. According to the latest figures, about 45,000 Turks own a house or a flat in Germany, a figure that is likely to double by the year 2000.[23] Presently there are more than 135,000 Turks who hold a savings contract with a building society.

The recent rise in racist violence in Germany has made some Turks reconsider the option of returning. However, return migration is no longer a realistic or even feasible option for a significant portion of Turks. The majority of Turks see Germany as their country of settlement for two main reasons. The first is that the economic opportunities in Turkey for returnees are not promising. The disappointing experience of the former returnees has discouraged many others. Secondly, many Turkish families are rooted in Germany by the education of their children, jobs, and social security rights. In a survey conducted by the Center for Turkish Studies in 1985 it was revealed that 39.4 percent of Turks in the Federal Republic of Germany had no plans to return to Turkey; 21 percent considered the possibility of returning in ten years at the earliest. Thus, 60.4 percent of the Turks living in Germany had intentions to remain in the country for

Table 10.8

Turks Entering and Leaving
the FRG between 1973-1989

Years	Enters	Returns	Balance
1973	249,670	87,094	+ 162,576
1982	42,713	86,852	- 44,139
1983	27,830	100,338	- 72,558
1984	34,114	213,469	- 179,355
1985	47,458	60,641	- 13,183
1986	62,161	51,934	+ 10,227
1987	66,247	45,726	+ 20,521
1988	78,402	39,876	+ 38,526
1989	85,679	37,666	+ 48,013
1990	84,346	35,535	+ 48,711
1991	82,536	36,638	+ 45,898

Source: Statistisches Bundesamt (Federal Statistics Office), Wiesbaden; Yurtdışı İşçi Hizmetleri Genel Müdürlüğü (Office for Workers' Services Abroad), 1991 Annual Report, Ankara, 1992

at least ten years.[24] Another study conducted by the Center for Turkish Studies in 1988 showed that 83 percent of the Turkish citizens living in Germany no longer considered returning to Turkey.

Status and Problems of Turkish Communities in Europe

The Turkish population in contemporary Europe presents Turkey with many economic and political opportunities. In the thirty-two years of the migration process the structure of the Turkish population in Europe, as well as its needs and objectives, has greatly changed. Today second and third generation Turks in Europe are heading for other positions than their parents. This is best illustrated by the increasing self-employment pattern among Turks and the increasing tendency to complete university education.

Turkish Employment and Self-Employment in Germany

Turks constitute 35 percent of the foreign labor force in the Federal Republic of Germany. The majority are employed in the manufacturing sector. The sectors with the next highest concentration of Turkish workers are services, construction, trade, and energy-mining. Of the 649,855 Turkish workers employed in Germany, 387,806 (60 percent) were working in the manufacturing sector as of 31 March 1992, while 16 percent were employed in the services sector. In 1973, 89 percent of the Turks living in Germany were male and 91 percent were employed as workers eligible for social security. However, in 1993 only 29 percent of the Turks in Germany were employed as workers eligible for social security. The remainder consists of dependent family members and some 37,000 self-employed businesspeople.

After many years of wage-earning employment, many foreign workers are making a transition to self-employment. According to the findings of the Center for Turkish Studies, the number of self-employed Turks in the Federal Republic of Germany has increased from 33,000 in 1990 to 37,000 in 1993. The total volume of investments made by Turkish self-employed businesspeople is about eight billion DM and their total annual turnover is approximately thirty-one billion DM. Self-employed Turks have created about 135,000 employment opportunities. The enterprises range from small family businesses to larger ones with 600 employees.

According to the findings of the Center for Turkish Studies, Turkish entrepreneurs generally own a significant amount of private capital for their investments but establish businesses in sectors requiring intensive labor power. At the same time, they refrain from increasing their knowledge and experience through consultant services.[25] Thus, two different types of Turkish entrepreneurs can be observed. While the first and smaller group is well-informed and educated, the remaining large portion encounters problems in many areas of business management. Similarly, while the capacities of the businesses are either too small or too large, the number of mid-scale businesses is significantly small. Despite all of these developments, the transition of the Turks from employee to employer status is an undeniably important development.

According to a survey conducted among fifteen cities by the Center for Turkish Studies in August 1990, 61.1 percent of the entrepreneurs

Table 10.9

Sectoral Distribution of Turkish Workers in Germany as of 31 March 1992

Employment Sector	Number
Agriculture, forestry, fishery	5,394
Energy, mining	20,332
Manufacturing sector	387,806
Construction	41,603
Trade	46,450
Transportation	25,182
Insurance, banking	1,959
Services	104,657
Non-profit organizations	5,355
Social insurance, etc.	11,023
Others	94
TOTAL	649,855

Source: Yurtdışı İşçi Hizmetleri Genel Müdürlüğü (Office for Workers' Services Abroad), 1992 Annual Report, Ankara, 1992

surveyed planned to establish connections with firms in east Germany and 54.8 percent have already taken an initial step in this direction. Turkish businesspeople seeking cooperation opportunities in the east German market with a capital ranging between 50,000 and 3 million DM especially look toward large cities such as Leipzig, Berlin, Dresden, Magdeburg, and Rostock. These types of developments are very significant for the creation of employment opportunities in the newly developing, former East Germany. However, regardless of the extent to which Turks establish private businesses, their opportunities to

Table 10.10

Self-Employment of Turks in Germany (billion DM)

	1981	1985	1990	1992	1993
Number	10,000	22,000	33,000	35,000	37,000
Total Volume of Investments	-	3.8	5.7	7.8	8.0
Total Annual Turnover	-	17.2	25.0	28.0	31.0
Employment (x1000)	-	77	100	125	135

Source: Zentrum für Türkeistudien, Essen

participate in political developments within society are almost non-existent.

The fact that Turks, whose businesses generally target customers from their own country, obtain the goods they offer their customers from German firms when necessary, procure credit from German banks, and even employ German personnel, is an indication of the extent to which the two cultures work together. It should be mentioned that, as financial opportunities improve and as Turks begin to integrate into German society, their tendency to return to Turkey decreases.

The economic integration of Turks, especially their initiative in setting up their own businesses, has aroused considerable interest not only in the Federal Republic of Germany but also in Turkey. Turkish businesspeople and official authorities have recently taken an interest in the economic potential of this business community, as well as its possible contributions to the Turkish economy through investments in as well as imports from Turkey.

While Turkish firms represent an important factor in the German economy, they represent an even greater potential for Turkey. Up to 20 percent of Turkish firms are engaged in international trade for their supplies and three-fourths of this group import goods from Turkey.[26] Turks have invested in fifty-five different sectors including detective bureaus, publishers, restaurants, travel agencies, grocery stores, and manufacturing firms.

Education

Since the Turkish population in Europe is fairly young, this inevitably implies the presence of large numbers of Turkish children in school. As of 1992 there were about 440,000 Turkish children in the German educational system alone.[27] In total there are about 640,000 Turkish children in the educational system (excluding universities and academies) in Germany, the Netherlands, Belgium, France, Denmark, Austria, Switzerland, and Sweden.

During the 1980s university education has become more important for Turkish young people, particularly in Germany. The number of Turkish students attending German universities has increased from 4,000 in 1975 to about 13,000 at the beginning of the 1990s and to 14,700 in 1993.[28] The majority of Turkish university students, however, believe that after graduation they do not have equal opportunities with Germans in attaining employment or in being promoted at work.[29] In total there are about 16,000 Turkish university students in the countries mentioned above. These university students have recently come together in a number of European cities to establish the European Association of Turkish Academics, which might be seen as the first sign of a future Turkish lobby in Europe.

Political Integration and Participation of Turks in European Societies

The political dimension of the incorporation and integration of Turks into western European societies also requires considerable attention. The fact that many European countries have become countries of immigration is still not officially acknowledged, even though this issue has become highly politicized in Europe today.

At present, Turks have very few possibilities for political participation in Germany. Aside from advisory councils, current laws allow few other opportunities for political co-determination. However, Turkish residents are showing a steadily increasing interest in membership in German political parties.

Although migrants are required to pay taxes, obey the law, and fulfill other civil duties, and although their lives are as affected by government as any other residents, they have no say in the decision-making process. In the words of Sarah Spencer, "the existence of such disenfranchised groups in significant numbers throughout Europe undermines democracy and must be rectified, either by encouraging widespread take up of citizenship, dual nationality or the extension of the right to vote to long term residents."[30] As there are valid reasons why acquiring citizenship in the immigration country is not attractive or acceptable for some immigrants, western European governments should consider dual nationality and granting the right to vote and stand in local elections. If a substantial number of permanent residents cannot vote, the legitimacy of the political decision-making process is impaired.

Formal political participation, as carried out in a representative democracy by means of voting, was denied to foreign "fellow citizens" in the ruling of the Federal Constitutional Court in 1990. In Article 20 of the German Constitution it is stated that "sovereignty belongs to the people." The Constitutional Court claimed that the word "people" referred to "people of German descent." Therefore, the decision of the Social Democratic Party (SPD) and Free Democratic Party coalition government of the Federal State of Hamburg in 1987 to give foreigners the right to vote and stand as candidates in local elections was overruled by the Constitutional Court.

The advocates of the local voting right say that foreigners and Germans are equally affected by decisions at the local level. On the other hand, the political interest of foreigners, which is presently oriented mainly towards events in the home countries, could be directed, with the introduction of a local voting right, toward events in Germany. Political participation is an effective means toward integration, and a concession of the local voting right to non-Germans could produce an effective and carefully considered integration policy. In the process, the positive experiences of other countries which have already instituted the local voting right for foreigners (including the Netherlands, Denmark, and Ireland) can be considered.

The fact that the decision of the Federal Constitutional Court does not further influence, and indeed expressly keeps open, the possibility of the introduction of a local voting right for citizens of EU-member states makes clear that there are two different ways of assessing the entire problem; citizens from EU-states are treated differently than those from non-EU states. This is because, along with numerous other regulations, a so-called "Union Citizenship" is introduced within the framework of an agreement on the establishment of the EU through Article 8-I of the Maastricht treaty. A citizen of the Union is, accordingly, "one who possesses the citizenship of a member-state." In addition; "Every citizen of the Union residing in a member-state of which he is not a national shall have the right to vote and to stand as a candidate at municipal elections in the member-state in which he resides, under the same conditions as nationals of that state."

According to the results of a survey conducted by the Center for Turkish Studies in the Federal Republic of Germany during September

1994 among four nationalities (Turks, Greeks, Italians, and former Yugoslavs) the right to vote and stand in local elections is considered very important by 46 percent of the foreigners who were interviewed. The total number of interviewees in the survey was 1412; 601 were Turkish, 212 were Greek, 239 were Italians, and 360 came from former Yugoslavia.

Analyzing Turks as a separate group, the results of the survey show that for 62 percent the right to participate in local elections in Germany is considered to be very important and for 21 percent it is considered to be important. Altogether, 83 percent of the Turks consider this right as being important.

As can be seen from Table 10.11, the SPD is the preferred German political party for Turks. The fact that the SPD is the traditional workers' party and that it pursues a more friendly policy towards migrant workers and foreigners than the other German parties led to these results. Yet it must also be mentioned that the SPD has to some extent lost its potential in the last ten years. According to a survey conducted by the *Kommunalverband Ruhrgebiet* in 1983, the SPD could have received 88 percent of the total votes in some neighborhoods which were densely populated by Turks. Another survey made by the Center for Turkish Studies in 1986 indicated that the SPD would have received 63% percent of all the Turkish votes provided that the right to vote in local elections was recognized. Compared to Greeks, Italians, and former Yugoslavs, Turks show a greater interest in this kind of political participation. Greeks and Italians already have the right to participate in local elections based on their EU status.

Voting is only one means of expressing political preferences. Additional means of political participation are essential if immigrants are to exert influence over public policy. For instance, public services could and should recruit staff who are themselves of migrant origin and apply equal opportunity policies in their personnel management. Public service jobs should be open to non-nationals as much as possible. It should be stressed again that citizenship is the key to participation in the political system, where many decisions affecting migrants are taken. "Residence rather than citizenship ought to be the major criterion for the attribution of rights and obligations by the state and offering state protection."[31]

Dual Citizenship

Dual citizenship could be another means to promote the integration of foreigners, and especially of Turks, in Germany. The question of dual citizenship is discussed especially in the situation of migrants, partic-

Table 10.11

Which Political Party Would You Vote For If There Were Federal Parliament Elections Next Sunday?

Political Parties	Turks
Social Democrat Party (SPD)	49%
Grünen/Bündnis 90	11%
Free Democrats Party (FDP)	10%
Christian Democrats Party (CDU)	6%
Democratic Socialist Party (PDS)	1%
None	9%
No answer	15%

Source: Zentrum für Türkeistudien, Essen

ularly Turks who stay in Germany for many years, often a decade or more. Numerous Turks who could apply for German citizenship ultimately do not because this would mean a loss of their original citizenship. Renunciation of Turkish citizenship often means more than the loss of certain rights in the homeland; it is also felt as the renunciation of one's cultural identity and the complete detachment from the homeland. Some states, such as Iran, do not release anyone from citizenship.

According to the results of the survey mentioned above, conducted by the Center for Turkish Studies, 55 percent of the interviewees have stated that they would be ready to accept German citizenship provided they could keep their present citizenship. While two-thirds of the Turks and the former Yugoslavs say yes to dual citizenship, less than one-third of the Greeks are interested in dual citizenship. Taking into consideration the populations of Turks and former Yugoslavs (1.92 million and 920,000 respectively), these results show that approximately 1.6 million foreigners would apply for German citizenship if dual citizenship was recognized.

The tendency among Turks to accept the citizenship of immigration countries was not very high in the 1980s. Beginning with the 1990s there

Table 10.12

Would You Take Up German Citizenship
If You Could Keep Your Present Citizenship?

	Total	Turks	Greeks	Former Yugoslavians	Italians
Yes	55%	62%	29%	69%	47%
No	21%	14%	34%	24%	23%
Do not know	17%	14%	37%	5%	14%
No ans.	8%	10%	0%	1%	16%

Source: Zentrum für Türkeistudien, Essen

has been a clear increase in the number of those who apply for foreign citizenship. The second generation Turks who were born and have been brought up in western European societies play a significant role in this increase. Though minor compared to the Turkish population living in Germany, the number of naturalizations among Turks living in the Netherlands is as high as and sometimes higher than the number in Germany. This result is a product of the difference between immigration policies and the kind of polity immigrants enter into in the two countries.

Although dual citizenship has been on the political agenda in Germany lately, the protocol of the new coalition government that was elected in the general elections of October 1994 has not lived up to expectations. According to the coalition protocol, new arrangements are planned to be introduced concerning the naturalization of foreign children. Thus, if a couple has been living in the Federal Republic of Germany for at least ten years and has an unlimited residence permit, and if their child was born in Germany, the child is granted an option for obtaining German citizenship. The child has the right to "German child citizenship" along with the citizenship of his or her parents. "German child citizenship" terminates when the child is 18 years old and automatically becomes German citizenship if the child does not take up any other citizenship within one year. As can plainly be seen, Germany is far from recognizing dual citizenship and such arrangements are far from meeting the needs of the foreign population.

Table 10.13

Naturalization of Turks in the Netherlands
and Germany (1984-1992)

Year	Netherlands	Germany
1984	310	1,053
1985	2,245	1,310
1986	1,480	1,492
1987	1,410	1,184
1988	820	1,243
1989	3,365	1,713
1990	1,952	2,016
1991	6,105	*4,969
1992	**4,492	9,682

* Applications for naturalizations at Turkish consulates in Germany
** January-July

Source: 1) Yurtdışı İşçi Hizmetleri Genel Müdürlüğü (Office for Workers' Services Abroad), 1991 and 1992 Annual Reports ; 2) Statistisches Bundesamt (Federal Statistics Office), Wiesbaden, different years; 3) Hürriyet (Turkish newspaper), 5 December 1992

One further legal means of allaying some of the problems encountered by Turks and other foreigners in Europe would be to enact anti-discrimination laws, such as those that have been passed in England and Italy. Such enactments would provide a more reliable framework for the legal enforcement of counter-measure designed to deter and to punish racist attacks. Legal regimes by themselves, however, are unlikely to be adequate if public attitudes and perceptions remain unchanged. In a certain sense, all of the measures outlined above can only be partial solutions so long as these core problems are not addressed.

The Single Market

After a long period of preparation, 1 January 1993 brought into effect the free movement of capital, services, and labor for 345 million citizens among the twelve countries making up the EC at that time. With the Single Market, any citizen of a member country who was able to find a job and living quarters in another member country of the EC within a period of ninety days thereby gained the right to work and live in that country. On the other hand, there are seventeen million foreigners living in the EU and approximately nine million come from countries beyond EU borders. Turks, making up 25 percent of this population, are the largest foreign group, followed by Algerians and Tunisians. They and other third country citizens living in the EU are unable to take advantage of these freedoms.

It can thus be said that invisible borders have come into existence for these people in Europe. For this reason, it is necessary that the right to free movement be granted to third country citizens legally residing within the borders of the EU. The Schengen Agreement, intended and designed to be a solution to this problem, has not yet fully been put into effect. Additionally, the agreement does not contain the conditions that would be necessary fully to solve the problem.

The Schengen Agreement

The Schengen Agreement was dually initiated by France and the Federal Republic of Germany in 1985. This initiative was later joined by the Benelux countries. The aim was to abolish borders in common on a step-by-step basis before the Single Market took effect. This agreement was initially formed only as a statement of intent and did not include concrete measures. It first gained substance with the signing in June 1990 of a supplementary agreement consisting of 141 articles. By this time, the number of countries that were party to this agreement rose to nine, including the Benelux countries, France, Germany, Italy, Spain, Greece, and Portugal. The main terms of the Schengen Agreement are as follows:

- The free movement of citizens of the countries having signed the Schengen Agreement within the borders of these countries and without any checks, accompanied by a commitment to take common measures against the probable consequences of an influx of refugees from beyond the region.
- The application of a common and single visa at the borders of the Schengen region.

- The identification and application of common policies regarding the pursuit of criminals.
- A common effort among security organizations regarding the pursuit of criminals.
- The establishment of a common information system among the countries having signed the Schengen Agreement and the common exchange of information.

Looking at what the Schengen Agreement will bring to citizens of third countries, we can see both negative and positive aspects. First, one can observe discrimination against and a certain classification of people from third countries. The Schengen countries are planning to use visa applications as a means of blocking an expected influx into the region from the southern hemisphere. A distinction is made by two lists, marked negative and positive. The negative list comprises over one hundred countries foreseen to be subject to visa applications. The positive list, on the other hand, comprises just a handful of countries for which visas are not required. Thus, three separate categories come into being:

1. Citizens of the Schengen countries.
2. Those who are not members of the Schengen countries and who may enter without visas.
3. Those who are subject to visa requirements and who come from undesirable countries.

One positive aspect of this application, however, is that a person who has been able to obtain a visa for a Schengen country and who comes from one of the undesirable countries on the negative list does not have to obtain additional visas for the other Schengen countries. Nevertheless, there are various conditions for obtaining a visa:

1. Ownership of a currently valid passport.
2. The certification of one's livelihood during the period of stay.
3. Not being listed as an unwanted person on the Schengen Information System (SIS).
4. Not being a person who will endanger internal or international security.

However, even if an individual has been able to fulfill each of these conditions, has obtained a visa, and is able to travel in and out of the other Schengen countries without one, this person is still required to declare his or her entry either at the border or at the first available police station within the border. Upon this declaration, the official in charge may make an inspection by obtaining information through the SIS. A person who enters the country without declaring entry may be recorded in the SIS as an unwanted person and may be immediately expelled from the borders of the country. In these situations, it is not possible to make any legal objection.

Persons who have been listed on the SIS and who possess the right to reside in another Schengen country may lose their residence permit pending a review in their country of residence. The Schengen agreement does not include a right to objection for the citizen of a third country in this situation.

According to Article 96 of the agreement, if citizens of third countries do not fulfill stated responsibilities and do not conform to regulations, these persons are to be declared unwanted persons and will be recorded as such on the SIS. Member countries are requested to deny issuance of a work permit to foreigners whose names appear on the SIS list.

Free Movement of Turks in the EU

According to Article 12 of the 1963 Association Agreement between Turkey and the EC, both sides are mutually responsible for bringing free movement into effect step-by-step. However, Article 60 of the Additional Protocol, which came into effect in 1973, placed limits on this and gave both sides the authority to take certain economic and financial measures, causing dire, large-scale problems. Article 60 also states that the countries are responsible for taking measures which will do the least damage to the implementation of the Association Agreement. Moreover, Articles 48 and 49 of the Treaty of Rome contain an escape clause, allowing free movement to be limited by bureaucratic and economic measures. Thus, for example, only a country's own citizens can work in state offices and free movement applies solely to existing work places.

The Additional Protocol foresaw the step-by-step granting of the right of free movement to Turkish workers, starting on 1 December 1976 and to be completed by 1 December 1986. However, by 1986 this right had to be suspended. Only a few improvements have been made in terms of the rights of the Turkish workers within the EU, and equality between Turkish workers and EU citizens does not exist.

The following is the response of the Federal Republic of Germany to the requests of the Turkish government concerning the free movement of its workers:

1. The regulations in the Association Agreement concerning free movement are only directionally indicative and its contents are

only tentative. Free movement cannot be put into effect on this basis.

2.   Under these conditions, it is not possible for Turkish workers to enter without limitations.
3.   The decision regarding permission to enter should be up to individual countries.
4.   Regulations concerning the free movement of Turkish workers will initially take the form of an improvement in the conditions and status of the Turks already residing in the EC.

The German government additionally stated that free movement was impermissible from an economic and social policy perspective. Parallel to these developments, the Court of Justice made the decision that "Turkish workers will not have the right to claim free movement on the basis of the Association Agreement" and stated that the Association Agreement was merely the outline of a plan and did not include any concrete regulations.

Cooperation in the Field of Migration
Between Turkey and Western Europe

Worldwide economic and social disparities cause migratory flows. Therefore, the question to be answered is "how we can control and manage migration flows?" Turkey is presently not only a country of emigration but also a country of immigration and serves as a bridge to Europe for migration flows. At present in western Europe family migration (formation) is becoming the largest source of legal migration, but other forms such as asylum-claims (whether political or economic) and irregular migration take on significance as well. Once the determinants of migratory flows are known, then the impact of migration and development policies—including aid, trade, and investment issues—should be discussed.

One way to prevent migratory flows is to support developing and transitional countries. Today it is commonly acknowledged that the imbalance between population dynamics and economic and social development as well as the perceived impacts of such differences leads to migration movements and to an interdependency between different world regions.

Migration has far-reaching political, social, economic, and cultural consequences and therefore requires a comprehensive policy based on a broad political consensus. Immigration should be limited to a level compatible with the infrastructure of the receiving country in terms of the labor market, housing, education, and health services. Migration should also conform with the justified interests of both the receiving countries and the exporting countries as well as with respect for human rights. Promotion of human rights, population and health programs, protection of the environment, promotion of human resource development, and job creation are necessary to reduce migration pressures. Governments of countries of origin and destination should seek to reduce the causes of migration by these types of actions. This will, of course, not only require financial assistance but also an adjustment of the commercial, tariff, and financial relations in order to revitalize the economies of the countries of origin.

In Turkey's case, the high population growth rate seems to be a major reason for migration flows. Therefore, population (family planning) programs and job training are appropriate responses to mass emigration in Turkey.[32] Strengthening the enterprising middle class is another measure likely to achieve success.[33] Other strategic elements to reduce emigration pressures include improved terms of trade for exports in exporting countries, reduced costs of borrowing, and better planning through improved local government decision-making.

In the future, migration from Turkey will largely depend on the socio-economic development in the country and on the admission policies and needs of the European countries. Many experts agree, particularly given the recent demographic trends, that migrants have become indispensable for the western European countries and that there is need for migration to Europe in the future.[34]

International income disparities are not easily resolved. Even though Turkey has shown a remarkable economic growth in the last ten years, it will probably take much more time before the disparity between the income levels of Turkey and the EU narrows down. Last but not least, we should also remember that migration not only responds to crude economic differences but also to perceptions of comparative advantage and social and political pressures.

According to projections by the Organization for Economic Cooperation and Development, the populations of the Federal Republic of Germany, Italy, Belgium, and Denmark will decrease in the next ten years. A decrease in population will also be observed in the Netherlands, Portugal, and Greece between 2010 and 2020, while the rate of increase of population will stagnate in France, Luxembourg, and Spain.[35]

Between 2030 and 2040 only Ireland will have a positive rate of increase. As negative demographic trends and population ageing are undesirable, controlled immigration to Europe from Turkey and other countries can be most useful in order to retain present economic growth and levels of welfare in Europe.

Table 10.14

Projection of Average Annual Population Growth Rate of EU Countries (1990-2050)

	1990-2000	2000-2010	2010-2020	2020-2030	2030-2040	2040-2050
BRD	-0,2	-0,6	-0,7	-0,8	-0,7	-0,8
F	0,2	0,1	0,0	-0,1	-0,2	-0,3
GB	0,1	0,1	0,1	0,0	-0,2	-0,2
I	-0,1	-0,2	-0,4	-0,4	-0,5	-0,7
B	-0,1	-0,1	-0,1	-0,2	-0,4	-0,4
DK	-0,3	-0,4	-0,6	-0,6	-0,6	-0,7
GR	0,2	0,2	-0,1	-0,2	-0,3	-0,4
IRL	0,6	0,4	0,3	0,3	0,2	-0,4
L	0,2	0,0	0,0	-0,1	-0,2	-0,1
NL	0,3	0,0	-0,2	-0,2	-0,5	-0,5
P	0,3	0,1	-0,1	-0,2	-0,4	-0,5
E	0,3	0,1	0,0	0,0	-0,2	-0,3

Source: OECD, Aging Populations, The Social Policy Implications, Paris, 1988

Integration vs. Incorporation

In the Europe of the 1990s, which recently took the first practical step toward creating an economic area and political union without borders, migration and the presence of foreign populations have taken on special significance. Migration will be, and indeed already has become, one of the most challenging issues, one which has been increasingly linked to the concepts of democracy and human rights. The extent to which foreign populations are incorporated into the social life and decision-making bodies is an important element in furthering democracy, pluralism, and human rights in Europe.

Migrants and foreigners are expected by the indigenous population to integrate into the host societies. However, integration demands the establishment of legal safeguards. Against the background of restrictive immigration policies, discrimination, and racism, migrants can hardly feel secure in their private lives. The uncertainty about their status undermines the efforts for integration.

Very often, the cultural and religious elements of the migrant's country of origin are used to explain integration into the host societies. However, such a one-sided approach often misrepresents why migrants adjust differently to various host countries. A broader, macro-level approach of incorporation, rather than integration, takes into account the kind of polity migrants enter into to explain the degree of integration and participation in the society. Incorporation should lead immigrants to develop a sense of belonging to their new society, and this depends largely on the availability of opportunities for responsible participation and on the extent to which racist attitudes are discouraged.

Racism and Xenophobia in Germany

Europe is presently facing a confrontation. On one hand, the protection of human rights has gained weight in public discussion and political negotiation. On the other hand, aggressive nationalism, racism, and xenophobia are gaining ground. Increasingly migration has been linked to the concepts of democracy and human rights. Simultaneously, efforts are being made to develop a European Union with obvious deficiencies in regard to the rights of migrants.

International bodies such as the Conference on Security and Cooperation in Europe (CSCE), the Council of Europe, the International Labor Organization, and the United Nations have been holding conventions concerning the legal status of migrant workers and the elimination of all forms of racial discrimination. At the same time, the establishment of the EU points to the creation of a "Fortress Europe" with defenses set up against mass immigration from less developed countries.

Despite the restrictions on entry into western European countries, reality moves in a different direction. First of all, classical labor migration continues in the form of selective recruitment for special professions on a bilateral basis. Second, refugees continue to immigrate. In fact, the acceptance of refugees has become a major gate of entry by which gaps in the labor market are filled. Third, the acceptance of diaspora immigrants continues (particularly in Germany) and creates serious conflicts between the locals and the newcomers.

These contradicting developments, and the lack of corresponding social policies, is notably felt by migrants and ethnic minorities living in Europe. Furthermore, Europe is confronted with growing xenophobia and racism as well as ethnic conflicts. The dimensions of aggressive racist behavior are reflected in the figures. In 1992 there were 2,584 aggressions against foreigners resulting in the deaths of seventeen persons in the Federal Republic of Germany. This was an increase of more than 65 percent from the previous year. The major targets were homes of asylum-seekers, but targets also included migrants settled in stable communities and even handicapped persons. Seventy percent of the perpetrators were under twenty years of age. In the first seven months of 1993, a total of 1,223 aggressions against foreigners was registered in Germany. Forty-three percent of the perpetrators were students, 31 percent were skilled workers, 1 percent were unskilled workers, and 19 percent were unemployed. Fourteen percent were affiliated with a right extreme group or were known to have a violent past. Not only Germany, but other European countries including Sweden, the Netherlands, France, and Belgium have also registered increasing animosity against foreigners, particularly Asians, blacks, and Muslims.

It is surprising that the increase in xenophobia in Germany was not taken seriously by the responsible authorities until 1992. Only after open attacks were carried out against foreigners—first in Hoyerswerda, then against asylum-seekers in Rostock, and then in the form of arson attacks on houses inhabited by Turks in Mölln and Solingen in 1992 and 1993— did the authorities realize that the danger from the extreme right was being underestimated.

However, the roots of xenophobia and racism can be traced back to the early 1980s. The process started then but was visible only in the field of social science, through texts about Turks which were widely circulated. In these texts Turks were often ridiculed because of their different tastes in food and dress. In some texts, to a lesser extent, violence against Turks was depicted where they were run over, stabbed, incinerated with technological efficiency, or boiled in hot water. These jokes were actually an expression of widely shared attitudes and values in German society. They revealed deep-seated fears and latent aggression, and signalled a potential for an eventual outbreak of overt hostility.

Instead of openly discussing the issue of immigration and integration of foreigners in the Federal Republic of Germany, the German government adopted a more restricted policy towards foreigners by introducing legislation for limitation of immigration and an amendment to the constitution with regard to the right of asylum. Unfortunately, no short or long-term policies were developed which emphasized the concepts of coexistence and multiculturality.

Particularly following the unification of Germany, in the region of what was formerly East Germany and now the so-called new federal states, hostility towards foreigners has taken on greater dimensions. First of all, individuals in the former East Germany, with a population of eighteen million, were unaccustomed to living with foreigners. Secondly, the expectations from the unification of Germany have clearly not been realized in the short-run. It was initially believed that unification would bring about a rapid rise in the standards of living in East Germany. As it became obvious that this would not occur right away and that a balance between the conditions of east and west Germany could only be achieved by the second half of the 1990s at the earliest, racism found a breeding ground in the new federal states. In particular, the asylum question has been exploited by German politicians and has been made a scapegoat for increasing social and economic problems.

What are the motives for racist behavior in European societies? Do the ideological gaps in the world have an effect on racism? Is the resurgence of ethno-nationalism in eastern Europe and the Balkans a consequence of the spiritual and mental "black hole" left after the dissolution of the communist system? Does the formation of the EU—considered to be a Fortress Europe by many—influence racist tendencies in these countries? Will we have a moral crisis in the West in which tolerance becomes synonymous with indifference, or a crisis in European humanist values? Is there an economic crisis which leads toward the marginalization of an increasing part of Europe's population?

There are obvious limitations on the mechanisms of formal democracy in combating xenophobia, aggressive nationalism, racism, and other manifestations of the extreme right. But there are, nevertheless, many legal, social, and economic actions one can take to combat racism and xenophobia. Recognition of dual nationality, easing naturalization, recognition of the right to vote and stand in local elections, equal opportunity policies, enactment of anti-discrimination laws, and finally stronger control over extreme right-wing organizations are a few very important ways of improving the situation of migrants in European societies and combating racism.

The existing educational systems in most European countries are not equipped to train the coming generations for international mobility and cultural diversity. The socialization process carried out by families, schools, and peers needs recasting, including measures such as a review of textbooks to strengthen the teaching of anti-racist values. Teaching of foreign cultures and history, for instance, would lead young people to develop a sense of respect and understanding for the migrant populations and minorities living in their countries.

Islam in Europe

Within this context, Islam has a significant meaning. Since the immigration of Muslim workers within the framework of the recruitment agreements, Islam became the most widespread religion after Christianity and the second largest religious community in Europe. For instance, presently there are 2.2 million Muslims living in Germany. A large number of them, about 80 percent, come from Turkey, and the rest from Iran, Morocco, Lebanon, Tunisia, and Pakistan. One should also mention the small but increasing number (about 50,000) who are of German origin.

Islam is an important element in the life style of many Turks. It goes beyond belief and becomes an expression of identity as well as a way of protection, especially for those who are disillusioned by their migration experience.

At this stage, the policies of the receiving countries concerning Islam and their Muslim populations is of great significance. So far, questions such as religious lessons in school for Muslim children and permission for building mosques have been generally approached with skepticism by the indigenous populations. As a result of an obvious deficit in fulfilling the religious needs of migrants, privately organized religious teaching in the form of Koran courses has attracted great interest. However, such a development may become dangerous due to the extremely radical nature of such organizations, a factor which should be considered when developing policies in education and culture.

The religious needs of the Turkish population, coupled with the indifferent attitude of German authorities towards these needs, have also paved the way for the establishment and development of Turkish-Islamic organizations in Germany. These organizations presently enjoy great support among all Turkish groups in Europe. This fact alone makes clear that in order to achieve peaceful coexistence between different communities in Europe it will be necessary to establish a permanent dialogue with Islam and other distinctive cultures.

Notes

1. *Statistisches Bundesamt* [Federal Statistics Office], (Wiesbaden, 1992).

2. Yurtdışı İşçi Hizmetleri Müdürlüğü [Office for Workers' Services Abroad], *1992 Annual Report* (Ankara, 1993).

3. Philip J. Muus, *Sopemi Netherlands 1991* (Amsterdam, 1991), p. 49.

4. Ibid., p. 49.

5. Faruk Şen, *Problems and Integration Constraints of Turkish Migrants in the Federal Republic of Germany* (Geneva: International Labor Organization, 1989), p. 12.

6. Ibid., p. 10.

7. *Statistisches Bundesamt* [Federal Statistics Office], Wiesbaden.

8. Zentrum für Türkeistudien, *Migration Movements from Turkey to the European Community* (Essen, January 1993), p. 118.

9. Çağlar Keyder and Ayhan Aksu-Koç, *External Labor Migration from Turkey and Its Impact* (Canada: IDRC, April 1988), p. 11.

10. Zentrum für Türkeistudien, *Migration Movements from Turkey to the European Community*, p. 118.

11. Village Development Cooperatives were set up in 1962 to promote rural development and give priority to members who wished to migrate abroad for employment. However, they failed to promote the expected rural development because they functioned to help members jump ahead in the emigration queue instead of launching viable development projects.

12. Zentrum für Türkeistudien, *Konsumgewohnheiten und wirtschaftliche Situation der türkischen Bevölkerung in der Bundesrepublik Deutschland* (Essen, September 1992), p. 1.

13. Zentrum für Türkeistudien, *Lebenssituation älterer Ausländer in der Bundesrepublik Deutschland—Zwischenbericht* (Essen, 1992) and Zentrum für Türkeistudien, *Konsumgewohnheiten*, p. 1.

14. Zentrum für Türkeistudien, *Zur Lebenssituation und spezifischen Problemlage älterer ausländischer Einwohner in der Bundesrepublik Deutschland—Kurzfassung des Abschlußberichtes* (Essen, October 1992), p. 4.

15. Zentrum für Türkeistudien, *Zur Lebenssituation und spezifischen Problemlage älterer türkischer und griechischer Einwohner in ländlichen Gebieten des Landes Nordrhein-Westfalen* (Essen, October 1992).

16. Philip L. Martin, *The Unfinished Story: Turkish Labor Migration to Western Europe* (Geneva: International Labor Organization, 1991), p. 65.

17. Ibid.

18. *Bundesanstalt für Arbeit* [Federal Institute for Labor], Nürnberg.

19. *Migration News Sheet*, Brussels, December 1991.

20. *Migration News Sheet*, Brussels, December 1991, p. 4. See also Arne Gieseck, Ullrich Heilemann, and Hans Dietrich von Loeffelholz, eds., *Economic and Social Implications of Migration into the Federal Republic of Germany* (Essen: Rheinisch-Westfälisches Institut für Wirtschaftsforschung, March 1993).

21. Zentrum für Türkeistudien, *Konsumgewohnheiten*.

22. Ibid.

23. Ibid.

24. Şen, *Problems and Integration Constraints*, p. 5.

25. Zentrum für Türkeistudien, *Turkish Entrepreneurs in the Federal Republic of Germany and Their Contributions to National Socio-Economic Developments* (Essen, September 1991).

26. TÜSİAD [Turkish Industrialists and Businessmens Association], *Federal Almanya'daki Türk İşadamlarının Ekonomik Potansiyeli ve Türk Ekonomisine Katkıları* (Istanbul, 1988).

27. Yurtdışı İşçi Hizmetleri Genel Müdürlüğü [Office for Workers' Services Abroad], *1992 Annual Report* (Ankara, 1993), p. 26.

28. Zentrum für Türkeistudien, *Türkische Studenten und Hochschulabsolventen mit besonderer Berücksichtigung der Bildungsinländer* (Essen, September 1992), p. 19.

29. Ibid., pp. 88-89 and 108.

30. Sarah Spencer, "The Social and Political Objectives of Immigration Policy," paper prepared for the seminar *The Economic and Social Impact of Migration,* organized by the Institute for Public Policy Research and the Friedrich Ebert Stiftung, London, 6-7 March 1993.

31. Council of Europe, *Final Report of the Community Relations Project* (Strasbourg, 1991), paragraph 109.

32. Ercan Uygur, *Foreign Aid as a Means to Reduce Emigration: the Case of Turkey* (Geneva: International Labor Organization, 1992).

33. Günther Schiller, *Reducing Emigration Pressure in Turkey: Analysis and Suggestions for External Aid* (Geneva: International Labor Organization, 1992).

34. Zentrum für Türkeistudien, *Migration Movements from Turkey to the European Community* (Essen, January 1993), pp. 158-162.

35. Zentrum für Türkeistudien, *Türkei und Europäische Gemeinschaft* (Opladen: Leske and Budrich, 1992), p. 13.

About the Editors and Contributors

Clement H. Dodd is professorial associate in the School of Oriental and African Studies at the University of London, where he established the Modern Turkish Studies program. His latest book on Turkish politics is *The Crisis of Turkish Democracy*, 2nd edition, 1990. Professor Dodd is currently working on a study of Turkey and the Cyprus issue.

N. Bülent Gültekin has been a professor at the Wharton School of the University of Pennsylvania since 1981, where he is a member of the Finance Department. He has served as governor of the Central Bank of Turkey, chief advisor to the Prime Minister for Turgut Özal and Mesut Yilmaz, and president of the Turkish Privatization and Housing Development Agency.

Kemal H. Karpat is distinguished professor of history and chair of the Turkish and Central Asian programs at the University of Wisconsin-Madison. He is also the founder and former president of the Turkish Studies Association and the Middle East Studies Association. Professor Karpat is the author of numerous works dealing with aspects of Ottoman and Turkish history.

Heinz Kramer is senior research fellow at the Research Institute for International Politics and Security of the *Stiftung Wissenschaft und Politik* at Ebenhausen, Germany. He was a visiting professor of International Relations at Bilkent University in Ankara during 1990. His publications include *Die Europäische Gemeinschaft und die Türkei: Entwicklung, Probleme und Perspektiven einer schwierigen Partnerschaft*, 1988.

Bruce Kuniholm is professor of history and public policy at Duke University. He is the author of *The Origins of the Cold War in the Near East: Great Power Conflict and Diplomacy in Iran, Turkey, and Greece*, 2nd edition, 1994.

Vojtech Mastny is professor of international relations and director of the Research Institute at the Bologna Center, Paul H. Nitze School of Advanced International Studies of The Johns Hopkins University. His most recent publication is *The Helsinki Process and the Reintegration of Europe, 1986-1991: Analysis and Documentation,* 1992.

Ayşe Mumcu is a Ph.D. candidate in economics at the University of Pennsylvania. Her research topics include Organizational Theory of the Firm, Public Economics, and Information Economics.

R. Craig Nation is associate professor of international relations and coordinator of the Russian area and East European studies program at the Bologna Center, Paul H. Nitze School of Advanced International Studies of The Johns Hopkins University. In 1992, he published *Black Earth, Red Star: A History of Soviet Security Policy, 1917-1991.*

Ziya Öniş is associate professor of economics at Boğaziçi University, specializing in the political economy of development with an emphasis upon privatization, reform of the state, and the politics of structural adjustment. He co-authored *Economic Crises and Long-Term Growth in Turkey,* 1993.

Faruk Şen is director of the Center for Turkish Studies in Essen, Germany and holds a chair at the University of Essen. He has published numerous articles and studies on the Turkish community in the Federal Republic of Germany, and on modern Turkey and its relations with Europe.

Duygu Bazoğlu Sezer is professor of international relations at Bilkent University and lecturer at the Nato Defense College in Rome. Her recent publications include "Turkey's Grand Strategy Facing a Dilemma," *International Spectator,* 1992, and *Turkey's Political and Security Interests and Politics in the New Geostrategic Environment of the Expanded Middle East,* Occasional Paper, Henry Stimson Center, 1994.

İlkay Sunar is professor of political science and dean of the Faculty of Economics and Administrative Sciences at Boğaziçi University in Istanbul. His research and publications focus on contemporary Turkey and its Ottoman past.

Index

About the Book

Modern Turkey has consistently aspired to integrate with the West. Its efforts have borne considerable fruit, and in the wake of the break up of the Soviet Union the leading western powers enthusiastically held up the Turkish experience as a model for the newly emerging states of the Caucasus and Central Asia. But the "Turkish Model" of secularism, democratization, a pro-western geostrategic orientation, and free market economics has increasingly come under fire at home. Frustrated with its failure to achieve full membership in an expanding European Union, traumatized by a sharp economic recession following the boom years of the 1980s, and challenged by a host of new domestic and foreign policy dilemmas, the Turkish Republic has been pressed to revise its aspirations and reappraise its goals.

The contributors to *Turkey Between East and West* agree that association with the western economic and security communities remains Turkey's essential long-term priority. That priority will be pursued, however, on the basis of a sharpened sensitivity to Turkey's own distinctive character, including the Ottoman and Islamic legacies and its stature as a bridge between East and West. These essays examine Turkey's process of adaptation to the realities of the post-Cold War world in the political, economic, and international domains and offer challenging assessments of the forces that are shaping the future of an increasingly independent and assertive regional power.